How Structure~ ''

Design and Beha\
from Bridges to Buil

For Louise, Jane, Julia and my sister

How Structures Work

Design and Behaviour
from Bridges to Buildings

David Yeomans

WILEY-BLACKWELL

A John Wiley & Sons, Ltd., Publication

This edition first published 2009
© 2009 David Yeomans

Blackwell Publishing was acquired by John Wiley & Sons in February 2007. Blackwell's publishing programme has been merged with Wiley's global Scientific, Technical, and Medical business to form Wiley-Blackwell.

Registered office
John Wiley & Sons Ltd, The Atrium, Southern Gate, Chichester, West Sussex, PO19 8SQ, United Kingdom

Editorial offices
9600 Garsington Road, Oxford, OX4 2DQ, United Kingdom
2121 State Avenue, Ames, Iowa 50014-8300, USA

For details of our global editorial offices, for customer services and for information about how to apply for permission to reuse the copyright material in this book please see our website at www.wiley.com/wiley-blackwell.

Wiley also publishes its books in a variety of electronic formats. Some content that appears in print may not be available in electronic books.

Designations used by companies to distinguish their products are often claimed as trademarks. All brand names and product names used in this book are trade names, service marks, trademarks or registered trademarks of their respective owners. The publisher is not associated with any product or vendor mentioned in this book. This publication is designed to provide accurate and authoritative information in regard to the subject matter covered. It is sold on the understanding that the publisher is not engaged in rendering professional services. If professional advice or other expert assistance is required, the services of a competent professional should be sought.

Library of Congress Cataloging-in-Publication Data

Yeomans, David T.
  How structures work: design and behaviour from bridges to buildings / David Yeomans.
       p. cm.
  Includes index.
  ISBN 978-1-4051-9017-6 (pbk.: alk. paper)   1. Structural engineering.   I. Title.

  TA633.Y46 2009
  624.1—dc22   2009007675

A catalogue record for this book is available from the British Library.

Set in 10/12 pt Minion by SNP Best-set Typesetter Ltd., Hong Kong

1   2009

Contents

Preface

The dedication of this book requires some explanation because, although it has been written to be suitable for architectural students, it was not originally conceived as such. The dedicatees include two archaeologists and an antiquarian book dealer. The idea for the book goes back further than I care to remember. Visiting an archaeologist friend, I picked up a book on Greek architecture, and it became apparent that the author's understanding of structure and construction lacked something. 'Don't you think, Louise, that it would be a good idea for archaeologists to learn something about building structures?' 'Yes it would' – and so the seed was sown. The idea was simply that something on building structures might be useful for people with little or no mathematics but whose work or subject of study involves understanding buildings.

Many years later Jane Grenville asked me if I could give some classes to her master's course on buildings archaeology at York University. 'Structures for archaeologists? I've always wanted to try teaching that.' And so the text for this began with the notes for that class. Working up the text into this form was pushed aside by other things until Julia, a dealer in antiquarian engineering books, said that she had asked the late Professor Skempton if he could teach her some structures. He'd claimed it would be difficult because the subject is highly mathematical. She thought this nonsense, pointing out that she frequently heard engineers discussing structures but they never used any mathematics. Of course she's right, we seldom do when thinking about structures. The general experience is that one manages with a few simple concepts. Given the rule for static equilibrium, the triangle of forces, and some ideas about moments and elasticity one has the basic bag of tools that will cope with most situations. What one needs to add to this to make a designer, rather than a mere stress analyst, is an understanding of the properties of the materials that make up the structures we build, because no real understanding is possible without that. How then to provide the simple bag of tools? Goaded by Julia's demands I determined to tackle the problem.

What started as something for archaeologists, architectural historians or even the interested layperson (represented by my sister), and still remains suitable for that audience, was then developed at the suggestion of my commissioning editor to include material that would make it an architectural students' text. Here we see what might be described as a non-threatening approach to something that is normally seen as a highly technical subject, the idea for a method coming from my experience of starting to learn Spanish.

I was taught French and Latin at school, starting with the grammar; and that is how we commonly teach the 'theory of structures'. We begin with the 'grammar' and only apply it to real structures afterwards, the transition sometimes being difficult for students. Today languages are often taught through communication. The Spanish teacher introduced herself in the first class with 'Me llamo Maria. ¿Como te llamas?' Tone of voice indicated a question and one quickly grasped what the reply should be without realising one was using a reflexive verb – a difficult piece of grammar because it is something that does not exist in English. Why then not teach structures in a similar way? Begin with simple structures that are easy to understand from common experience and build up the grammar, i.e. the theoretical ideas, only as necessary. This might even be something that would appeal to engineers because it sometimes seems as if they have learnt a number of abstract concepts without grasping how they apply to real structures.

I only wish I had thought of this approach while I was teaching architectural students because no matter how simple we tried to make the subject for them they probably regarded structural analysis as a series of mind-numbing routines. The evidence was there in what I called my Christmas test. In the last class before the Christmas vacation I would present first-year students with a puzzle that I first came across in *Meccano Magazine* when I was ten years old:

I have to weigh a lorry, but it is too long for the weighbridge. I put the front wheels on the weighbridge and take a reading. I then drive it forwards so that only the back wheels are on and take another reading. I add the two readings together. Do I have the weight of the lorry?

Half the students would answer 'yes' and half would answer 'no'. Clearly a lot of guessing was going on. I would then draw a picture representing the situation (see Figure 0.1; arrows represent forces). By the time it was complete all would realize that the answer was 'yes'.

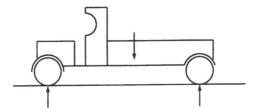

Figure 0.1 The force supporting a lorry.

They had worked with simple diagrams, happily writing down, as they had been taught, a formula that said that the sum of the support reactions must equal the sum of the loads, but this clearly had no real meaning for them. At least, it was not something that they could relate to a real situation. And that is just the problem; whatever the abstract theories – the grammar of structural analysis – they have to be related to real-life situations. It is the real situations that a designer, or someone trying to understand an actual building, begins with, which then has to be described in terms of abstract diagrams. That is the approach here. We will begin with real situations and learn to draw diagrams that represent the forces and explain how those forces work.

Some time ago I discovered a teaching film that featured a guide to one of the French cathedrals, demonstrating the action of the vaults and flying buttresses to parties of tourists. This was done by lining up the men in two rows to represent the columns of the nave. They then raised their arms to represent the ribs of the vaults, linking hands with their neighbours

Figure 0.2 A human model of a Gothic cathedral.

and those opposite at what would be the bosses that often decorate the meeting of the ribs. The women then stood behind their husbands with their hands on their shoulders to act as the buttresses and flying buttresses (Figure 0.2).

The guide then placed his hands over the 'bosses' at the meeting of the ribs and lifted his weight off the ground hanging from the outstretched arms of the men. The result was that all could feel the forces thus created. To support his weight pressing down on their hands the men would be pushing upwards with their arms. But their arms pushed downwards on their shoulders, and because their arms were inclined inwards they pushed outwards. Except for the wives pushing inwards from behind the men would have staggered backwards and the edifice would have collapsed. The tourists at the cathedral, perhaps with no previous knowledge of building structures, were given an experience they would not forget and an immediate understanding of the structural behaviour of Gothic cathedrals.

Similarly, many people will be familiar with Baker's demonstration of the way that the Forth Bridge works (see Fig. 1.4). Baker was the designer of the bridge, and the photograph of his assistant being supported by two men with the aid of a couple of chairs and some struts is probably the most famous explanation of a structure. We can all imagine the forces in both these demonstrations because we all feel weights and forces when we lift or move something. We have all weighed something using a pair of scales, carried shopping, moved a piece of furniture and perhaps fixed a bracket to a wall. Some of us have played rugby and pushed in a scrum. All of these activities give us knowledge and experience of forces in action and so we can imagine the forces in structures in a similar way. Thus we all have the first requirement for understanding structures. Both demonstrations also illustrate what we will discover are called components of forces, but such knowledge is not necessary if all we want to understand is the cathedral or the bridge. However, if we want to go beyond these simple demonstrations we need to develop some general concepts to make up the bag of tools. In fact there are not that many, as will be shown by a glance at the Appendix, which sets out the elements of the grammar.

The other aspect of this approach is that it is about how we look at structures. It would be foolish to assume the ancients had no understanding of structural behaviour even though they did not have the panoply of mathematical tools that we use today. Of course, structures have changed since the ancients, and the way that we look at them has also changed, but design is often dependent upon the way that we look at things. The word 'truss' means something quite different to a present-day engineer compared with its meaning to an eighteenth century carpenter, in spite of similar principles applying to both. So much so that engineers who have not looked at early structures have sometimes been confused by the terminology. There are historical examples of engineers who have made imaginative leaps in design by looking at structures in a different way from their contemporaries. A tendency to plunge into calculations before developing a good qualitative understanding ties one to standard solutions. Work is no substitute for thought – but it's often so much easier to let the computer do the work.

This then is a book for architectural students but also one that can be read by anyone who might want or need to understand the basics of building structures but has little or no mathematics. It will help archaeologists and architectural historians for whom an ignorance of the subject must limit interpretations of their material because this is such an important aspect of building. It might equally be useful for those who work with engineers in dealing with historic buildings, and, being a book that is simple to follow, perhaps for all who are interested in understanding the nature and history of the built world around them. My sister, who once asked me about the jettying of timber-framed buildings, might find that it answers the question for her. Being able to understand the structure of buildings might have practical use for administrators of historic buildings but it may simply provide a richer insight for those whose leisure involves visiting and looking at them. It might also be of use to engineering students, who might well benefit from a glimpse at real structures.

The approach adopted within each chapter is to develop a structural idea using very simple examples and then to use those ideas to explain apparently much more complex structures. For example, we begin with the Forth Bridge likened to a simple wall bracket. Many of the examples used are of historic structures but this is not intended to be a history of structural ideas nor of structural design. (Readers who want to go on to explore those subjects will find recommended reading in footnotes.) It could not be that kind of book because the structures used as examples are not dealt with in chronological order but simply as they serve to illustrate the structural issues and, as the Forth Bridge shows, some very basic structural ideas have been used in some comparatively recent structures. The cantilever bridge is a later development than truss bridges, arched bridges or suspension bridges, which all require more complex ideas for their understanding. The reader will have to bear with some jumping backwards and forwards historically so that the structural ideas can be developed simply with interesting examples.

In this book we are going to look at how buildings behave and worry about the theorems afterwards. But like the language books designed for the communication approach that have summaries of the grammar in an appendix, the same has been done here with some basic concepts that one can look up as one needs to. The first step in the process is to turn the structures that we want to understand into simple line diagrams – a process of abstraction that at the very least simplifies the drawing. The human models are developed into line diagrams with arrows showing the forces. The weight of the cathedral guide pulls downwards on adjacent 'bosses' formed by the clasped hands. The men's arms push upwards against this but there is a downward force on their shoulders that is also trying to push them back while their wives push inwards. Similarly, the weight of Baker's assistant is carried by tension forces in the men's arms and compression forces in the wood struts and, as we shall see, these forces can be represented by arrows showing their direction, reducing the drawings to much simpler line drawings. Much of the book will be about developing the skill to reduce complex structural situations to such simple line diagrams in order to help understanding.

Teachers might find that subjects are not treated in the order normally found in structures texts. As I wrote, I discovered that the more normal order did not suit my approach. The buckling of columns had to be dealt with in the first chapter to understand the events described. Normally it is something that would be left until much later in a course, and is something that requires a certain amount of mathematics. Here it is only dealt with in a qualitative way because anything more than that would require mathematics that I assume the reader not to have. The order that I have chosen is to begin with bridges because these can be treated as two-dimensional structures – and little more than simple structures. I then go on to buildings where what is structure might not be immediately obvious. There the order is to look first at walls and then frames, the support structures, and then the parts of the building that they support, the floors and the roof. This does not entirely divide the subject neatly by the structural ideas used because, while floors are structures in bending and the chapter is used to introduce that subject, there is also bending in frames. Readers might well find that a strict sequential reading of the text is neither necessary nor perhaps desirable.

This ordering has a supplementary message, which is that the structure of a building is not something apart; it is intimately associated with the construction of the building. It is not something to be added on at the end but should be thought about as the design progresses. Of course engineers are often involved with buildings where the structure is only thought about when it has to be, and so when irrevocable decisions have already been made. This is usually to the detriment of the design and incurs unnecessary costs for the client. Perhaps this is something that clients should be aware of, that money spent on early structural advice is well worthwhile and could save them money in the end. Thus, this is not just about the analysis of structures, it is also about how they are designed, the forces that shape the design and the choices that designers make, taking into account the nature of the task to be performed, the materials that they have to hand and, in some cases, the skills to work those materials.

There are technical issues to be understood but technical terms are explained as they are encountered in the text. They are also defined in a glossary, which may provide handy revision notes for students or as a reminder to others if they forget something. The words are identified in the text by being in italics the first time they are used. Some are simply words used for components of a building, commonly understood by those in the building trade but not necessarily by those outside it. Others are the names given to structural ideas.

A little simple algebra is required, but do not be afraid because this is no more complicated than the balancing of a seesaw. When a child sits at one end, its much heavier parent knows to sit much closer to the pivot to be able to balance it. Again this is something we have all experienced so that a simple algebraic description of the principles should not be a problem, and that is the only algebra needed in the book. The other mathematics is a little geometry and the drawing of graphs; but perhaps I have said too much here. Many readers might not recognise the understanding of such diagrams as mathematics and might be frightened off if they thought of it as such. But we all see graphs presented to show the rise and fall of prices or the stock market, and surely we can all play with a ruler and compasses. Occasionally there may be a few algebraic manipulations and a little trigonometry, but working through these is not necessary for an understanding of the general ideas and so they may be omitted. To make this clear some passages are set in boxes within the text to identify those that can be ignored if you wish. There will also be some structural concepts that are for the more mathematically able reader but these are treated in the same way and may also be ignored. As a teacher I am also aware that people see things in different ways so that some approaches will not appeal to all. If there is repetition in the explanations that is why; it is to provide alternatives that I hope will accommodate the needs of different readers.

Something needs to be said about notation because the forces, shown by arrows, need to be identified as do some of the dimensions. There is something of a convention in this. Loads are generally given the letter W (W for weight presumably). Reactions, the forces supporting a structure that respond to the load (i.e. react to it), may be given the letter R. Where there are both horizontal and vertical reactions they get the letters H and V. The letters P and Q are also commonly used for forces. Of course the letter F is also used from time to time to stand for a force. In many diagrams there will be more than one of the same kind of force, for example two horizontal forces or two reactions. To distinguish them a number is placed after the letter as a subscript – thus R_1 and R_2 (R one and R two). Occasionally, it is simpler to add a mark above the letter, thus H and H′ (H and H prime). If you wish to draw your own diagrams you are of course free to invent your own notation, C for compression and T for tension, for example. Stresses get the lower case f and deflections the Greek ∂ (delta).

Dimensions are also given letters. While the span of beams is given the letter l (l for length?) the height of a roof structure or arch is given a lower case h. This is probably the only letter that appears in one form as a force and in the other as a dimension; normally convention keeps the two distinct. Other symbols found for dimensions are d and a. Note that if there are two diagrams next to each other where the same letters are being used this is not to imply that they represent the same numerical values (unless the text specifically says that this is so). For those unfamiliar with the notation it is also necessary to note that I have used the convention of a full stop to represent multiplication. This is to avoid any possible confusion between the multiplication sign and the letter x. Thus A multiplied by $B = A \times B = A.B$.

A word about the writing style. I am a teacher and used to standing in front of a class and speaking to them. That is how I imagine you, my reader, and so there are no third person circumlocutions, and not that much use of the third person otherwise. The first person has been liberally used, mostly in the plural. A former student who read my first draft said she could hear me speaking and I have tried to keep to that spirit. And that brings me to my acknowledgements. The first includes all the students in the first classes that I taught at what was then Oxford Polytechnic, many of whom were older than me and who taught me the rudiments of building construction while I taught them the rudiments of structural design. It was there that I learnt of the relationship between construction and the structural principles involved. My former student who was to do the drawings sadly died before being able to do the work and her younger son made drawings for me. I have only been able to keep a few but thank him for those I have used. I need to thank all those, and there are many, who, when I mentioned the idea of this book, told me that it was just what they needed and so encouraged me to continue with the idea. And of those, I need to thank Aylin Orbasli, who put me in touch with my editor and his appreciation of the publishing possibilities. Finally, Charles Goldie deserves thanks for checking one or two pieces of mathematics that I drew upon but which you, my reader, will not have to worry about.

David Yeomans

1 Brackets and Bridges

Figure 1.1 Failure of the Dee railway bridge, 1846.

When civil engineers in Canada graduate they are given a steel ring, to be worn on the little finger of their writing hand, which identifies them as graduate engineers. No doubt those who wear it see it as a kind of badge of honour, but they should see it as a constant warning because traditionally it was made from the steel of the first Quebec Railway Bridge, which collapsed during construction. The warning is simple; no matter how experienced you might be as an engineer – and Theodore Cooper, the consulting engineer for the Quebec Bridge, was very experienced – you can still have a failure. When the Dee railway bridge collapsed in England in 1846 (Figure 1.1) it might well have destroyed the reputation of Robert Stephenson, then Britain's leading railway engineer. Instead it led to a major enquiry because at that time the behaviour of iron railway structures was little understood. The same cannot be said of the Quebec Bridge – the story of its collapse is a human drama and a human tragedy. It involved no complex technical issues, as some engineering failures have, and Cooper's career ended in disaster rather than triumph. Most of the technical issues were very simple, with a structural type similar to the successful Forth Bridge, built just a few years earlier, so what could have gone wrong? To understand this involves understanding something of the process of design and having some very simple technical understanding of the structural principles involved. This collapse is an excellent introduction to the latter.

Cooper's tragedy

Theodore Cooper began his career as an assistant to another famous engineer, James Eades, on the St Louis Bridge, another very significant structure in the history of engineering. This elegant three-span arch bridge over the Mississippi River, completed in 1874, was the first all steel bridge; bridges up to then had been in cast and wrought iron. Cooper then had a long and successful career as a bridge engineer, but he had never built a really long span, so that his appointment by the Quebec Bridge Company as consulting engineer for a railway bridge over the St Lawrence River must have suited both him and the bridge company. The bridge company had the services of the leading North American bridge engineer, while Cooper had an opportunity to build what he would surely have seen as his crowning achievement. Instead it was to be a disaster, and his career ended with a major failure instead of a record-breaking span. This was to be a cantilever bridge rather like the Firth of Forth Bridge, with cantilevers extending from either shore and a suspended span between them. With the south side cantilever completed and the suspended span under construction, the cantilever suddenly collapsed and over 80 men working on the bridge at the time lost their lives.

By then in his early 60s, Cooper had been reluctant to travel frequently from his New York office to Quebec to inspect the work in progress and instead relied upon the services of a young assistant, Norman McClure, just as Eades had relied upon him in the construction of the St Louis Bridge when he was a young man. Unfortunately this assistant proved too inexperienced, or perhaps lacked sufficient self-confidence, and when things began to go wrong there were conflicts of opinion in which his voice was insufficiently firm. But at the same time all was not well within Cooper's office. He was understaffed for the magnitude of the task so that the true situation was not appreciated. The result was fatal delays in taking the action that might have prevented the collapse and saved those lives.

Of course, failures are not unknown. There had been bridge failures before and there were to be failures to follow, but of the most famous failures that of the Quebec Bridge stands out because it did not involve any principles that were unknown at the time, something that has not been true of some other significant collapses. The Dee Bridge on the Chester and Holyhead Railway collapsed when a train was crossing it and there was some loss of life. This bridge used a combination of wrought and cast iron in a form that had been used on other bridges but was in principle simply wrong. What was significant about that collapse was that it led to a government enquiry into the use of cast iron in railway bridges. Railway construction then involved longer spans than had been built before and much heavier loads so that engineers were stepping into unknown territory. While the design of this bridge was wrong in principle it was not obvious to engineers at the time that this was so, and the report of the commission of enquiry provides a good insight into contemporary engineering knowledge.[1] Stephenson's career survived this failure and he went on to complete the spectacular Conway and Britannia tubular bridges on the railway line to Holyhead, and the Victoria Bridge over the St Lawrence at Montreal.

Sir Thomas Bouch was not so lucky when his Tay Bridge collapsed in a storm in 1879, taking with it a train and the lives of all those on board. The bridge had scarcely been com-

---

[1] *The Report of the Commissioners appointed to inquire into the Application of Iron to Railway Structures*, 1847.

pleted and the inquiry into that disaster revealed a story that included poor construction, and irresponsible use by the engine drivers, who were in the habit of ignoring the speed limit and racing the ferry across the river.[2] But it also became clear that Bouch had not taken wind loads into proper account in his design. This was not something that bridge engineers had taken much note of until then, but the failure now concentrated minds on the issue, and it was certainly taken into account in the design of the Forth Bridge.

It was wind that was also to bring down the Tacoma Narrows Bridge in 1940, although it was not a particularly severe wind that caused the problem, nor was the bridge a particularly long span. It was, however, the most slender suspension bridge that had been built up to that time, and the wind produced aerodynamic effects that had not been previously recognized. Because of its slenderness it twisted in the wind (Figure 1.2) in a way that exaggerated the effect of what became known as vortex shedding, until the bridge was destroyed. The replacement bridge was made much stiffer and since then engineers have been aware of the need to guard against this kind of failure, sometimes using wind tunnel tests to explore the behaviour of their bridge decks.

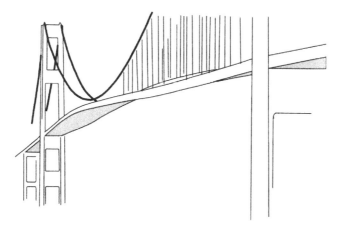

Figure 1.2 Tacoma Narrows Bridge twisting in the wind.

These three failures all occurred when engineers were pushing at the boundaries of what was then known. When buildings are built higher, or bridges have longer spans, there is always the possibility that one will discover some aspect of the structure's behaviour that was not previously recognised. But the span of the Quebec Bridge was not that much greater than that of the Forth Bridge, less than 10% longer, so that should not have been an issue. What Cooper also did, however, was to design for higher stresses in the steel than had been used previously, something that will be dealt with in more detail later in the chapter, and

[2] *The Inquiry into the Tay Bridge Disaster*, 1880.

this in part was his undoing. But the structural issues come down to too much load on members that were too weak – and it is the reason for this that needs to be explained.

The Forth Bridge

In building a bridge across a wide body of water an engineer has to balance two difficulties: the difficulty of having a long span (or several long spans) and the difficulty of making foundations in the river. The simplest iron or steel bridge structure is just a series of girders resting on piers. The ill-fated Tay Bridge had been just that, and so is its replacement that is still in service today, but these designs required a great many piers and so a great many underwater foundations. When Baker came to bridge the Firth of Forth he chose to limit his foundations to shallow water and an island and build gigantic cantilever structures to span across the gaps between them (Figure 1.3). A cantilever is a structure that is supported at one end only, unlike a beam, which is supported at both ends. A simple example is a shelf bracket, but Baker's design involved cantilevering out in both directions from each of the supports, double cantilevers, like brackets fixed back to back.

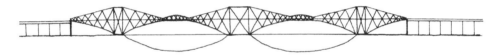

Figure 1.3 The Forth Bridge.

To explain this design Baker made a now famous demonstration to show exactly how it would work. He had his assistant, Kaichi Watanabe, sit on a board to represent the weight of one of the suspended spans supported between the cantilevers. The board was supported by a pair of inclined wooden struts while two men sitting on chairs with their arms held out grasped the ends of these struts. The men, their arms, the struts and the chairs they sat on represented these massive double cantilever structures and, with counterbalancing weights, they were able to support the weight of Baker's assistant on the suspended board.

This has become such a well-known demonstration because we can all understand it by imagining the forces in our own bodies if we were one of the men sitting on the chairs helping to support Watanabe's weight. The wooden struts must be there; pushing upwards or the men would not be able to hold their arms out to support his weight. Their arms must be holding the ends of the timber struts and pulling inwards on them or these struts would collapse downwards, rotating about their supports. The counterweights at either end must be there or the two men, the struts and their chairs would topple into the centre.

Figure 1.4 is based on the photograph of the time, reducing it to a simple line drawing, but we could reduce it still further to a diagram of forces, by simply removing the drawings of the men and leaving the lines representing the forces. That is how engineers represent structures. In the diagram, Watanabe's weight is represented by an arrow that pushes downwards on the suspended board. The struts are pushing upwards against this weight and the forces in these struts can also be represented by arrows. As they push upwards against the

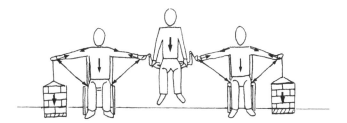

Figure 1.4 Baker's demonstration of the Forth Bridge.

board on which Watanabe sits they push downwards on the chairs, but they also push outwards against the hands of the men holding them and whose arms pull inwards against this force. Again arrows represent the forces in the men's arms: they pull inward on the ends of the struts but at the same time are pulling on their shoulders in the other direction. Of course the counterweights produce similar forces on the other side of the men and adding more arrows there completes a diagram of forces within the demonstration structure (ignoring for the moment the forces in the men's bodies and their own weight). All that is now required is to add in the upward forces from the ground under the chairs because all structures are eventually supported by the ground.

Rather than do that with Baker's demonstration we can do it with a diagram of the structure of the bridge. The cantilevers were built first; Figure 1.5a shows what the structure looked like before the suspended spans were added, the weight of the structure being equally distributed across the foundations.

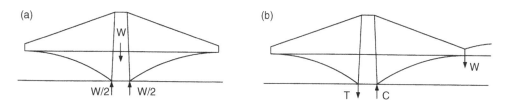

Figure 1.5 The cantilever support forces with **(a)** self-weight alone, and **(b)** load of the suspended span alone.

In the demonstration Watanabe's weight is balanced at either end by heavy weights, and the simple diagram of the bridge shows why these were needed. If the main structure weighed nothing, a suspended span would put a load on the ends of the cantilever arms that, if not counterbalanced by some weight on the other side, would lift the structure off the opposite foundation and it would have to be tied down – as shown by the arrow marked T. The weight of the main structure itself, and the span on the other side prevent this from occurring.

We can see from this that there are two ways of looking at a structure. We can consider its overall behaviour, as in Figure 1.5, and think about the forces at the ground that are necessary to support it, or we look at what is happening inside it, as in Figure 1.4, looking at what happens at the ends of each member. This second way of thinking about a structure, taking each of the joints between members in turn and imagining which way each member is pulling or pushing at it, is a fairly standard way of analysing a structure and drawing the forces in it. Notice that apart from the applied loads, Watanabe's weight and the two counterweights, the other forces, those in the members of the structure, are in pairs. The arms have pairs of arrows pointing inwards and we know that the arms are in tension as they pull inwards. The timber struts have pairs of arrows pointing outwards, and we know that these are in compression as they push outwards and upwards. Tension involves pulling and compression involves pushing.

Some grammar – actions and reactions

At this point it is appropriate to introduce a little grammar in the form of a term that we shall need later. The forces shown in the arms of the men and the timber struts would not exist if it were not for the loads that have been applied: Watanabe's weight on the suspended span and the counterweights. These loads are sometimes referred to as *actions* upon the structure, the forces generated in the members being *reactions* to them. This calls into mind Newton's third law, that for every action there is an equal and opposite reaction. This equality of action and reaction might not be so apparent here but we shall see how that works in the next chapter. But note that because the word 'load' is so commonly used we shall continue to use it, so that the forces generated in the structure are reactions to the applied loads.

Baker's design for the Forth Bridge required three of the double cantilever structures. The suspended spans between them were simple girders, and we shall look at how they work in the next chapter. The tension members of the cantilevers are straight lattice members, while the lower compression members are curved tubes. As the structures were cantilevers, once the foundations in the river had been completed and the central support structure erected above them, the equivalent of the chairs and the bodies of the men, the cantilevers could be built out on either side. At every stage the weight on one side of the central support would be balanced by the weight on the other. Moreover the cantilever arms would be working exactly as they would when the bridge was completed, i.e. with the top members in tension and the bottom in compression. Sometimes the forces in a structure during construction are different from those once it is completed, and that was so for the girders spanning between the cantilevers. They were designed so that when completed they would span like beams between their ends, but they were built by cantilevering from the ends of the main cantilever structures. When they met in the middle they could be joined together to form a beam. How exactly that was done need not concern us here; sufficient to say that it was successfully accomplished at the Forth, but over the St Lawrence, it was while this suspended span was being constructed that the collapse occurred.

Members in compression

The collapse at Quebec occurred because of failure of compression members. Members in compression cannot be made too small or they will collapse through buckling, something that can easily be demonstrated with some simple struts; garden canes will serve the purpose. Take a long thin garden cane and load it in compression. The cane will bend sideways under this load, as shown by the dotted lines in Figure 1.6, and if enough force is applied it will eventually break. One can readily imagine that if the struts of Baker's demonstration were made progressively smaller they would eventually collapse in the same way. Some simple experiments illustrate how the properties of a column affect the load that it can carry – changing the length of the cane for example. Garden canes are sold in different lengths and thicknesses. By cutting canes down to the lengths we want we can have two thin canes of different lengths and two long canes of different thicknesses. By applying loads to the ends of these until they buckle, it will immediately be apparent that the longer the cane the smaller the force that has to be applied to produce this buckling effect. The long thin cane will buckle under a smaller force than the short cane of the same thickness. A thicker cane of the same length will take a much larger load before buckling occurs.

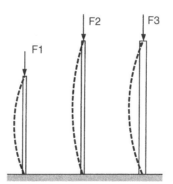

Figure 1.6 Column buckling.

If the forces shown in Figure 1.6 are those that cause the cane to buckle then F_2 is less than F_1 (normally represented as $F_2 < F_1$) because the second cane is longer. But as the third cane is thicker than the second, F_2 is less than F_3 ($F_2 < F_3$). (The symbol $<$ is read as 'less than' while the symbol $>$ is read as 'greater than'.)

Garden canes are almost solid circular columns and can bend just as easily in any direction. If a thin lath were used instead it would bend about the narrow dimension, and if this were progressively reduced it would eventually be unable to support even its own weight, just as a piece of paper cannot. Since a lath always buckles about its smaller dimension we might reasonably assume that a symmetrical section was the most efficient as a column, i.e. for the same cross-sectional area a square column would be better than a rectangular one. For a given cross-sectional area of material a circular tube is the best shape for members in compression, something that one might demonstrate by rolling a piece of paper into a tube. A sheet of paper that cannot support its own weight can be easily folded into a square tube or taped to make a circular one and will then stand upright and might even be made to carry a small load.

In Figure 1.7 a column shaped like 'a' will carry more weight than 'b' although both have the same cross-sectional area and so will have the same compressive *stress* for the same load. Column 'c' has twice the cross-sectional area of the other two but will carry more than twice the load of 'a' simply because of its shape.

Figure 1.7 Column cross-sections of equal area.

This shows clearly why tubes were used for the compression members of the Forth Bridge. The tension members at the top of the cantilevers are built up to the required size as square lattices with rolled angle sections riveted together. This would have been the simplest way of building up sufficient material to carry the forces. In contrast the tubes of the compression members at the bottom would have been more difficult to make but were known to be much more efficient in carrying the compressive load. The diagonal members between these are also tubes in one direction but lattices in the other so it is clear that the designer intended one set to work in compression while the others worked in tension.

The Quebec Bridge

The original design for the Quebec Bridge produced by the Phoenix Bridge Company was for a span of 1600 ft (480 m) but Theodore Cooper recommended increasing the span to 1800 ft (540 m), the intention being to move the bridge piers into shallower water, which would speed construction and so reduce the costs. This was important in a river that froze in winter, and it was a sensible suggestion, although all involved were aware of the fact that it would make the span greater than those of the Forth Bridge and therefore set something of a record; as such it would have been a fitting culmination to Cooper's distinguished career as a bridge engineer. The eventual dimensions are shown in Figure 1.8. The central span was to be 675 ft (205.74 m) with the cantilever arm supporting it 562 ft 6 in long (171.45 m). The landward cantilever span, called the anchor span, was slightly smaller at only 500 ft (152.4 m). Unlike the Forth Bridge, where lattice girders were used for the tension members, the Quebec Bridge used much simpler eye bars for the top chord of the cantilevers and the diagonal tension members. These are flat bars with holes at either end through which there were pins to join the bars together. Each 'member' would be built up from a number of such eye bars. The compression members comprised plates built up to form four flats then connected together with a lattice to make them all act together, rather than the tubes that Baker had used. From what has been said this might seem a strange decision. It is clearly not as structurally efficient as tubes but easier to make.

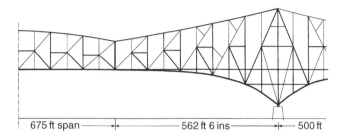

675 ft span ─────────┼─────────── 562 ft 6 ins ───────────┼── 500 ft

Figure 1.8 Quebec Bridge showing dimensions.

There had been some warning of the impending failure because deflections of the compression members had been noticed by McClure, who was overseeing the construction on Cooper's behalf, but his concerns were not acted upon. This was partly because of differences of opinion about the cause of the deflections, partly because of poor communications between the parties involved, and also because of lack of adequate authority on site. Cooper was in his office in New York and only receiving letters from his young assistant, expressing his concerns. The Phoenix Bridge Company, who were making the components for the bridge, claimed that what McClure saw as deflections in the members was simply because the members were not quite straight when brought to the bridge. But deflections measured on different days had shown that they were increasing: the bridge was beginning to collapse. At one stage the foreman of the construction crew had become concerned about the state of the structure and ordered his men off the bridge, but was then persuaded to let them back. Eventually McClure travelled to New York to discuss his concerns, and it then became clear that the weights of the suspended span that was in the process of being built was too great for the strength of the cantilevers. It seems that the weight had crept up in part because the connections between the members proved larger and therefore heavier than had been anticipated. Last-minute instructions from Cooper to stop work so that no more load was put on the structure arrived too late and at the end of the shift on 29 August 1907 the compression members on the south anchor span failed. Of 88 men on the bridge at the time only 11 survived the collapse.[3]

Forces in a bracket

The forces on the compression members were clearly larger than the members could have withstood, so either there was an error in calculating them or Cooper had been optimistic about the stresses that the steel could carry. Whatever the strength of the steel there was certainly an error in calculating the forces in the members, but this requires some explanation because it is not a difficult figure to find. If we knew the weight that the cantilever

[3]This can only be a brief account of the collapse. For a fuller account see Eda Kranakis, 'Fixing the Blame: Organizational Culture and the Québec Bridge Collapse', *Technology and Culture* 2004:45.3; 487–518; and William D. Middleton, *The Bridge at Québec*, Indiana University Press, Bloomington, IN, 2001.

had to carry we could estimate the forces ourselves. Cantilever bridges are rather like shelf brackets writ large, and most of us have had some experience of putting up a shelf bracket, and perhaps having one fail, when the forces acting become only too apparent.

To fix a bracket to a masonry wall, holes are first drilled in the wall to take the fixings. These take the form of plugs, nowadays made of plastic, with screws fixing the bracket to them. Each screw grips the plug but also forces the plastic against the sides of the hole in the masonry to develop the friction forces that hold it in place. But it is not always as simple as that. Sometimes, perhaps if we drill into soft mortar rather than into a brick, the top fixing fails, pulling out of the wall and allowing the bracket to rotate about the bottom fixing. The dotted lines of Figure 1.9 show the movement that will occur.

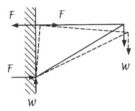

Figure 1.9 The virtual movement of a bracket under load.

This failure clearly shows the forces involved, and imagining the mechanism of failure is a useful way of understanding most structures. If it fails, how will it fail? In which direction will it move? Therefore what forces are required to prevent this movement? We can see from the bracket failure that the load on the end of it is trying to rotate it one way about the lower fixing (clockwise in the drawing) while the force in the upper fixing is trying to prevent this with a force that is producing a rotational effect in the other direction (counterclockwise). The two forces are different in magnitude but if the bracket is successfully fixed they must be producing equal but opposite rotational effects about the bottom fixing.

The forces are of different magnitude because their distances from the pivot are different. This is something that we should be familiar with. It occurs when a parent balances their child on a seesaw. The parent has to sit closer to the pivot than the child in order to balance the seesaw simply because of the difference in their weights. If the weights and distances are represented by their initial letters then a large **W**eight multiplied by a small **d**istance is balanced by a small **w**eight multiplied by a large **D**istance, i.e. W.d = w.D (W × d = w × D) (Figure 1.10). This is exactly the arithmetic of the bracket and the bridge. The turning, or rotational effect of a force about a point is called the *moment* of the force, i.e. 'moment' = 'turning effect', and it is convenient to use this word simply to avoid the longer two-word phrase. The moment (turning effect) of any force about a point is simply the product of that force and its distance from the point in question, sometimes called its lever arm (often but not always the pivot about which it might rotate). Notice that to complete the diagram of forces the force at the pivot has been included. Ignoring the weight of the seesaw itself this must be the sum of the weights of the two people sitting on it.

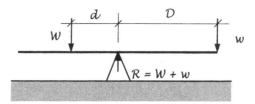

Figure 1.10 The forces on a seesaw.

The steelyard

There is a measuring device called a steelyard that uses just this principle. As heavier loads are placed upon it so the moveable weight has to be slid further along the arm to balance the device. Weights placed on the pan are indicated by distances along the arm.

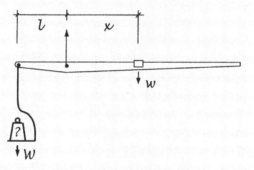

Figure 1.11

On one side there is an unknown weight W at a fixed distance l from the pivot while the fixed weight, w, is at a variable distance x from the pivot. The product W.l = w.x.

In the seesaw and the steelyard all the forces are vertical and the structure connecting them is a simple beam, whereas in the bracket one of the forces is horizontal and its distance from the point about which rotation is occurring is measured vertically up the wall (Figure 1.12a). Nevertheless, the principle remains the same. If the horizontal force is represented by the letter F and the height of the bracket by the letter h, then W.l = F.h, precisely the same arithmetic as the seesaw. The bracket also has the same forces in it as the cantilever bridge, although one of the members is horizontal and the other inclined. The lower member must be in compression pushing out on the end of the upper member and inwards on the wall. The upper member is pulling inwards on the end supporting the load and outwards on the wall. There also needs to be an upwards force at the wall to balance the downward force of the load on the end of the bracket.

Anyone who has difficulty with this might usefully read the first few pages of Chapter 8, which describe the process of putting up a ladder. This is the closest that we come to experiencing ourselves the effect of moments of forces with the forces in different directions.

Before leaving the simple bracket we should note that there is another way of arranging the forces. In Figure 1.12b a wooden shelf is assumed to be supported by a simple loop of string at either end. The string passes under the shelf, up the wall to some fixing and then down to the front of the shelf. The weight on the shelf is represented by the shaded area and we can assume that it acts in the middle of the shelf as shown. The string is naturally in tension, nothing else is possible, and it is the shelf that is providing the compression force at the bottom. If the weight to be carried is the same as before and the geometry is the same, the forces at the wall are half of the forces in Figure 1.12a simply because the weight has shifted inwards to the middle of the shelf.

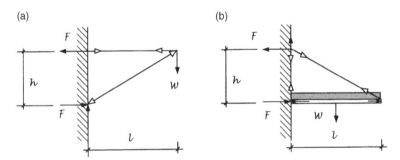

Figure 1.12 Two different brackets.

In the Forth Bridge, and in the design for the original Quebec Bridge, both of the bracket members are sloping and the lower member is curved. The latter, an aesthetic decision, complicates things a little but we can still treat the structure like a simple bracket. The compression in the lower member can be found if we know the weight of the suspended span and the geometry of the structure. In this case to find the compression in the lower member we need to consider moments about the top of the bracket, the point marked 'a' in Figure 1.13. This point rather than the bottom is considered as the pivot. The weight on the end of the bracket multiplied by its length is balanced against the force in the compression member multiplied by its distance from the pivot. Note that the distance is measured at right angles to the member, something that will be dealt with in more detail in Chapter 8. The horizontal line simply represents the internal viaduct, which plays no part in carrying the load of the suspended spans. In fact it places additional loads on the structure, which for the moment we shall ignore.

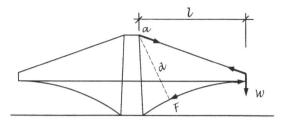

Figure 1.13 Principal forces in a bracket of the Forth Bridge.

It is possible to turn the verbal description into a simple equation. If the span is l and the load on the end of the cantilever is W then the moment about a is W.l. The resisting moment is the force in the bracket multiplied by its lever arm d, so that F.d = W.l and therefore (dividing both sides by d) F = W.l/d.

If the calculation is that simple then how was it that Cooper got it wrong? The answer to that is that he did not know accurately enough the weight of the suspended span, i.e. the magnitude of the weight W. Of course it was a little more complex than that because there was also the weight of the cantilever itself, which doubtless had also been underestimated, but the overall principle is the same. To understand how that happened we need to look at the process of the design.

The design process

'Begin at the beginning,' the King said, gravely, 'and go on till you come to the end: then stop.'

Alice's Adventures in Wonderland

If only it were that simple. Just as the design of the Quebec Bridge demonstrates a small number of structural principles it also shows some of the features of engineering design. The principal cause of the collapse was the failure of the engineers to make a proper estimate of the weight of the suspended span. While the function of a bridge is to carry some load across a gap, a great deal of what it is carrying is its own weight, which may be many times that of the load to be imposed upon it. The ideal is to start at the top and work down so that one knows the weight of each part before designing the structure to carry it, but the engineer cannot always do that, as the case of the Quebec Bridge shows. Any structure is built from the foundations up so that the first things required by the contractor are the drawings for the foundations, ideally the last thing to be designed – but engineering designs are seldom carried out under ideal conditions.

The Quebec Bridge Company was initially short of funds but when it was eventually known that there would be funds for the bridge it wanted work to start as soon as possible – it is always thus. As so often happens this means that detailed design and construction are proceeding at the same time. How then are we to be sure that the overall design is adequate, especially in a bridge where most of the load to be carried is its own weight? The answer is to make a guess – or rather an estimate, which is the word that engineers prefer to use.

Making an estimate like this might seem to be a rather crude way of determining the forces in a structure but it is something that engineers often do and is an essential part of the design process. In the early stage of a design the engineer has some ideas of what forms the structure might take and wants to know whether or not any particular idea is practical. Will it result in acceptable forces that can be accommodated or will they simply be too large? The engineer will probably have more than one idea and would like to compare them. To do this what is needed are simple 'back of an envelope' calculations just to give some idea of the forces involved. Such calculations might quickly rule out some impractical ideas, hence the engineering adage that 'a job worth doing is worth doing badly'. Of course the estimates used for such calculations are important and if they are wrong there can be problems later in the design process as the engineer has to find ways of dealing with unexpectedly large forces.

A similar process is carried through into the design proper as estimates are made of the foundation loads on the assumption of the weights of the superstructure. One of the more recent buildings where this caused a serious problem was in the design of the Sydney Opera House. It originally assumed that this would comprise relatively thin shell structures and the foundations were designed on the basis of the weights of such shells. In the event that was not possible and a much heavier structure based on arches was adopted. Thus the already constructed foundations had to be strengthened.

There is clearly a certain amount of engineering judgement in such early estimates, dramatically demonstrated by the Quebec Bridge failure. The superstructure of the Quebec Bridge can be divided into two parts, the structure of the cantilevers and that of the suspended span between them. Just as the foundations had to be designed before the superstructure, so the cantilevers had to be designed before the designs for the suspended span were completed. Therefore the cantilever design had to be based upon an estimate of the weights coming onto them. As the design proceeds the calculations should be refined but, in this case, even though the suspended span had been designed and was being constructed no one had checked the weights to compare them with the original estimate, which in the event proved disastrously low. With detailed design and construction pressing ahead after initial delays, accurate figures were not produced until rather late, and it was only when McClure had pointed out the buckling of the members that mistakes were realised. Long before Cooper sent the telegram ordering work to be stopped, so that no more load should be put on the cantilevers, the latter were already carrying a much larger load than the structure was designed for.

Stresses

The problem was exacerbated by Cooper's assumption of high stresses in the steel. The question is: how much stress will a material carry before it fails? It is possible to ensure low stresses simply by using more material, but one of the definitions of an engineer is someone who can do for a shilling what any fool can do for two. The idea is to use as little material as possible. As the Quebec Bridge Company was short of funds, Cooper, as well as increasing the span, proposed to allow high stresses in the steel as an economy measure. By designing for a higher stress he reduced the quantity of material needed and so saved money, and as this is such a central aspect of engineering design it is sensible to tackle the definition of stress.

If we stand on a piece of blackboard chalk it will crush under our weight, but use a block of chalk large enough and it will carry our weight. It is not the force that a material carries that causes it to fail but the stress within it, which is defined as the force per unit area. If we wanted to suspend a heavy load we would all be aware that it would be better to use a steel wire than a piece of string of the same diameter. The steel wire would be capable of carrying a higher stress and therefore a greater load. Figure 1.14 shows how stress is measured. The column has a compressive force in it that is acting along the column. The area, A, the cross-sectional area of the column, is at right angles to the direction in which the force is acting and the stress is the magnitude of the force divided by this area.

The stress is simply the load divided by the area of material that is carrying it. In Figure 1.14 the weight on the column exerts a force P on the column, which has a cross-sectional area A. Therefore the stress in the column is simply P/A.

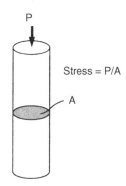

P

Stress = P/A

A

Figure 1.14 Stress.

If the engineer begins by knowing the forces in a member the question is then how much stress might be safely allowed in the material that is to carry that force, something that is found by loading materials to failure. The results provide the data that engineers use for sizing the members of their structures. The problem is a little more complex than that because excessive deflection might be regarded as a failure. Also, as we have already seen, failure of long members in compression occurs because of buckling, which involves a more complex calculation of behaviour than we can deal with here. Nevertheless the allowable stress is still the place to start.

At the time of the construction of the Quebec Bridge, steel was still a relatively new material in structures. True it had been used by Eades, Cooper's former employer, on the St Louis Bridge, but the tendency had been to use the same safety factors for steel as those that had been used for wrought iron.[4] If higher stresses could be allowed then the quantity of steel used, and hence the cost, would be reduced. This was Cooper's strategy, but here he was sailing into the unknown, and seems to have gone beyond what other engineers were to regard as prudent. When the bridge was redesigned, both lower stresses and a different profile were used, resulting in a much greater weight of steel. But there was also the form of the compression members that did not behave as assumed. Tubes were more difficult to fabricate but the lattice joining the steel flats together was inadequate for its task. The collapse led to concerns about the design of the Queensboro Bridge, New York, which was then under construction; consequently its loading was reduced by having fewer train tracks across it than originally intended. Engineers either learn by their own mistakes or by the mistakes of others.

[4]Pugsley, Sir Alfred, *The Safety of Structures*, Edward Arnold, London, 1996, pp. 34–35.

2 Stiffening a Beam – Girder Bridges

Figure 2.1 Todentanzbrucke, Lucerne, by Frank Brangwyn (copyright David Brangwyn).

An obvious question to ask of the Forth and Quebec Bridges is why are they so large and complex? What is the reason for throwing all that steel into the air? Could it not have been simpler? The ill-fated Tay Bridge, built just a few years before the Forth and Quebec bridges, had been a simple matter of piers in the river and girders spanning between them, and other girder bridges, not that dissimilar in design, were successfully carrying railways over deep valleys without any problems. The Forth Bridge was not a response to what had proved to be an unsuccessful design; Bouch, who had designed the Tay Bridge, had already produced a design for a bridge over the Forth every bit as complex as the one actually built. The principal lesson learnt by engineers from the Tay's collapse was the need to take proper account of wind forces, and although that would have affected the detailed design of the Forth Bridge it does not account for its overall form. Instead, what is evident from the site of the bridge was the way in which Baker managed to make use of shallow water and an island of rock in the Firth for his foundations. The balance to be struck by all bridge engineers is that between the difficulty of building long spans and that of constructing the supports. Using these places for support was an attractive approach in an otherwise deep tidal estuary, and it was a similar consideration that had caused Cooper to lengthen the proposed span of the Quebec Bridge. He wanted the brackets to be closer to the shore and in shallower water in a river that froze in winter.

The balance is simple to understand; the shorter the spans the more supports one requires. Conversely, the fewer the supports the more complex must be the structures spanning between them. When the task is to cross a river and the foundations have to be built in the water there is a problem of scour around the foundations as well as the difficulty of building in water. Scour was a particular problem for early masonry arch bridges where the supports were large compared with the spans between them. In some situations the supports within the river may also be vulnerable to damage by debris being carried downstream in times of flood. It is no wonder that designers looked for larger spans.

The simplest kind of bridge that we can imagine is just to span a beam across a gap, perhaps in its earliest form a tree trunk thrown across a stream. In more sophisticated times timber has been converted to rectangular shapes, and several timbers laid side by side to form a deck that is easy to walk upon or take a cart across. Such a simple structure is limited to the length of timbers that can be obtained, and the load it can carry depends upon their strength and stiffness, but it nevertheless formed the basis of some simple bridges. The earliest recorded was Caesar's military bridge across the Rhine, but Caesar only provided a written account of it, so the drawings that we have are those made several centuries after the event and based on his description. Figure 2.2 is Palladio's interpretation of Caesar's text, the best known of the drawings made. The bridge comprised a series of beams over trestle supports. What Caesar wanted was a rapidly built structure that was as simple as possible, and driving piles into the river at intervals was the way to achieve this. The bridge would only be temporary and the loads on it not that great.

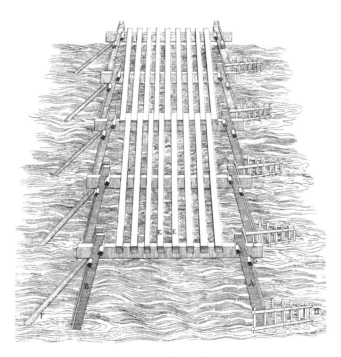

Figure 2.2 Caesar's military bridge according to Palladio.

Palladio's reconstruction shows simple frames of three members buttressed downstream by the members marked F against the pressure of the water. One of the important aspects of the bridge was the way in which the cross beams were keyed to the piers by the simple timber blocks, marked D, set in notches cut into the timbers to be joined. The upstream supports A were protected by fence-like structures. They would forestall the possibility of an enemy launching logs into the river above the bridge in an attempt to damage it. Even for such a simple timber structure longer spans would have been preferable but as the span increases so too does the deflection of the beams. There is also a practical limit to the size of beam that one can use, either because of the availability of timber or the problems of handling large and therefore heavy pieces during construction. The simplest way of reducing the deflection of a beam is simply to strut it from below. Here is another compromise the designer must make, that between complexity and weight of structure, the former presenting problems of design, the latter practical problems of construction. Caesar's simple construction provides nowhere from which the beams could be strutted, but strutting was adopted in a large number of timber bridges and is such a simple device that Caesar must surely have known of it. Simplicity of supports, which would have facilitated rapid construction, seems to have been his intention.

The simplest strutting arrangement is to have a pair of struts from either side propping the centre of each span (Figure 2.3a). The struts must be in compression to stop the beams from deflecting and they must be attached to the piers to stop them from sliding down them. This is not very efficient because longer spans can be achieved by separating the struts so that the beams are each supported at two points along the span (Figure 2.3b), in which case the distance between the piers is more than three times as long as an unassisted beam of the same *scantling* can span with acceptable deflections. Obviously, there will need to be a pair of struts for every beam in the deck, and in both arrangements shown the function of the struts is to push upwards against the underside of the beams.

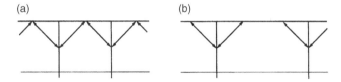

Figure 2.3 Strutting of a simple timber deck.

To achieve this requires appropriate construction details, the complexity of design that has been referred to. Imagine first a single span bridge between masonry piers where the beams are strutted from the piers. Obviously the struts need something to support them, and the simplest arrangement is to project small corbels from the masonry for them to sit on. If the struts are pushing upwards against the underside of the beams they must be pushing downwards against the corbels as shown (Figure 2.4). But because they are sloping they will also be pushing outwards against the faces of the masonry. We know this from the fact that if we try to lean on an inclined walking stick it will tend to slide away from us. Only friction or some convenient stop will prevent this from happening. Thus we can imagine the compressive force in the struts being resisted by two forces at each support, an upward force

Figure 2.4 The forces at the end of the struts.

from the corbel and a horizontal force pushing inward from the masonry. At the top of the struts there must also be some arrangement to stop their ends from sliding inwards along the beam and also to hold them in place and stop them falling into the river. This might be done by notching the beams so that the struts rest against the notches or perhaps more simply by putting another horizontal strut under the deck between the ends of the two inclined struts (Figure 2.5). The latter is simpler because it avoids the need for the carpentry of the notches.

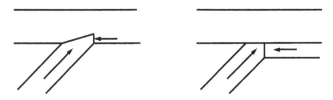

Figure 2.5 Restraining the top of the struts.

Some grammar – components of forces

The inclined struts are supported by corbels built into the masonry. As the struts push down on the corbels, so the corbels push up to support them. But at the same time the struts push outwards against the walls of the abutments that prevent them from sliding along the corbel, so the walls must be pushing back against the struts. Thus, an inclined force in a strut results in two resisting reactions, one vertical and the other horizontal. These can be thought of as resisting two *components of the force* in each strut, i.e. the inclined force in each strut can be thought of as having a vertical and a horizontal component, each of which is resisted by an equal and opposite reaction in the support. We have seen the components of a force in the bracket. The force in the inclined leg of the bracket has vertical and horizontal components. At the wall these are resisted by vertical and horizontal reactions produced by the fixing (Figure 1.12). At the outer end the vertical component of this inclined force is the reaction to the load hung on the bracket, while the horizontal component is equal and opposite to the tension force in the top member of the bracket. We will deal with this in more detail in the next chapter.

This was exactly the structure of the Bassano Bridge designed by Palladio (Figure 2.6). This bridge, with its roof supported on an arcade of columns, is a little more elaborate than most but strip off the superstructure above the deck and it has the same basic structure; beams stiffened by inclined struts with short horizontal struts to keep the inclined struts in place. Notice that Palladio shows how the struts are prevented from sliding down the posts by what appear to be collars. The result is as if the beams were being supported by 'arches', each comprising three pieces of timber all in compression (Figure 2.7). However, the beams that form the deck are not simply passive elements applying loads to these three-member arches, they are also a necessary part of the structure because if they were removed the struts could not stand by themselves.

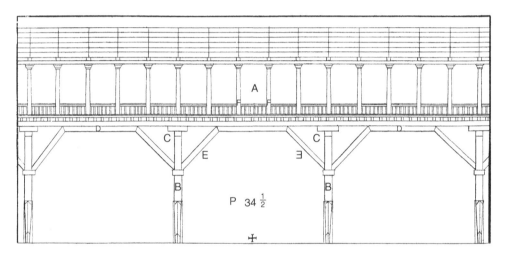

Figure 2.6 Bassano Bridge designed by Palladio.

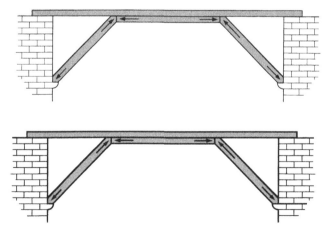

Figure 2.7 Strutting a simple beam bridge.

What we have without the deck is a mechanism rather than a structure (Figure 2.8), something that can freely distort. This particular mechanism is called a four bar chain (the ground being the fourth bar). Placing a deck beam over the top prevents this combination of struts from moving feely. For the struts to move in this way the deck would be bent downwards under the load and upwards over the other support (Figure 2.9). Clearly, there is going to be a little movement when load is applied because the deck beams are not infinitely stiff, i.e. they will bend a little, but this demonstrates that the deck is as much part of the structure as the supporting struts.

Figure 2.8 Four-bar chain.

Figure 2.9 Deflections caused by a point load.

If the structure has no weight the deck tries to rise upwards at the end farthest from the load and the strut at that end will have to go into tension. There will also need to be some hold-down force at the supports at that end. If the self-weight of the bridge is large compared with the load there will already be compression in the struts so that all the load does is reduce the forces a little in the struts on one side. This is shown in Figure 2.10, where the shaded area represents the self-weight of the bridge and the struts are drawn at different thicknesses to suggest different forces.

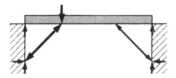

Figure 2.10 Effect of a point load on the strut forces.

Clearly, it is important that the deck beams are continuous where they are supported by the inclined struts, and one might wonder why this is different from a pair of brackets supporting a suspended beam between them. The difference is that the brackets would require the supporting masonry to provide horizontal forces at the top, i.e. at deck level, pulling outwards with the deck being in tension just as in Figure 1.12a. Instead there are only vertical forces at the top to support the deck and any load on it.

The simple truss

The Bassano Bridge survives to this day but the timbers there now are not those of the original bridge. The disadvantage of bridges that rely upon piers in the river is that both the piers and the struts below the deck are vulnerable to debris carried down the river during floods, with the result that the Bassano Bridge has been damaged and repaired a number of times. Thus, while this simple structural arrangement is ideal if the bridge is high above the water, and if the abutments can resist the outward thrust of the inclined struts, there are many situations in which it is better to raise the supports above the deck where they are no longer so vulnerable. This means that the deck must be hung from some kind of structure, which involves a radical difference in the structure of the deck itself. Now, instead of every beam being strutted from below they must all be carried on cross beams, rather like the trestle beams of Caesar's bridge, and it is these cross beams that are supported by the main structure.

If the strutting arrangements, i.e. compression members, are placed above and either side of the deck instead of below it, the cross beams can be supported by hangers from the junctions of these members. The deck of the bridge is tied up to the compression structure, and this explains the use of the term 'truss' to describe this kind of structure – to truss simply means to tie up. In this arrangement the abutments no longer have to resist the outward thrust of the struts because these can be connected to the beam across the bottom, which therefore has to act as a tie. Engineers apply the term 'top chord' to the assembly of compression members in such a truss, while the tension members are the bottom chord. (Of course, in a cantilever structure it is the top chord that is in tension and the bottom chord that is in compression.)

This is not only a more complex structure but also one that involves much larger forces because only two arch-like arrangements of struts are carrying a load that was previously carried by as many sets of struts as there were beams in the deck. As the deck beams forming the bottom chord of the truss are now in tension they either have to be single members or means must be found to join timbers together in such a way that tension forces can be transmitted across the joints. But the structure in Figure 2.11b also needs the continuity of the deck beam if it is to work as a structure as did the beam with the three-member arch below it. The framework now comprises two triangles and a rectangle. Fasten three members together to form a triangle and it will be rigid, but four members pinned together to form a rectangle will not be – it will be a four-bar chain. One can imagine this structure distorting

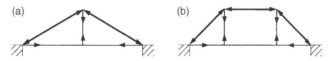

Figure 2.11 **(a)** Two-member and **(b)** three-member top chords.

just like that in Figure 2.8, so that the stiffness of the bridge deck must again be restricting its movement. If the lower chord beams cannot be made sufficiently stiff, the solution is to put diagonal members across the rectangle to form stiff triangles.

These two basic structural forms also appear in roofs, where they are called respectively king post and queen post trusses. We will therefore be returning to these structures in Chapter 8; the basic queen post truss was used in some bridges, as can be seen in the wood-block print of the Todentanzbrucke, Lucerne, shown in Figure 2.1.[1] Although partly clad to protect the structural timbers, the inclined struts, the posts and the straining beam between the posts can be clearly seen. In this case there are three spans visible so the builder considered it simpler to place more piers in the river than to have a more complex structure. The sizes of the timbers used can be gauged against the figures on the bridge; they are clearly massive. However, it is likely that the lower chord of the truss was built up from two or more timbers keyed together as in the bridge shown in Figure 2.14.

These simple bridge trusses would have a rather limited span, but longer spans can be achieved with more complex trusses. The design for the Cismone Bridge, by Palladio (Figure 2.12), used a combination of king post and queen post trusses that can be understood by deconstructing Palladio's drawing of the bridge.

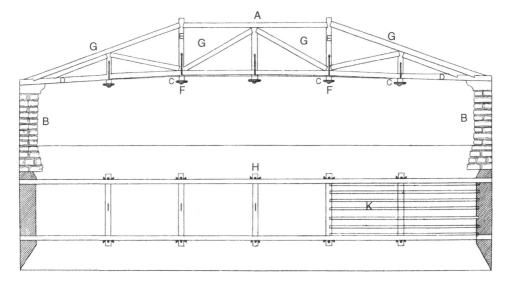

Figure 2.12 Cismone Bridge, by Palladio.

The plan shows the deck carried by five cross beams, which are supported by five hangers. The hangers were attached to the cross beams by bolts and metal connectors, but Palladio's drawing is not clear about that. He shows the metal straps but not how these supported the deck beams.

---

[1] The name derives from decorations on the bridge depicting the Dance of the Dead.

'These [posts] are bound with the beams with iron which we will call cramps, passing through a hole made for that purpose in the heads of the said beams, in that part which advances beyond the beams that form the sides.

These cramps, because they are in the upper part along the said upright and plain [posts], are perforated in several places. And in the upper part, near the said thick beams, by one hole, sufficiently large that they are driven into the [posts], and flattened afterwards underneath with iron bolts . . . .'

The inclined struts are notched into the hangers so that if the latter tried to drop under the action of the loads on them, they would pull on the ends of the struts. The apparent complex arrangement of these struts can be simplified by dividing it into two structures (Figure 2.13). First there is a queen post truss with three timbers in compression and two hangers to support two cross beams. Then, inside these, and so supported by the hangers, are three smaller king post trusses that support the other three cross beams. This is certainly how Palladio would have envisaged his structure.

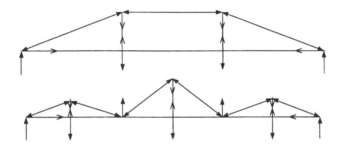

Figure 2.13 Deconstruction of the Cismone Bridge.

Palladio claimed that the horizontal beams at the bottom of this framework were single pieces of timber. In this structure there was no need to have a stiff beam to form the lower chord of the truss because the framework is an assembly of triangles that cannot be distorted into any other shape. However, the lower chord has to transmit tensile forces and while this could be managed with several pieces of timber, suitably joined together, a single timber would have simplified construction.

This system of assembling small trusses together to make a long-spanning bridge was adopted by others. In the late eighteenth century the Grubenmann brothers in Switzerland built bridges like this on a much larger scale and roofed over for durability, so successfully that some survive to this day. They used a variety of structural arrangements but many relied upon combining king and queen post trusses in much the same way that Palladio had done. Moreover, many of these were more than simple footbridges and had to cope with large moving loads.

In the example shown in Figure 2.14 the sequence of queen post–king post–queen post across the span is overlaid with a much longer queen post-like arrangement, although one might imagine it as a kind of arch. This is deconstructed in Figure 2.15. This was a theme

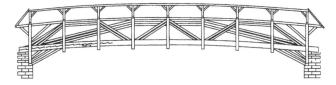

Figure 2.14 A bridge by the Grubenmann brothers.

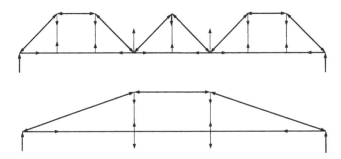

Figure 2.15 Deconstruction of the Grubenmanns' bridge.

that they used for many of their bridges, adopting whatever combination of trusses was convenient for the length of span. For more moderate spans they might use three king post trusses, or for longer spans three queen post trusses. In each case these would have a long overlapping truss that always used multiple timbers. Some of the Grubenmanns' bridges used what are called *funicular arches* in which a series of members are arranged in an arch-like form (Figure 2.16).

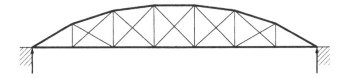

Figure 2.16 Squire Whipple's bridge.

They were not the only bridge designers to adopt an arch for the basic structure of a bridge with the deck hung from it. In 1841 Squire Whipple in America patented a design for cast and wrought iron bridges, which was much copied, although few now remain. Whipple called his structure a suspension bridge because the deck was suspended from what was essentially an iron arch. We might call it a bowstring truss because the deck is in tension acting like the string of an undrawn bow. Clearly the top chord is in compression and the lower chord in tension with vertical tension members between the two. The diagonal members will come into play when loads move across the bridge and the loading is not symmetrical, and because they are thin 'wires', they can only work in tension. However, what was important about the bridge was not that it led to a new family of structures, although the bowstring truss has since become an important structural type, but this arrangement changed the way in which bridge structures were perceived.

When the German theorist Carl Culman[2] drew Squire Whipple's truss form he saw it quite differently from the arch and hanger arrangement. In an article that described the bridge he drew the overall shape but with a single braced panel (Figure 2.17). This was because he saw the structure as an assemblage of similarly braced panels. The point of this is that a panel braced in this way cannot be distorted (at least not without failure of one of the members) and so if a series of such panels is put together the structure so formed will have the same property. None of the panels can be distorted so the structure will span from one end to the other providing the members are all strong enough to resist the forces that come onto them. This was a complete transformation in the way of looking at trusses and it is how engineers see such structures today; so much so that the idea of a truss as a series of arch-like structures is quite foreign to current thinking. There has been a complete shift in the way these structures are seen.

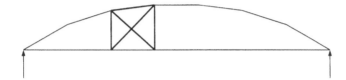

Figure 2.17 A braced panel of Squire Whipple's bridge.

The important result of this change in thinking is that not only can we dispense with the idea of a truss as a series of arches but it also allows us to design trusses that simply cannot be seen in this way. Instead a truss is simply thought of as a series of braced panels joined together, each panel being a quadrilateral with a single brace dividing it into two triangles. Squire Whipple's cross bracing was not strictly necessary; one brace between each pair of verticals would have been quite sufficient providing he had them all the right way round.

Tension trusses

Timber structures work best in compression because it is difficult to get tension forces into timber members; Palladio used metal strapping at the bottom of the hangers in his bridge. That meant that designers of timber trusses had to think in terms of strutting up the hangers. But when wrought iron became available, and members could be joined together with rivets or bolts, having tension members was no problem. In fact because of the buckling problem dealt with in Chapter 1, it was the handling of compression forces that now became more

---

[2]This change is discussed by Tom Peters in 'Bridge technology and historical scholarship,' *Proceedings of the First International Congress on Construction History*, 2003; Vol. 1, pp. 61–67.

difficult. Nevertheless, some of the structures that were then built had a family resemblance to the earlier timber trusses because they took much the same form in reverse. Compare the two structures of Figure 2.18. The first is the simple queen post truss described above while the second is the same structure turned upside down. Note that the effect is a simple reversal of the forces in all the members; those that were in tension have gone into compression while those that were in compression have gone into tension.

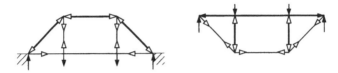

Figure 2.18 Turning a structure upside down reverses the forces.

The trusses of timber bridges were built up by adding a number of king and queen post trusses together, but recognising that trusses can be assembled of braced panels produces a much simpler means of designing them. Imagine a bridge that consists of a series of square panels each braced with a diagonal. A square panel alone is a four-bar chain, but putting a brace across it turns it into two rigid triangles. The bridge is arranged to be symmetrical so that the diagonals change direction at the centre (Figure 2.19).

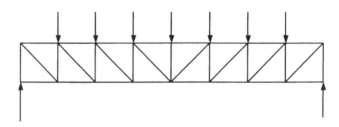

Figure 2.19 A simple girder.

To determine the forces in the members of such a truss imagine first removing a member from either the top or the bottom of one of the panels. This might happen if a member or a joint failed. The bridge would then fail by the two parts either side of the break rotating as shown in Figure 2.20, the points that had previously been joined by the member that has been removed either moving apart or coming closer together. If the former, that member must have been pulling the two sides towards each other, i.e. it was in tension. If the latter, the member must have been holding the two parts apart and so must have been in compression. This exercise can be carried out for all the members along the top and bottom chords with the same results, i.e. the whole of the bottom chord is in tension and the whole of the top chord is in compression.

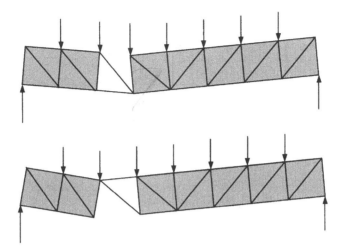

Figure 2.20 Movement of the girder following failure of either a lower chord member or an upper chord member.

If one of the internal members is removed, either a diagonal or a vertical member, what was a square panel distorts into a parallelogram (Figure 2.21). Again, whether the member is in compression or tension can be seen by whether the points at either end of the member move apart or towards each other. Using this logic it is clear that in the truss shown the diagonal members are in tension and the vertical members in compression.

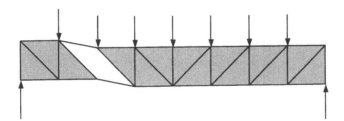

Figure 2.21 Movement of the girder following failure of an internal member.

We could repeat this exercise with all of the internal members of the truss and we would find that all the diagonals were in tension and all the verticals in compression. This does not mean that it is always the diagonal members that are in tension and the verticals that are in compression. Consider the truss shown in Figure 2.22, in which the diagonals are the other way round. By imagining the removal of one of the end diagonals one can see that it must be in compression, as must all the other diagonals. It is the vertical members in this truss that are in tension. This might appear to be a better arrangement as it eliminates a couple of members at either end. However, it has the disadvantage that the compression members are longer than the tension members. We saw from the exercise with the garden canes in

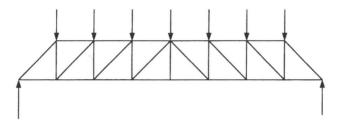

Figure 2.22 A girder with diagonals in compression.

Chapter 1 that longer compression members carry less load for the same area of cross-section and so it is to the designer's advantage to reduce their length.

What can be deduced from this exercise is that in symmetrically arranged trusses like these the internal members will be alternately in compression and tension, but this only works if the load is also symmetrical. Whipple might have had the problem that a cart going over the bridge might be very heavy compared with the self-weight of the bridge, and American railway engineers who built trussed bridges of various designs were certainly faced with this problem because of the considerable weight of a locomotive. With a very large asymmetrical load one would want these compression diagonals to change from one direction to the other at the point where the load is applied. The solution for large rolling loads was to have two sets of diagonals. In Whipple's case, where the diagonals could only take tension, whichever diagonal was required to carry the tensile force would do so. For the railway bridge engineers it was easier to detail the timber to take compression and whichever member was required to do that could do so. In these railway bridges iron tie bars were used for the vertical members, which would always be in tension. By tightening the tie bars the diagonal members could be put into compression with no load on the bridge so that when load was applied the effect on those diagonals that might have gone into tension was simply a reduction of the compressive force that had been put into them. This is a technique called prestressing, which will be discussed more fully in relation to concrete structures in Chapter 7.

In order to go beyond this simple qualitative understanding and find the forces in the members we need first to be able to find the support reactions for an asymmetrical load on the bridge, the kind of thing that would be produced by a heavy load passing across it. The situation is shown in Figure 2.23, where there is a load distance 'a' from one end and 'b' from the other. We all know that if two people pick up something the person nearest the centre of gravity of the object has the larger portion of the weight to bear; the question here is how much will each be carrying?

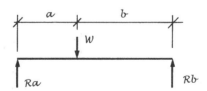

Figure 2.23 A beam and point load.

This can be solved by observing that Figure 2.23 is essentially the same as Figure 1.10 turned upside down. R_b is clearly the larger force. Transposing these forces for the values of the forces on the seesaw we know that $W = R_a + R_b$ and that $R_a.a = R_b.b$. In fact the way that this is actually worked out, rather than considering moments about the load, is to take moments about one end of the beam. Then $W.a = R_b.(a + b)$.

Ignoring for the moment the self-weight of the bridge, the forces in the top and bottom chords will be greatest at the point where the load is applied. What we can now find is the increase in the force in the chords as a result of the live load. Figure 2.24 shows the left-hand part of Figure 2.20a with the broken member replaced by the force F. If moments of the forces are taken about the hinge under the load then the reaction R_a is trying to rotate the end of the bridge clockwise. Preventing this is the force F that acts through a lever arm equal to the depth of the bridge truss, d. Thus, $R_a.a = F.d$, or $F = R_a.a/d$. If we imagined the member in the top chord removed and repeated the calculation we would get a similar result. This very simple approach avoids finding the forces in all of the members just to find the ones that we want, i.e. the maximum forces in the top and bottom chords. (It is called Ritter's method of sections after August Ritter who suggested the technique.) The largest force will occur in the chord members at the centre of the truss when the load is in the middle.

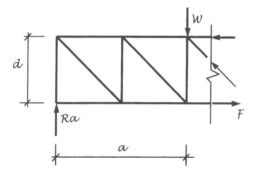

Figure 2.24 Use of the method of sections to find the lower chord force.

This method of sections can also be used to find the forces in the diagonal members by considering the vertical equilibrium of a part of the truss after it has been cut through. With the cut as shown in Figure 2.25, the tension in the vertical member is simply equal to the

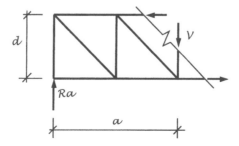

Figure 2.25 Use of the method of sections to find the force in an internal member.

reaction R_a. If the cut is made through a diagonal the vertical component of the force in the member will be equal to R_a – but finding the values of components of forces will be dealt with in Chapter 3. The largest force in these members of Figure 2.19 will, of course, occur next to the supports.

The self-weight of the structure can be handled in two different ways. It can be treated as a series of separate loads applied at each panel point or it can be treated as a single distributed load concentrated at the centre of gravity of the section of the structure being considered. We shall use the second of these approaches when considering the structure of a suspension bridge in Chapter 3. More arithmetic is involved in the first method but the principles remain the same, we are balancing moments produced by the loads against the moment produced by the supports.

Girder bridges: the Forth Bridge

We are now in a position to look a little more closely at the structure of the Forth Bridge. So far it has been seen just as pairs of brackets supporting the suspended spans, but the railway track runs through these brackets and has itself to be supported. The internal framing of the brackets comprises a series of diagonals, tubes in one direction to take compression, shown as the thicker lines of Figure 2.26, and lattice girders in the other to take tension forces. The horizontal girder carrying the rail track is described on the original drawings as the internal viaduct and stands on a series of what were described as trestles supported on the main tubes where the long tension and compression diagonals meet. The diagram of Figure 2.26 is a simplification because the distance between the main tubes becomes progressively greater towards the supports, so that the track structure is narrower than the width of the lower chord of the bracket. It thus resembles a bridge within a bridge and the term 'internal viaduct' is appropriate. Where the main diagonals cross there are other verticals supports described as ties.

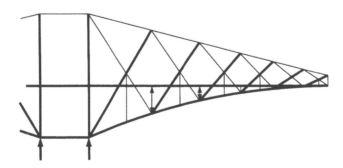

Figure 2.26 The Forth Bridge, distinguishing between compression and tension members.

What this exercise demonstrates is that a structure can be considered at quite different levels of detail. A simple overview can be taken, ignoring the details of construction, perhaps to find the load on the foundations or the forces in the main members of the structure. It can then be examined more closely to determine the internal forces within the structure. How closely you choose to examine it depends upon the purpose of the exercise, but it is normal to begin with the overview in the initial stages of the design process and then progress to the details.

3 Arches and Suspension Bridges

Figure 3.1 Ponte Rotto by Frank Brangwyn (copyright David Brangwyn).

As hangs the flexible line, so but inverted will stand the rigid arch.

Robert Hooke

At first sight arch bridges and suspension bridges might not seem to have much in common. The former, constructed of rigid materials, give every appearance of weight and solidity while the suspension bridge is humanity's equivalent of the spider's web, stretched seemingly weightless across space. The masonry bridge might appear to leap across between the banks but to do so the materials of the arch, whether brick or stone, visibly press against the abutments from which they spring. More expressive of the forces, by virtue of the fact that they are concentrated in the cables, a suspension bridge hangs in the air under clear tension. And yet in spite of this physical difference the same laws shape both. That they share the same structural principles was first discovered by Robert Hooke in the seventeenth century long before the suspension bridge was invented. His observation, quoted at the head of this chapter, simply means that the shape taken by a line supporting a number of weights is the mirror image of the ideal shape for an arch supporting the same weights disposed at the same horizontal intervals. However, this was simply a theoretical finding; it was not something that could be applied by designers at the time, nor for some time to come – bridge designers still had to work by trial and error.

Just as the last chapter looked at the change that occurred in the way in which people saw the behaviour of trusses, so this chapter deals with the way that designers came to understand the behaviour of arches. A useful way to approach this is to look at two bridges that were built in the mid-eighteenth century and the ideas that shaped them. One is an example of learning from one's mistakes while the other displays some faulty thinking about arch behaviour. These were both structures that deviated from what had been the norm for centuries, the semicircular arch that had been used by the Romans for bridges and aqueducts and developed as vaulting in the construction of buildings. Its use in vaulting will be dealt with in Chapter 9 but the obvious place to begin is with these Roman bridges.

We do not know how the arch was invented. Roland Mainstone has discussed a number of possibilities but without coming to any conclusion.[1] He has pointed out that while rock arches sometimes occur naturally, man-made arches are not used in places where these are found. However, we sometimes find arches forming within masonry walls where there has been some partial collapse. This sometimes happens because the movement of a poor foundation results in some masonry falling away and leaving the material above spanning across the gap. Also the collapse of the outer skin of a thick wall can occur near its base as a result of pressure from the core material (see Chapter 5) and again the material above will take an arch-like form, but we have no idea if this kind of thing inspired some early inventor.

The Roman use of semicircular arches might possibly have been because of some kind of sympathetic reasoning about the way that an arch ought to be shaped in order to best carry its load. Did they perhaps think that the best shape would be one that came down vertically onto the supports in order to bring the loads down that way? One still finds this kind of sympathetic thinking about structures although it is not usually very helpful, and in this case such an idea would simply be wrong. The shape could also have been derived from the way that they set out and constructed their arches, but whatever the reason semicircular arches continued to be built into the eighteenth century. The designs for Westminster Bridge as late as 1750 had semicircular arches, although elsewhere in Europe things were a little more advanced and shallower arches were already being built. These are called *segmental arches*, their form being the segment of a circle. A segmental Roman bridge survives in Spain, but the best-known early segmental bridge is the Ponte Vecchio over the River Arno in Florence, dating from 1345. The advantage of this type of arch is that the bridges require fewer piers in the river than semicircular arches, and it seems curious that they were not adopted earlier in Britain. Whatever the reason for this British backwardness it has the advantage for us today that we can follow the development in thinking and design as better designs were adopted in the eighteenth century.

Building an arch

The masonry of an arch requires some temporary support while it is being built, and this is called *centring*, normally constructed as a timber framework. This raises an issue that we

---

[1] Roland Mainstone, *Developments in Structural Form*, Allen Lane, London, 1975, Chapter 6.

have not considered so far, that of temporary works, which nearly all construction methods require in some form. The strength and stability of such structures need to be considered just as much as the permanent structure because they will sometimes be carrying considerable loads. A masonry arch could either be propped up from below or carried on some timber structure that spans across much the same gap as the masonry, perhaps a timber arch spanning the opening. In most cases this was the most convenient as it avoided supports in a river or a deep gorge and the timber centring could simply be supported on the masonry piers. Often the supports for the centring were incorporated into the masonry and remained as a permanent feature. Many Roman aqueducts, comprising a series of arches on tall piers, have corbels at the top of the piers. These were almost certainly there to support the timber centring on which the arches were built. In fact it makes more sense for the arch to be corbelled out slightly with nibs to carry the centring a little way above the springing of the arch. This is what was done for the two lower tiers of arches of the Pont du Gard (Figure 3.2). With this arrangement of supports, when the centring is lowered it comes clear of the sides of the supports as well as from the underside of the arch.

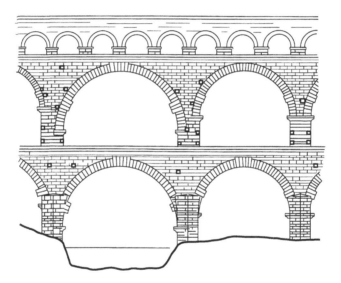

Figure 3.2 The Pont du Gard.

It was no doubt for dramatic effect that the artist Frank Brangwyn used a view from underneath for his etching of the Ponte Rotto in Rome, shown at the beginning of this chapter (Figure 3.1), but in doing so he shows clearly the projecting nibs at the bottom of the arch that would have supported the centres on which it was constructed. One may deduce from this that a framework of timber spanned across between each corresponding pair of nibs. Timber boarding called *lagging* would then have been laid between these frames on which the masonry would have been placed, beginning with the ring of slightly tapered stones called *voussoirs* that formed the arch ring. These form the basic structure of the bridge and once complete would carry the load of the material placed above. The filling above that formed the *spandrels* can simply be considered a dead weight upon the arch ring.

Centrings for bridges were major feats of engineering in themselves because they had to span as far as the masonry (or nearly so) and carry the weight of the masonry arch until it was completed. As they were temporary, economy of means would have been a consideration in their design, and if they were to be used repeatedly in several arches they would also have to be light enough to handle. They clearly had to be capable of removal once the masonry was completed, and removed without damaging the masonry or becoming dangerous structures in the process. What form these temporary supports took is most often a matter of speculation because by their very nature they have not survived. Nor is the construction of centring described in manuals or books on architecture, and there are very few illustrations of it until the drawings and descriptions of bridge construction produced in the eighteenth century. The shape of the centring naturally determined the shape of the arch but presumably as circular curves were the simplest to set out this affected the choice of arch shape for a long time.

One can imagine that getting the centring in place would be relatively easy because it would have been possible to handle it from above. Hoists of some sort, possibly just *shear-legs* or *gin poles*, could have been mounted on the piers and the centres lifted into place. But with the arch complete the centres would have to be handled from below and from the side. If they were just to be dismantled that might not be too much of a problem, but it would be more difficult if they were to be moved intact from one arch to the next. At the Ponte Roto this was solved by having a series of nibs with spaces between. With no load on them the centres could perhaps have been moved sideways and dropped down between the nibs.

Working out how to build a bridge would have been part of the designer's task. When Mylne produced his design for Blackfriars Bridge in 1759 one of the admired aspects of his proposals was his design for the centring (Figure 3.3). Note the way in which it is supported on folding wedges, i.e. pairs of opposing wedges that would allow the centres to be accurately levelled. But, equally important, the folding wedges also allowed the centres to be eased away from the arch once it was complete by driving them back in the other direction. The centring might at first look rather complex but the arrangement of overlapping timbers can be broken

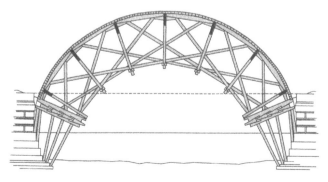

Figure 3.3 Mylne's centring for Blackfriars Bridge.

down into simple overlapping frames, each comprising a plate directly under the arch supported by a pair of struts from the piers on either side. It is these that define the shape of the *intrados* of the timber arch that is thus formed. John Rennie used much the same arrangement for Waterloo Bridge half a century later.

If these historical issues seem to be irrelevant in today's world of concrete bridges, bear with me. Some of the issues raised in the next historical examples have relevance to a recent failure of a concrete arch structure that we will be able to discuss in the light of the lessons that these provide.

Blackfriars Bridge

A competition had been held for the design of this bridge and when the various designs were made public there was considerable debate about them. Mylne's design was opposed on the grounds that he was proposing to use 'elliptical'[2] arches. Some felt that elliptical arches were not as strong as arches based on the simple circular curves that had been used until that date. The rather public debate about the strongest shape for an arch, carried out in journals and pamphlets, was fuelled by the various contenders for the bridge contract who would like to have seen Mylne's design rejected. The arguments put forward show something of current thinking, not all of it technically sound. It was Samuel Johnson who led the attack against Mylne's proposal to use an ellipse, doubtless put up to this by the author of a competing design. Observing first that the most important characteristic of a bridge is its strength he argued that:

> Any weight laid upon the top of an arch has a tendency to force that top into the vacuity below; and the arch thus loaded on the top stands only because the stones that form it, being wider in the upper than the lower parts, that part that fills a wider space cannot fall though a space less wide; but the force which laid upon a flat would press directly downwards is dispersed each way in a lateral direction.

That was certainly true, but it was the argument that followed that led Johnson into an error.

> If the elliptical arch be equally strong with the semicircular, that is, if an arch, by approaching to a straight line loses none of its stability, it will follow that all arcuation is useless, and thus the bridge may at last, without any inconvenience, consist of stone laid in straight lines from pillar to pillar.

Johnson does not seem to have been very observant because in his day he could have seen lintels over window and door openings formed as flat 'arches' in brickwork. If he had noticed such an arch he would surely not have been able to add what followed.

---

[2] The shape was not a true ellipse but what we would call a three-centred arch, i.e. composed of three circular curves.

But if a straight line will bear no weight, *which is evident to the first view* [my italics], it is plain likewise than an ellipsis will bear very little and that as an arch is more curved its strength is increased.

A flat arch built as a lintel in masonry is called a *plate bande*, and not only were they deliberately built to span openings in masonry but one sometimes sees them formed by accident. Dry-stone walls are commonly capped with a row of stones along the top placed vertically. The walls themselves are seldom very well founded and the effects of frost on the ground below them sometimes causes a collapse of a short section of the wall. When this happens the wall can sometimes collapse leaving the coping stones above spanning across the gap (Figure 3.4a), a miracle that Dr Johnson would probably have had difficulty believing in. We need to ask how this is possible.

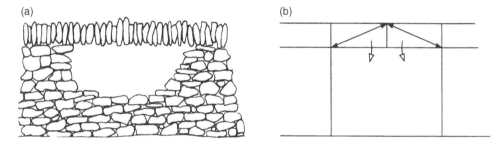

Figure 3.4 A flat arch formed accidentally in the coping of a wall.

In fact the flat arch is perhaps easier to understand than the curved arch. Dr Johnson imagines the stones falling into the space beneath and unlike the normal arch these coping stones are not larger at the top than at the bottom. The only thing that is preventing the coping stones of a wall from falling in this way is the friction between them. Without that the whole of the spanning section of coping stones might simply slide down relative to the rest just as Johnson imagined. The fact that they do not is because they are being squeezed together just as when we pick up a row of books by squeezing them between our hands; relax the pressure and the books will fall in a heap onto the floor. Pressing them together increases the friction between them. If there is a compression force between the stones they can behave as a single body rather than as separate stones. The question with the stones is what is doing the squeezing.

The other possible mode of failure is for the coping to rotate as two masses of stone with the centre falling downwards (Figure 3.4b). But observe how this happens; each half will have to rotate about its bottom edge while at the centre the two moving masses of stone will rotate about a kind of hinge at the top edge. Drawing lines between the points about which rotation might occur makes it clear that their total length is longer than the gap. The only way that failure of this kind can take place is if the coping stones beyond the gap were to move apart slightly giving room for the two masses of stone to rotate as described.

As the stones are trying to fail in this way they are pushing out against the coping stones at either side and these, unable to move, are pushing back. Meanwhile the stones at the central hinge are also pushing against each other. The result is a large compressive force in the stones between the hinges, producing the friction that is preventing them from sliding. The mistake that Johnson made was to separate the arch from its supports. It is the stability of the whole structure that we are concerned with. A flat arch will not work unless the abutments resist the outward thrust of the two halves as they try to rotate, and it is the same with any arch. Both the shape of the arch and the forces at the abutments need to be considered, not just the shape of the arch alone.

Pontypridd Bridge

In 1746, William Edwards, a 27-year-old mason and local preacher, contracted to build a bridge over the River Taff at Pontypridd in Glamorganshire. The bridge he built had piers in the river and after two years it was brought down in a flood, clearly a result of scour that undermined it. As the contract included a clause that he would maintain the structure for its first seven years he was obliged to replace the bridge, and given the fate of his first structure decided to build a bridge without piers in the river. This meant a single arch of very long span that could clearly not be a simple semicircular arch or it would be too high; something rather flatter was needed. Unfortunately the centring for this collapsed when the bridge was nearing completion. Edwards tried again, this time making the arch very thin, almost certainly very like the one that survives there to this day. The lightness might have been for financial reasons, as he must have been incurring a loss on this structure, or simply to reduce the load on the centring. This time the arch stood for a while but then collapsed after six weeks by breaking upwards at the crown. In 1756, ten years after his initial contract, the present bridge was completed, and with a span of 42 m remained the longest arch in Britain for 40 years.

How was it that his bridge failed, and how did Edwards modify his design so that it then succeeded? People had been building arches for centuries; they were a tried and tested method of bridging a gap. The Pontypridd Bridge is simply one of those examples where increasing daring in structural design eventually led to a failure because the behaviour of the structure was not properly understood. In this case, as often happens, valuable lessons were learned from the failure, which could then be applied to the revised design. In designing his final version Edwards obtained advice from Rennie, the leading engineer of his day (and one of the contenders for building Blackfriars Bridge), but we do not know exactly what that advice was. What we can do is to explain why the present design succeeded and why its predecessor failed in the way that it did. This involves a more general understanding of the forces in arches.

The forces in an arch

From the description of Johnson's misunderstanding of arch behaviour, a consideration of the outward forces produced by an arch seems to be a good place to start. We also need to recognise that the effect of friction between the voussoirs is such that they do not have to be considered separately. We can group a number of voussoirs together and consider them as a single structural element, which is how we thought of the coping stones of the dry-stone wall.

This is a considerable advance on some early thinking about arches, where the vous-soirs were thought of as spheres with a single frictionless point of contact. With the forces between them at this point of contact a 'line of thrust' could be drawn between the contact points. However, this only allowed one such line to be drawn, ignoring the possibility that the load on the arch might change requiring a quite different line to be drawn (see below).

Voussoirs can be grouped together so that the arch is divided into two parts, which has the advantage that it creates a symmetrical arrangement, assuming for the time being that the loads are also symmetrical. Because the structure is symmetrical there can only be horizontal forces at the apex as each side leans upon the other. Newton's third law – that for every action there is an equal and opposite reaction – tells us that the vertical forces at the abutments of the arch must both be equal to W, the weight of each half of the arch, but also that there is a horizontal force at the abutment equal to the force at the apex (Figure 3.5).

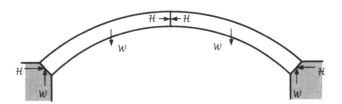

Figure 3.5 Simple forces in an arch.

One half of the arch could be removed and replaced with a horizontal force and it would make no difference to the remaining half. There was a nineteenth century demonstration by Attwood that did just that.[3] Attwood used models of half arches, with the force at the 'centre' supplied by a strap around the end and loaded with a weight over a pulley. This is shown in diagrammatic form in Figure 3.6, with dimensions added for two arches of different propor-tions. If the horizontal force at the springing must be equal to the force at the centre that is holding the arch in place, this makes finding that force rather important for the designer of an arch bridge, not so much to ensure that the masonry can withstand the compressive stresses but for the ability of the abutments of the arch to resist its outward thrust. To find this force we can take moments about an abutment for one half of the arch, i.e. considering

[3] Attwood, G. *A Dissertation on the Construction and Properties of Arches*. London, 1801.

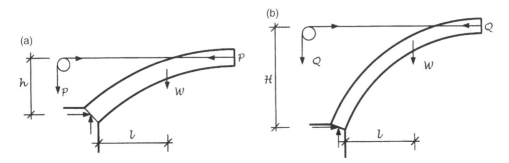

Figure 3.6 Half arches, supported by weights over pulleys.

the possibility of rotation about the abutment for that half of the arch if the other half was simply removed and replaced with a horizontal force. In each case the clockwise moment produced by the weight of the arch is resisted by the anticlockwise moment produced by the restraining force. If we assume the weights of the two arches are the same then, as the span is the same, so are the clockwise moments they produce. Therefore the anticlockwise moments produced by the restraints must also be equal. Put into mathematical notation this reads:

$$W.l = P.h = Q.H.$$

Because h is smaller than H, P must be larger than Q. In other words the shallower the arch the larger are the horizontal forces generated at the abutment.

Practical issues

The magnitudes of the forces within the arch are not particularly important because in most cases the contact area between the voussoirs is large enough for the stresses to be very low. For a bridge the question is whether the foundations are capable of carrying the forces imposed upon them. Edwards's bridge was a single span so that this load came directly onto either bank. In a bridge of several equal spans, once it has been completed, each span produces an equal thrust against its supporting piers, which therefore only have to carry vertical loads. It is true that there will be some change as loads pass over the bridge, but this will normally be a small force compared with that of the self-weight of the masonry. It is more of a problem in buildings, where an arch might be carried by a pier and not balanced by one on the other side. Then there is a question of how large the pier should be in order for it not to be pushed over by the thrust of the arch; but for the time being let us stay with bridges.

The diagrams so far have shown the loads at the centre of each half of the arch ring whereas these support a mass of masonry above and the centre of gravity of that will be closer to the supports. Clearly that is where the load should be applied in the diagrams, so we need to find the centre of gravity of that mass of masonry. Fortunately there is a simple mechanical way of finding the centre of gravity of any shape. If a model of the shape is made, perhaps by cutting it out of a thin sheet of plywood, and this model is hung from any point, then the centre of gravity, i.e. the point at which the weight may be considered to act, must be immediately below this point of suspension. It would be producing a moment about the point of suspension if it were not so and that would soon move the shape to the desired position. This is the principle that can be used. The apparatus is simple; it consists of a string with a weight on the end to act as a plumb bob and something to act as a pivot. Make a small hole in the shape whose centre of gravity is to be found and hang it from the pivot (Figure 3.7a). Mark the edge where the string passes, then the centre of gravity must lie on a line between the hole from which it is hung and the mark. Draw this line on the surface; the dotted line in Figure 3.7b. Repeat the process with a second hole to find a second line. As the centre of gravity must lie on both lines it is at their point of intersection.

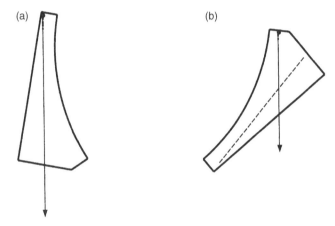

(a)   (b)

Figure 3.7 Finding the centre of gravity.

Having found the centre of gravity we can redraw Figure 3.5 to include the spandrels above the arch ring and with the load correctly placed (Figure 3.8). Nevertheless, as the spandrel is not part of the load-resisting structure, we will continue to leave it out of subsequent diagrams.

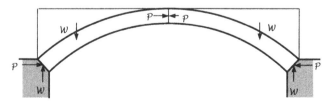

Figure 3.8 The arch weights correctly placed.

Thus far, we can see the variables that affect the forces at the supports and perhaps the size of the supports that might be needed to carry an arch. We do not know what rules Roman engineers might have used but in the fifteenth century Leon Batista Alberti discussed the overall proportions of the arch and its supports in his architectural treatise. He recommended that the width of the piers should be one-quarter of the height of the bridge; the clear span of the arches between six and four times the width of the piers; and the thickness of the voussoirs not less than one-tenth of the span.[4] This is a continuation of the rules of proportion that were used by Gothic architects but have little relation to the kind of understanding that we have today. Also, assuming that what he calls the height of the bridge is not the rise of the arch but the total height above the water he is probably describing a semicircular arch bridge.

Forces within the arch ring

Simplification of the arch ring into two rigid bodies has enabled us to find the forces at the springing of the arch and so the forces on the piers but it says nothing about the forces within the arch ring. It is these that we need to find in order to answer Dr Johnson's objections to the elliptical shape of the arch and to understand the failure of the Pontypridd Bridge. As the latter failed by springing upwards at the crown, we might propose a division of the arch into a number of rigid bodies with hinges between them that would allow that to happen. Assuming a symmetrical structure, there would have been a symmetrical mechanism of failure. To give this, three hinges are needed close to the centre allowing two pieces of the bridge to rotate upwards. Of course the heavy spandrels must be moving downwards and inwards to produce this movement at the centre, and the mechanism shown in Figure 3.9 seems plausible. But to relate this to the forces acting we need to be able to trace the line of thrust within the arch; in other words the shape of the analogous chain that Hooke described.

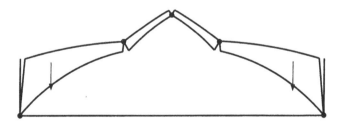

Figure 3.9 The failure mechanism of the Pontypridd Bridge.

In the diagram of coping stones of Figure 3.4 we simplified the line of force to two straight lines between the hinges. In fact it is a curve rather than a pair of straight lines, but we will come to that. The point is that an arch fails by forming hinges about which the various parts rotate and the line of thrust passes through those hinges. It can do nothing else because as

---

[4]Leon Batista Alberti, *Ten Books of Architecture*, 1485, Book 4 Chapter 6 and Book 8 Chapter 5.

the arch fails in this way the hinges are the only points at which the segments either side are in contact. As a prelude to finding exactly where the lines of thrust might be we need to look at another idea in structural analysis.

The triangle of forces

The assumption in the arch diagrams drawn so far is that there are two forces at each springing, one horizontal and one vertical. In the previous chapter the inclined forces in the timber bridge struts were each resisted by two forces at the abutments: a vertical force from the corbel and a horizontal force from the wall of the abutment. This seems reasonable given the nature of the construction, and it was pointed out that these forces opposed the vertical and horizontal components of the force in the inclined strut. In the diagram of Figure 3.8 two forces have also been shown at the abutment whose values we know because they must be equal to the vertical and horizontal forces acting on the half arch. But in this case the abutment is a sloping surface and it seems more reasonable to expect a single force to be acting across this surface. While the diagram shows the vertical and horizontal components of this inclined force it is better to find the force itself.

The direction of the inclined force can be found fairly simply because it can be shown that if there are three forces acting on a body then their lines of action must all pass through a single point. What this means in practical terms is that if the lines representing the two forces whose direction we know, that of P and W, are extended, as shown by the dotted lines of Figure 3.10a, they will meet at some point; in this case just above the *extrados* of the arch. If a line is then drawn from the abutment through this point then the reaction at the abutment must act along that line.

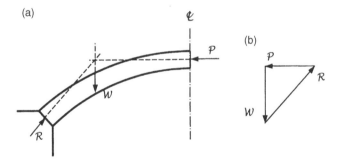

Figure 3.10 The triangle of forces applied to half of a bridge arch.

This leads to one of the most powerful tools in understanding structures, and yet one of the simplest if one can accept the limited amount of abstraction required. If the forces are drawn to scale, i.e. with the length of the lines proportional to the magnitudes of the forces, they can be rearranged into a triangle as shown in Figure 3.10b. The lines representing the forces form a perfect triangle and the arrows showing the directions of the forces all act in the same direction around the triangle.

The triangle of forces

Demonstrating that the forces must all pass through a single point is fairly simple. We know that if lines indicating the direction of P and W are extended they must meet somewhere. If moments are taken about this point for the three forces acting on the body (in this case the half arch) then the forces P and W produce no moment about this point. As there can be no net moment on the body, the force R must also produce no moment about that point. The only way that is possible is if the direction of the force also passes through the point, although that does not explain why the scale drawing works.

Forces are vectors, quantities that have both magnitude and direction. Velocities are also vectors, and both are added in the same way but it is simpler to imagine the addition of two velocities. Imagine a boat setting out across a river. The boat travels at a particular velocity in still water but to this must be added the velocity of the river (Figure 3.11). If the boat steers perpendicular to the shore with a velocity V_1, but the river is flowing with a velocity V_2, we know that the actual track of the boat will be V_3. These are distances travelled in a given time so that given the first two velocities the third can be found from a scale drawing. This is the simple addition of velocities, and we could add forces in the same way. But in the triangle of forces we are finding a third force that is equal and opposite to the first two forces added together, the equivalent of $-V_3$.

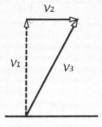

Figure 3.11

From what we know so far, a range of solutions to the arch problem is possible because it is not clear where along the contact surfaces the forces R and P are acting. They might be anywhere within the arch ring, i.e. anywhere between the top and bottom of the voussoirs they are acting on. To find exactly where, we need to consider what would happen if the arch were to fail.

If the arch fails under its own weight because an abutment gives way, i.e. the abutments move apart, it would do so by forming three hinges allowing the two halves to rotate about the abutment as they moved 'into the vacuity below', to use Dr Johnson's words. Dotted lines in Figure 3.12a show the supposed movement of the arch and the position of the hinges necessary for this to occur. These are at the intrados of the arch at the abutments and at the

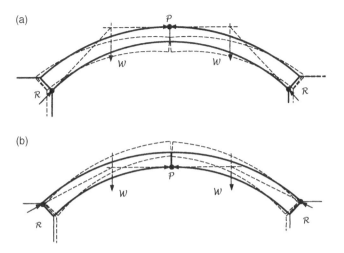

Figure 3.12 The effect of abutment movement on an arch.

extrados at its crown. Forces would have to be acting through these hinges, because they are the only places where the masonry is touching.

Inward movement of the abutments would result in hinges at the top of the lowest voussoirs and at the bottom of the arch ring at the centre with the arch moving upwards (Figure 3.12b). This might seem an unlikely possibility, but imagine a three-span bridge with two heavy vehicles approaching from either end. With both the end spans loaded, the centre span might not be able to resist their inward thrust and could possibly fail in this way.

The first assumption produces the minimum values that the forces P and R can take, the second the maximum values they can take. This is an approach that engineers might adopt when there is some uncertainty about the behaviour of a structure. We can assume contradictory models of behaviour that provide maximum and minimum values for the forces in question. The technical terms used for these values are *upper bound* and *lower bound* values. The formation of three hinges only occurs when there is movement of the abutments, and this need not lead to failure of the arch because a three-hinged arch is still a viable structure. For an arch to fail under a load without movement of the abutments at least four hinges must form, something that might occur if a heavy load were to pass over the bridge.

The hanging chain analogy might be used with the simplification of the bridge's weight to a pair of points to demonstrate what is happening with the upper bound condition. Lines of thrust drawn through the three hinges in Figure 3.13 lie within the masonry of the arch. It is not possible to draw such a line of thrust that passes through the three hinges that form for the lower bound condition, i.e. with spreading of the abutments, and which lies within the masonry. Nevertheless, there must clearly be such a line of thrust and the fact that it cannot be drawn in the same way is because the simplification does not allow us to. What we need is a more accurate model of the line of thrust; one that takes full account of the distribution of loads on the arch rather than assuming it is concentrated at a two points.

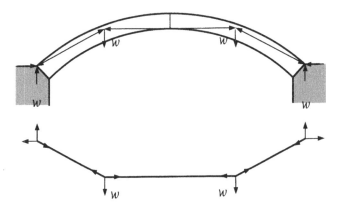

Figure 3.13 Lines of thrust in an arch compared with a hanging chain.

Having found the forces at the crown of the arch, and knowing where the hinges are assumed to form, both the arch and the masonry above it need to be divided into a number of 'slices' whose weights can be worked out. These constitute the loads on the arch. The weight of each section can then be represented as a line whose length is proportional to the weight. The total weight of the spandrel is simply the sum of all these smaller weights, i.e. $W = w_1 + w_2 + w_3 + w_4 + w_5 + w_6$ (Figure 3.14). Where the spandrels are solid the weights, and so the lines representing them, are proportional to the distance between the *soffit* of the arch and the level of the roadway at each point. Of course the spandrel is not always solid.

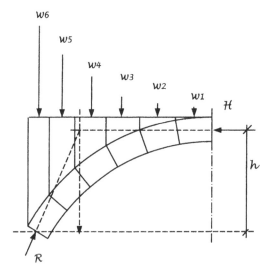

Figure 3.14 The loads and forces on a half arch.

In Figure 3.14 the horizontal force and the support reaction have been placed at arbitrary points but the first task is to find the centre of gravity of all the loads and hence the angle of inclination of the reaction at the abutment.

There is a numerical means of finding the position of the centre of gravity that depends upon taking moments. If the distances of all the separate loads, w, from some point, such as one side of the abutment, are known then moments can be taken for each about that point and added together. From the way that the centre of gravity has been defined the moment of the total weight of the arch about the same point must have the same value. Thus dividing the total weight of the arch into the sum of the moments that we have obtained gives the distance of the centre of gravity from the chosen point.

It might be sensible to find the upper bound for the forces in the arch, which means placing the horizontal force at the crown at the intrados of the arch and the reaction at the intrados. Starting from the top, add the thrust at the crown of the arch to the first part of the load w_1. This can be done using the triangle of forces and yielding the result r_1 (Figure 3.15a). Then add r_1 to the force w_2 to obtain the force r_2 with a second triangle of forces. Continue this process until all the components of the line of thrust have been found. Of course the process can also be begun from the bottom.

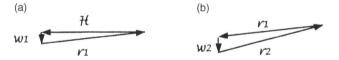

Figure 3.15 Successive addition of the arch forces.

Drawing a series of different triangles in this way is unnecessarily tedious as the starting point for each successive triangle is the line obtained as the solution to the preceding triangle. Therefore it is possible to combine them into a single diagram. Having drawn the triangle to obtain the forces H and R, divide the line representing W into smaller parts to represent the separate parts of the weight w_1 to w_6. Then the forces r_1 to r_6 can all be drawn from the origin of the force H. Having found the direction of each of the forces a diagram can be drawn that traces the line of thrust through the arch. This changes direction at the line of each of the loads w_1 to w_6, each segment of the load path being parallel to the corresponding force r. The resulting line must lie within the arch ring of voussoirs.

That is how it is done for the upper bound (Figure 3.16) but we should note that the line of thrust between the abutment and the nearest component of the weight must leave the arch a little. For the lower bound the same thing will happen at the top. Moreover, with the simple diagram here the load w_6 will be making no contribution to the total weight of the arch affecting the lower bound line of thrust. But remember that this sketch is for illustrative purposes only. In any case neither the upper bound nor lower bound solutions would

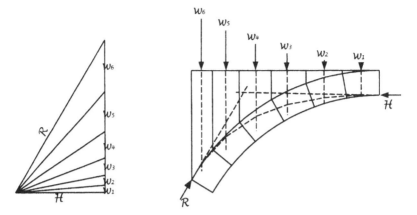

Figure 3.16 The diagram for adding all the forces on a half arch.

show the actual line of thrust in the arch, they simply show the extreme positions that it might take. The point is to show that some line of thrust can be drawn in this way that lies within the arch ring. Doing this by hand is rather tedious and there have been computer programs designed to carry out the task but these assume fairly regular geometries and certainly would not deal with Edwards's bridge, which we are now in a position to look at.

Edwards's failure

Armed with this theoretical background we should be able to understand why Edwards's first single arch failed and why his modification succeeded. If we imagine a line loaded with the self-weight of the bridge it would have very heavy loads towards the support and very little load in the middle. The effect would be to produce a shape that was steep towards the supports and very shallow across the centre where there was very little weight. This shape turned upside down would have to lie within the arch ring, but try as we might by adjusting the magnitude of the horizontal forces this is not possible. The line of thrust of Edwards's failed arch must have clipped the intrados of the arch rather like Figure 3.13. If it had passed outside it the arch would not have lasted five minutes. We can assume that very high stresses would have developed at the edge of the masonry, either with some crushing of the material or some compression of the mortar, and this changed the geometry of the arch sufficiently for the line of thrust to pass below the intrados, at which point the centre sprang upwards and the arch collapsed.

What Edwards did for the replacement bridge was to build holes in the spandrels to lighten them (Figure 3.17), thus lightening the load close to the supports. This resulted in a line of thrust that had a more uniform curve, less steep towards the supports, and so which fitted within the arch ring at the centre. Of course, he could have achieved the same result by thickening the arch at the centre so increasing the weight there, or even just adding weight to the arch over the centre section. The line of thrust would then have moved upwards in response to this additional load just as a loaded chain would move down in response to one.

Figure 3.17 Edwards's Pontypridd Bridge with holes to lighten the spandrels.

Yet another solution would have been to flatten the arch itself at the centre to conform more closely to the line of thrust, but we may suppose that had he thought of that he would have rejected the idea either on aesthetic grounds or because it would have complicated the construction of the centring. But the astute reader will realise that this suggests exactly the kind of elliptical form adopted for Blackfriars Bridge, the shape that Dr Johnson so objected to.

An unexpected failure

There was a recent failure of a new tunnel that was under construction. I confess that I was not a witness to this collapse and have not read any detailed reports about the cause. My knowledge of it comes from having travelled through the completed tunnel and from photographs following the collapse that were posted on the web. I was only in the position of an interested observer, but one armed with some knowledge of structural behaviour.

The story seems very simple: the railway went through a cutting in an area where land was at a premium so that if the cutting were to be replaced by a tunnel new land would be created over this that could be used for car parking, or something similar. To cause minimum disturbance to railway operations the tunnel lining was of precast units that could be quickly put in place. Pairs of arch segments could be placed from either side to lean against each other much like some of the sketches above but with an adequate rise to clear the trains. Soil could then be backfilled over the completed lining and brought up to the required level. That much of the designer's intentions was clear from what could be seen, and it seems like a simple enough plan. Unfortunately, something went wrong. During the backfilling operation the tunnel lining collapsed and many tons of soil were deposited onto what is a busy commuter line. What then went wrong? Short of the possibility that the components of the lining were poorly made, i.e. did not meet the designer's specification, there seem to be two possibilities.

The interest in Blackfriars Bridge was such that there were drawings made of it during its construction, from which it is clear that the centring was left in place until the spandrels over the arch rings had been completed. The arch therefore did not have to carry any temporary loads that might be different from the final load; any temporary out of balance load arising from the construction process could, if necessary, be transmitted to the centring. This was not possible with the tunnel construction. The whole purpose of the precast sections was to carry loads from the very beginning; centring would simply have obstructed the working of the railway. Therefore it was essential that they be designed to do this and it is quite possible, even likely, that the loads during construction would determine the design of the arch. As the fill is brought up on each side the loading must present a problem very similar to Edwards's bridge, with loads close to the springing of the arch and nothing over the crown. The line of thrust must pass though the hinge at the top of the arch where the two segments meet but elsewhere would clearly be well outside the thin concrete ring. This could only be accommodated by the bending resistance of the ring.

We may presume that the designers were aware of this and designed the arch accordingly. However, they would probably assume that the fill would be brought up evenly on both sides so that the arch would be symmetrically loaded. If for some reason this did not happen and there was an imbalance in the loads on either side of the arch, then the bending forces on the arch would be much greater – possibly greater than had been designed for – and the arch would collapse. One can imagine that it might not be an easy task to monitor the heights of fill on both sides of the arch at the same time. Of course, this is simply speculation, but speculation informed by the structural principles involved. Moreover, the possibility of uneven loading of the arch raises the problem of the uneven loading of old masonry arches by today's heavy traffic loads.

Arch with point load

It is possible to use the chain analogy to imagine what would happen to the forces in an arch if a heavy load passed across it. The forces in a cable, or the line supporting the weight of washing hung on a washing line, are very visible. The tension structure takes the shape of the forces in it because it can do nothing else. In contrast a masonry arch always remains the same shape because it can do nothing else. Nevertheless the forces within it are changing as they adapt to the applied load. Of course masonry arches were very heavy compared with the loads that came on to them, so until relatively recently there was little concern about these loads. Only recently, with large increases in vehicle weights, has the stability of masonry arches become a problem.

Using Hooke's analogy of the hanging chain, the line of thrust can be imagined for a heavy load placed on the arch. The position of the line has been chosen so that it exits the arch at each abutment where hinges are likely to form. A hinge is also likely to form immediately under the load. In Figure 3.18a the line lies within the arch and although three hinges might form this will not produce a failure of the arch. Increasing the magnitude of the force has the effect of producing lines with less curvature so that eventually that joining the load to the furthest point will touch the intrados of the arch (Figure 3.18b). If

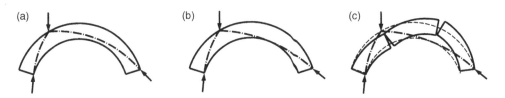

Figure 3.18 Increasing an eccentric load until sufficient hinges form to produce failure.

there is any increase in the load beyond that point four hinges will form and the arch will collapse.

Iron and concrete arches

Some iron bridges have been built exactly like masonry bridges, i.e. as a series of castings that act just like masonry voussoirs. The lead was set by the bridge over the Wear at Sunderland, built between 1793 and 1796. A century later the Pont Alexandre III across the Seine in Paris was also built of cast iron voussoirs. For that bridge there were 15 ribs formed

---

Finding the forces for a hinged arch

The forces on a three-hinged arch with a large point load can be found graphically. The forces at the supports can be found for the self-weight as before by drawing a force from each support to intersect the line representing the self-weight at the level of the crown. If the self-weight is known the magnitude of the forces can be found as before. The forces needed to support the additional point load are found separately. From the pin supporting the half of the arch not carrying the load draw a line through the pin at the crown and continue it to cut the line of the load (Figure 3.19). That force must pass through the central hinge if it is to have no moment about that hinge. The third force, i.e. that from the other support hinge, must pass through the point thus found. Note that 'pin' and 'hinge' are used interchangeably.

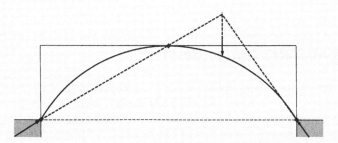

Figure 3.19 A three-hinged arch with a point load.

   We now have three forces in equilibrium whose directions are all known so that if the magnitude of the load is known a triangle of forces can be drawn to find the two support forces. It is clearly simplest to find the horizontal and vertical components of the support forces for both the self weight reactions and the reactions to this load so that they can be added together.

   The last step introduces an important principle. If we want to find the effect of a complex system of forces it may be easiest to find the effect of each force separately and then add them.

from castings that were each a little over 3.6 m long. This bridge has a rise of just over 6 m and a span of almost 110 m but differs from a masonry bridge in that it was designed with three hinges. This meant that the ribs sprang from a large diameter 'pin' with a similar pin at the centre. These pins allow some movement of the bridge to accommodate expansion and contraction of the metal, a common device for iron and steel bridges, which are affected by temperature changes. This is such an important structural type that for those who can manage the mathematics it deserves a little more detailed examination.

The diagram of Figure 3.19 has been drawn as if it were a masonry arch with deep spandrels, but an iron, concrete or even a timber arch is likely to be quite thin. If the arch is drawn as a thin line diagram, the line supposed to be the centreline of the arch, then the distance between the line of force and the line of the arch is a measure of the bending within the arch. Ignoring the effect of self-weight, this is largest under the load on one side of the arch and midway along the other side. (These are also the places where the hinges are likely to form in a masonry arch that fails under a point load.) Robert Maillart shaped many of his concrete arched bridges taking this form. He used three-hinged arches to allow some movement in the bridges and shaped the spandrels such that they were deepest midway between the abutments and the crown (Figure 3.20).

Figure 3.20 A Maillart bridge.

Robert Maillart's bridge designs

Maillart's later bridges may appear superficially similar to his early designs but there was a change in their engineering. His early designs seem to have been based upon ideas coming from the use of graphic statics (the methods we have been using here) with the arch as the only active part of the structure. In other words the deck and the vertical supports between it and the arch were simply passive loads upon the arch. However, if the arch carries a moving load, while the load is on one side of the arch, as shown in Figure 3.19, that side of the arch will deflect downwards while, at the same time the unloaded half of the arch will deflect upwards. That being so, if the deck itself is made stiff it will resist the upward movement of the arch on that side and so contribute to the overall stiffness of the structure. One might draw an analogy with the effect of deck stiffness in Figure 2.9. Maillart's later designs took the form of this deck-stiffened arch.[5]

[5] Billington, David P. *Robert Maillart's Bridges: the art of engineering*, Princeton, 1979.

Another form of arch that has been widely used is the two-pinned arch. Gustave Eiffel used this type for his Garabit Viaduct over the Truyère River, France, which for many years was the highest bridge in the world. This arch takes the form of a catenary, which is appropriate when the self-weight of the bridge is large in comparison with any live load that might come onto it. A catenary is the shape that a hanging chain adopts under its self-weight alone. Unfortunately, two-hinged arches cannot be analysed graphically and the forces in them will also change with changes in temperature. On a steel bridge these changes can be quite large as the steel warms up in the sun and would then want to expand. In a three-hinged arch this is possible because the arch can rise and fall slightly with rotation about the hinges, but it is not possible in a two-hinged arch as there is no central hinge to allow movement there. The effect is that the abutments will be called upon to restrain the arch and prevent its expansion, so there will be large inward forces that will induce bending in the arch. How much force and how much bending depend upon the stiffness of the arch, i.e. its resistance to bending.

In some ways like the Forth Bridge, the Garabit viaduct has long girders supporting the tracks that are simply picked up by the crown of the arch and a pair of columns on either side. Thus the arch is loaded with point loads from these columns. Figure 3.21 shows a simplified version of the bridge and assumes a large load coming down one of the vertical members that connects the girder with the arch. Such a load would be produced by a heavy locomotive crossing the bridge. Whatever the forces involved in supporting the self-weight of the bridge, the additional forces supporting this load must pass through the two hinges at the base of the arch. But with no other fixed point through which either force must pass it is clear that an infinite number of pairs of forces can be drawn to intersect on the load line. As before, the distance between the lines of thrust and the arch is an indication of the bending within the arch at any point, but note also that as the arch is deeper towards the crown its stiffness increases there also. The calculation of the forces on the arch must take into account not only the geometry of the arch but also its stiffness. There are also steel and concrete arches that have no hinges so that in these bridges there is bending at the supports. Of course that is just what a masonry arch is, except that the bending in a masonry arch is limited by the depth of the voussiors.

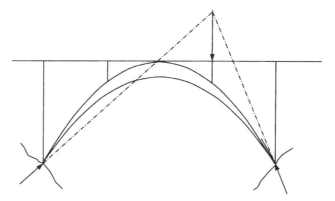

Figure 3.21 Effect of a point load on the Garabit viaduct.

The suspension bridge

How then does all this relate to suspension bridges? These were a nineteenth century development when large iron forgings could be produced to make the chains from which a deck could be hung. Rope bridges had been used by a number of civilisations for crossing very large distances, either over rivers or deep valleys. They were perfectly satisfactory while transport was by pack animals but they were not suitable for the wheeled carts and wagons used in Europe and North America. For these a flat deck was essential. But if the rope bridges seen by travellers could cross such large gaps it was reasonable to assume that something like that could be used to suspend a flat deck, except that iron chains or wire rope substituted for the natural fibres used in the rope bridges. We need not consider the technology of their construction but an important issue to be determined in their design was the relationship between the weight of the deck and the forces in the cables that are at the heart of the design.

James Finley designed the first suspension bridges in America, recognising that it would be a very cheap form of construction that might be widely used. His idea was to patent a design that others would pay to adopt, but if he was to make money out of this it was necessary to specify a method for determining the overall proportions of the bridge and the length of the hangers – a method that was simple for others to use. Knowing no mathematical techniques by which to calculate the forces in the cables of the bridge, or to determine the resulting shape that would give the hanger lengths, Finley resorted to experiment. He hung a number of weights on a cord that passed over a pulley and determined the tension force with a much larger weight (Figure 3.22a). He reasoned that this large weight would be equal to the tension in the cord either side of the pulley and, by symmetry, that the tension at the two ends of the cable would be equal. But what was the tension elsewhere in the cable?

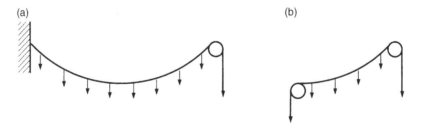

Figure 3.22 Finley's experiments to determine the forces in a suspension bridge.

He found the force at the centre by another experiment, dividing the cable in half and replacing the missing half by a second pulley and weight (Figure 3.23b). This looks something like Attwood's demonstration of the forces in an arch. As in Attwood's model, half the structure is used although the forces in it are in tension rather than in compression. Finley found that the second weight was smaller than the first so that the maximum force in the cable occurred at the supports. Because his intention was to patent a design that he could sell he needed a standard shape that all would use. This he decided should be such that the

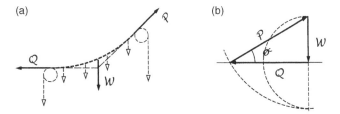

Figure 3.23 The triangle of forces and Finley's experiment.

tension in the cable would be equal to the weight of the bridge. Although that might seem rather arbitrary, it seems a reasonable starting point since one could presumably predict the weight of the bridge and test the chain to see if it would carry that load.

Finley found by experiment that this would occur when the sag in the cable was between 1/6.5 and 1/7 of the span. However, we could find this out by using the triangle of forces. Half of the suspension bridge can be represented by the diagram of Figure 3.23a, in which the weight of this half of the bridge, instead of being divided between the hangers, is combined into a single weight, W, acting halfway between the support and the mid-span. The force Q is the tension in the cable at mid-span, and the force P that in the cable at the support tower.

It is now a simple matter to draw the triangle of forces to scale, making the length of the inclined force P, the tension in the cable, twice that of the vertical force W, which is half the weight of the bridge. This can be done with a ruler and compass and will give the angle of inclination of the cable at the support. (Figure 3.23b includes the construction lines used to draw this diagram.) We know that the weight acts halfway along the half of the deck that we have drawn and that the line of inclination of the cable must intersect the deck at that point. Putting the forces back to where they actually act presents the full picture with the heavy broken line showing the suspension cable for the proportions of the bridge that Finley's method produces (Figure 3.24).

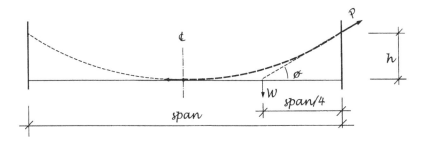

Figure 3.24 Proportions for the bridge using Finley's method.

Of course, for those with a little trigonometry this can be calculated rather than drawn and measured. Two methods are possible:

1 From the triangle of forces 2P sin $\emptyset$ = W but P = 2W
  Therefore sin $\emptyset$ = ½, from which $\emptyset$ = 30°
  $\tan\emptyset = 1/\sqrt{3} = h/(span/4)$
  i.e. $h = span/(4\sqrt{3})$
  From which h = span/6.93.
2 Again from the triangle of forces and using Pythagoras
  As P = 2W, the proportions of the triangle P : W : Q are $2 : 1 : \sqrt{3}$
  These are also the proportions of the triangle where h : span/4 = 1 : $\sqrt{3}$
  $h = span/(4\sqrt{3}) = span/6.93$

The behaviour of the suspension bridge was a little different from that of the rope bridge. While the latter weighs little and readily adapts itself to the loads that come onto it, suspension bridges have a relatively heavy and stiff deck that has to remain level. One does not want the bridge to have to adapt too much to the imposed loads so that it only works well if the load is small compared with the weight of the bridge. This was not immediately recognised. Some thought the suspension bridge could be used for railways, whose development occurred at much the same time, i.e. during the early nineteenth century. They were soon disillusioned. The weight of the train, or possibly just the engine, was sufficiently large compared with the weight of the bridge that it produced a considerable deflection in the supporting chain. This required the chain to rise in the unloaded part of the span taking the deck with it. According to Robert Stephenson the effect was like 'a wave before the engine ... just like a carpet'.[6]

We can see this effect in a line of washing. Hang an additional shirt on a line full of washing and there will not be much change in the shape of the line. But hang a wet towel on the same line and the change in shape will be more dramatic, the line being pulled down by the weight of the wet towel but rising up towards the far support. This analogy can then be applied to the suspension bridge. Assume that instead of having a weightless line a heavy chain hangs under its own weight taking the form of the dotted line shown in Figure 3.25. The weights are a combination of the weight of the chain and the weight of each length of bridge that a hanger supports. A weight representing a point load on the deck is now hung on the chain and it distorts into the shape shown by the solid line. The weight of the chain and deck are represented by a series of arrows of equal length distributed along the chain and the additional weight shown by the longer arrow.

Arches in buildings – flying buttresses

Before leaving the subject of arches we have to look at their use in buildings because they were so important in much early architecture. Arches in buildings did not spring from the

---

[6] Robert Stephenson's evidence to the *Report of the Commissioners Appointed to Inquire into the Use of Iron in Railway Structures*, 1849. Stephenson was reporting observations made by others.

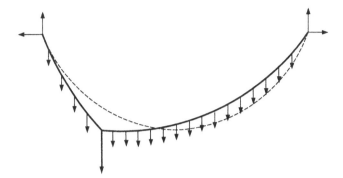

Figure 3.25 A point load on a heavy chain.

ground or from heavy piers, like those of a bridge, and the problem that faced their architects was that if an arch was used as the basis for a roof vault then how large should they make the supporting piers? This occupied the minds of a number of theorists. Wren's idea of balancing the weight of the vault with that of the pier was completely wrong. Others looked with varying success at the behaviour of the arch, success here being defined as the reasonableness of their theories compared with a modern understanding of the arch. The discussion above has provided some basis for determining the thrust of an arch, and in Chapter 5, which discusses walls and piers, we will look at the effect of a horizontal force applied to these structures. Then the overall stability is a matter of putting the two together. The matter that cannot be left till then is that of flying buttresses, not simply because they were referred to in the preface, but because they are a special case.

The vaulting of great churches is clearly arch-like in form and so equally clearly must thrust outwards. The three-dimensional nature of these vaults will be discussed in Chapter 9, but here we need to consider how the outward thrusts they produce at such prodigious heights might be brought safely to the ground. Just as the depth of an arch cannot be too shallow in relation to the span, so a buttress cannot be too small in relation to its height. Thus as cathedral builders went higher they had to bring the buttressing further out. The buttresses could hardly be solid over the aisle vaulting and so were built outside the aisle walls with arches flying across to where the builders supposed the vault thrust to be. Part of the problem was that these flyers had to be designed to resist a rather wide variation in loading. When first built they had simply to support their own weight because neither roof nor the vaults would be in place. As such they had to act as simple arches. When the roof was on they would have to resist wind loads when they occurred, although those on the windward side of the building would not be loaded. Eventually they would have to resist the thrust of the vaults, as well as occasional wind loads. The need to support its own weight and to act as a prop to the walls are conflicting requirements. The flying buttress needs to be at a steep angle to act as a prop but to support its own weight it acts as an arch producing vertical as well as horizontal forces at both supports.

This accounts for the shape of the buttresses, which have straight tops but are curved at the bottom. But although the shape of the buttress will accommodate this range of forces there is still one other problem. Under its self-weight alone there might not be sufficient compressive force between the voussoirs to prevent sliding at the upper end of the buttress, and studies have shown that many are close to this critical level of stress. To overcome this problem the flying buttresses were often propped at the end where they meet the wall by little columns, as suggested by the vertical arrow in Figure 3.26.

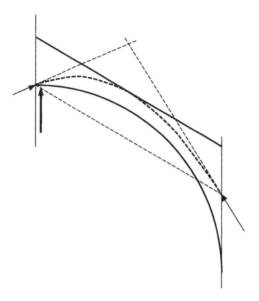

Figure 3.26 Lines of forces in a flying buttress.

What might be the ideal shape for the intrados of a flying buttress can be found by a graphic construction. The same construction would also suit a bridge arch where the deck was heavy in comparison to the rest of the bridge and the road needed to slope because the terrain required the ends to be at different heights. As we shall see it works better for bridges than flying buttresses. The construction depends upon two facts: that the ideal shape for an arch supporting a load distributed uniformly along a line is a parabola, and that if one joins the point of intersection of the tangents to any two points on a parabola to the mid-point of the chord drawn between those two points then the parabola itself bisects that line. If the second point is difficult to imagine the construction should make it clear (Figure 3.27).

We assume that the ends of the arch are given, this includes both the top line, which in a bridge would be the line of the roadway, and the springing points. Draw lines between the two springing points, which will be the chord of the parabola. From the mid-point of this chord draw a vertical line that cuts the line of the deck and extend it an equal distance above. From this point draw lines through the two springing points (the dotted lines of Figure 3.27b). These lines show the direction of the reactions at the springing points of the bridge. Divide the deck into a number of equal sections and, taking the mid-point of each, draw vertical lines to represent the loads. To one side (or below) set up the force diagram by first drawing a vertical line to represent the weight of the bridge divided into the same number of equal lengths as sections of the bridge deck. We shall call this the load line. From the ends

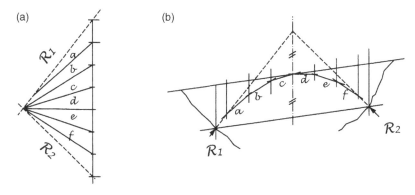

Figure 3.27 Finding the shape of a parabolic arch.

of this line draw lines parallel to the two reactions R_1 and R_2. From where these intersect draw lines to each of the points on the load line. Starting from one end and from the point where the line of reaction intersects the first vertical line representing the load, draw a line parallel to the line on the force diagram next to the reaction line. From where that intersects the next vertical line draw a line parallel to the next line of the force diagram, and so on. It is probably best to work from both ends towards the middle. If the drawing is accurate enough the curve traced out by these lines will be a parabola just touching the line of the deck.

Of course modern bridge engineers can set out a parabolic curve and cast concrete to that shape but Gothic builders were stuck with circular curves for their falsework. Therefore all that we can do is find a parabolic curve that can be drawn inside the shape of the flying buttress. There is a further point in that all of this depends upon the uniformly distributed load. As this will seldom be achieved in practice this simple construction can only be used as a starting point in design. The setting out of the flying buttress as a circular curve makes it heavier towards its ends and so the shape of the curve should be steeper at its ends than shown in Figure 3.26.

Arches in walls

This discussion of the flying buttress brings us to the question of arches within buildings, and while these first chapters have dealt largely with bridges in an attempt to keep to two-dimensional structures, we are now going to have to look at buildings. This is because arches were so commonly used in early buildings that it does not make sense to leave them aside only to have to return to them later. This will mean that for the first time we need to consider structures working in three dimensions.

The most common use of arches was simply to carry a wall over an opening, or a series of columns for an open arcade. Ideally an arch in a wall should be a segment of a circle, simple to set out and an appropriate shape for the load. But what happens if one wants a pointed arch to suit a Gothic style building? We know that a pointed arch is appropriate for carrying a large point load at mid-span rather than for a continuous load. The builders of the Doge's Palace in Venice cunningly combined both shapes.

The wall of the upper part of the palace is carried on an arcade of pointed, Gothic columns. To combine this choice of architectural style with the structural requirement for arches that were segments of circles, the first stage of the structure was a series of semicircular arches to take the load of the wall, clearly seen on the righthand side of Figure 3.28. These were supported by a second series of arches of the same span but displaced to one side. As the first row of arches produced a series of point loads (as shown) it was appropriate for this second row to be pointed arches. The supports for these were rather closely spaced so every other support was carried on a third set of arches, also loaded at the crown and so pointed. This enabled every other column to be removed. Finally the upper tier of arches was cunningly disguised as a circular decoration within the spandrels of the intermediate arches, seen on the left of the drawing. One needs to look carefully to appreciate the structure.[7]

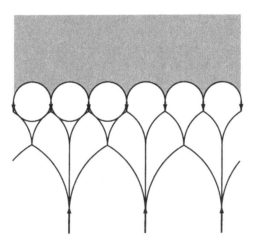

Figure 3.28 The arches of the Doge's Palace.

The architects of this building faced another problem. In a single-span bridge the abutments resist the outward thrust of the arch. In a building there is commonly the masonry wall either side of an opening that is able to resist the arch thrust. If there is more than one span, as there is in an arcade, then the thrusts of adjacent spans cancel each other out at each column. But there might be no adjacent span, something that was inevitable at the corner of an arcade, and it would be unfortunate if buttresses had to be built to resist the thrust. That is something seen in early arcades, but buttresses at the corner of the Doge's Palace in

---

[7]This structure was first described by Felix J. Samuely in 'Tricento mechanics', *Architectural Review*, 1950;108: 191–93.

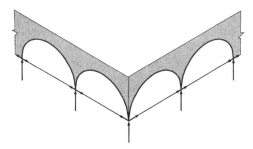

Figure 3.29 Restraining arches at the corner of a building.

Venice would hardly have been appropriate. In this case, and in many other examples in Italy at that time, the simple answer was to use tie rods across the tops of the columns to resist the outward thrust of the arches. This is seen in Figure 3.29, where there are pairs of semi-circular arches at the corner of a building.

A more interesting problem occurs at internal corners although it is a less frequent occurrence. This is the situation in cloisters where the vaulting (see Chapter 9) is carried by arches around the inside of the cloisters. The arches across the cloisters naturally thrust outwards on the arcade of columns but these are buttressed. Like the arcade of arches around the Doge's Palace the arches along the outside of the cloister thrust against each other until the corner is reached. There the corner column has thrusts from two adjacent sides and so two thrusts at right angles to each other. In the cloister of medieval cathedrals this was not a problem because the cloisters were vaulted and the vaults provided the counteracting thrusts required. Of course they did – these were the thrusts that elsewhere along the cloisters might have to be resisted by buttresses against the outside of the columns. But what if the roof was not vaulted?

In Spain there are a number of two-storey cloisters, vaulted on the ground floor but with the upper cloisters roofed with simple rafter and tiled roofs. These are carried on an arcade of arches just like those on the ground floor below, but the problem for their designers was

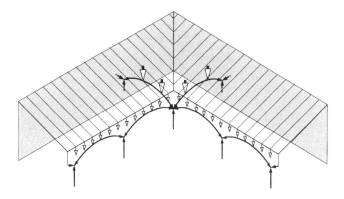

Figure 3.30 Upper cloisters of Toledo Cathedral.

how to cope with the thrusts of these upper arches on the corner columns when there was no counteracting force from a vaulted ceiling. All that they could do was to strut across the cloister to the mass of the building behind, the question being the form that these struts should take. Simple timber beams would have been an adequate, if inelegant solution. The ideal would be to construct something in masonry, continuing the arch form of the arcade. The difficulty with that idea is that the arches would have had horizontal thrusts at their abutments but no corresponding load on the arch itself. The result would have been the same kind of failure as Edwards's bridge; they would have sprung upwards in the centre. The solution was to provide each arch with the necessary load to ensure the line of thrust remained within it. To justify the arch shape some sculpture might be placed on it to provide this load (Figure 3.30); lions *couchants* might be suitable. The example that I have in mind is in Toledo where the arcade uses three-centred arches.

4 Bringing the Loads to the Ground – The Structural Scheme

Introduction

Bridges have been discussed in these early chapters because, apart from ensuring their resistance to wind loads, they are two-dimensional structures in which the structural components are clearly apparent. Buildings are more complex if only because the load-bearing elements are often not immediately distinguishable from those that are not load-bearing. Of course, this is something most people recognize because a common question asked by those who want to remodel their houses is whether or not a particular wall can be removed. Is it supporting the floor above? They know that floors are supported by walls but that not all walls serve this function. The difficulty is because walls have very different functional requirements: the bridge is there to support a load, to enable us to cross a gap, while a building is there to provide shelter. Apart from the very simplest buildings they are also divided by walls into rooms that have different functions, and in many forms of construction there is little difference between the walls that separate outside from inside or that separate various rooms, whether the walls are carrying load or not.

Buildings are also three-dimensional objects so that there can be different ways in which the loads are brought to the ground. In the simplest buildings the only load that the structure has to carry is the weight of the roof, although in some cases the wind loads can become significant. If the simple building of Figure 4.1a were built of masonry we might reasonably expect the roof to span across the building and so be carried by the two long walls. If that were so the gable walls might be removed and replaced with some non-load-bearing material, a sheet of glass perhaps, so looking like Figure 4.1b. But it is also possible, if a little more difficult, for the roof to span the length of the building and be carried by the gable walls. In that case it is the long walls that could be removed, or replaced with a glass wall, as in Figure 4.1c. In fact, as we shall see in Chapter 6, it is possible for the weight of the roof to be carried

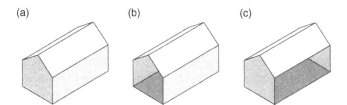

(a)   (b)   (c)

Figure 4.1 In a simple masonry building it is not always a straightforward matter to identify the load-bearing walls.

by the long walls while the wind load on the roof is carried by the end walls. In designing a building it is a matter of choice, while in understanding an existing one it is a matter of detective work.

These differences are just some of those that make building structures more difficult, or more interesting, depending upon how you see it. To summarise the differences between buildings and bridges, bridges are simple structures because: (i) they have a simple function, which is to carry load and the structure is clearly visible; (ii) they are two-dimensional, or can be divided fairly simply into two-dimensional elements; and (iii) they are generally made of a single material, such as timber, iron, steel or concrete. In contrast buildings are more complex because their principal purpose is to provide shelter and the structure is only there to support the shelter-providing elements. Therefore the structure is not clearly visible because walls might be used to perform either or both of these functions. Often the structure is hidden behind decorative elements, i.e. roof and floor structures are hidden above ceilings, and walls may also contain hidden structures. They are also assembled out of a number of materials that can behave quite differently and the interaction between these can be as important as the behaviour of each alone. They are three-dimensional, either because the load-carrying elements, while two-dimensional in themselves, are formed into three-dimensional assemblies, or because the individual elements might be three-dimensional in both form and behaviour. This last point is something that we will deal with in the final chapter.

How one chooses a structure is a matter of design skill and the development of this skill is not something that can easily be tracked through a book that is trying to develop analytical skills. Skill in design comes from recognising the available choices and being able to decide between them. Although students of design need to keep in mind the development of this skill, it is much simpler to explore the choices made by those in the past through what they built – which is the general theme of this book, suggesting ways of developing the detective skills necessary to understand existing buildings. That is the strategy adopted here.

The alternatives

As it might not be obvious exactly how a building is carrying its loads, the detective always needs to bear in mind the various possibilities. Consider for example a simple two-storey building with just two rooms on each floor (Figure 4.2a,b). The arrows show the direction in which the floors might span and there are two possible arrangements for that; either the central wall and the two short external walls are loadbearing (Figure 4.2a), or the joists span across between the long external walls (Figure 4.2b). Even if the joists span between the long walls the internal ground floor wall might have to support an internal wall on the floor above. It will certainly have to if the latter is masonry and might have to even if it were timber, depending upon how the wall above is built. A timber wall might simply rest on the wall below or be designed to span across between the walls on either side. Even if the internal ground floor wall were load bearing it is not impossible to remove it providing that a suitably sized beam is substituted.

One can see that even in the simplest building there is a range of possibilities, and we have not yet considered the roof, nor indeed how we might make a hole in the floor to

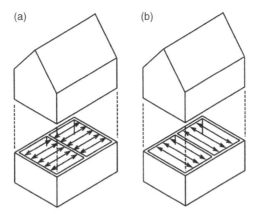

Figure 4.2 Alternative floor spanning directions.

accommodate a staircase. How then is one to distinguish between the two arrangements shown? It is the floor construction that will give the clue and, short of taking up the flooring to see, one might be able to tell simply by looking at the run of the floorboards. They must be at right angles to the direction of the joists that support them and so presumably parallel to the load-bearing walls. Would that it were so simple. In many cases the floor will comprise no more than boards and joists, as this suggests, but as we shall see in Chapter 7, there are other ways of constructing floors, so that occasionally some opening up of the fabric might be required – meaning in this case the lifting of one or two floorboards.

The roof might well pitch across the short distance onto the long walls, but if the building is part of a row of houses that would not be convenient because there would then be gutters over the party walls; better to pitch the roof front to back (Figure 4.3a,b). This does not mean that it is the external walls that are carrying the roof because, as we shall see in Chapter 8, there is more than one way to structure a roof. The two simplest and contrasting methods are for roofs to be based upon rafters that span across the building or to have purlins that span the length of the roof.

These very simple examples show how there are different structural possibilities in the simplest of buildings. Designing a building involves choosing a suitable *structural scheme*,

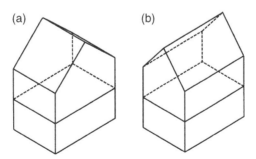

Figure 4.3 Alternative roof pitches.

i.e. the means by which the loads on the structure might be brought to the ground; understanding an existing building involves determining what its structural scheme actually is. The latter is in fact the task of the conservator, who often has to deal with buildings that are showing signs of distress. Then the task is to diagnose the causes of this distress and to prescribe an appropriate remedy. I choose these words deliberately because understanding the behaviour of existing structures, especially when they are showing signs of distress, can be likened to medical diagnosis.

Buildings show signs of aging and their present condition might be a reflection of little more than that. The aging can be exacerbated by a lack of maintenance, just as there are those who neglect their bodies. Distress might even be the result of deliberate alterations to the building by those who have failed to recognise the possible effects of such changes. It might be the result of some abuse of the building, its use for some unsuitable purpose for example, perhaps leading to an overloading of structural members, or it might be the result of some external agency. Just as the doctor has to determine the causes of an illness, given the symptoms, so understanding a structure involves a similar diagnostic process. The advantage the doctor has is that all his or her patients have the same anatomy, whereas buildings differ considerably. The result is that diagnosing a building problem requires a description of the anatomy first and perhaps rather more exploratory surgery than is necessary for a human patient. The advantage that the conservator has is that the building has rather simpler functions than a human body, simply to stand up and keep out the weather, and as the first of these involves resisting the loads that are imposed upon the structure; it is these we must discuss next.

Choices

If design of a structure is a matter of choice, how ideally should we choose? – 'ideally' because the design of a building's structure is naturally constrained by a variety of considerations other than the structural ones. One should ideally span across the shortest distance and bring the loads down to the ground by the simplest and most direct route. We can see how this works in my early nineteenth century house, which is quite small and has the joists on the first floor spanning from front to back (Figure 4.4). This is sensible for the larger room at the front simply because that is the shortest direction and there is a central load-bearing wall. It also avoids the joists having to be carried either by the party wall separating my house from the one next door or by the wall with the chimneys. However, this is not possible in the room at the back of the house (not shown here), which is too long for the same pattern to be repeated and so the joists span across the narrow direction. Neither is the pattern repeated completely for the ground floor, which is over cellars. The joists do span from front to back under the two ground-floor rooms but not across the ground-floor passage, where they run from side to side. This is almost certainly because the passage is paved with stone flags above boarding and the builders were concerned about the weight of the flags on a longer span.

This flooring layout was commonly used in semi-detached houses, as mine is, or in terraced houses (row houses) of the nineteenth and early twentieth centuries. But in Britain a form of construction called cross-wall construction became popular for terraced houses in

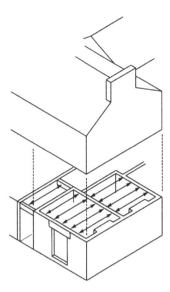

Figure 4.4 A simple arrangement of floor joists.

the 1960s. In this form the only load-bearing walls were those between the houses, so that the joists spanned across the building between these. Fixing into the party wall was no longer a problem because of another change in technology. The joists were supported on metal joist hangers that were built in to the masonry, so that the joists themselves were not built in. The advantage of this was that the front and rear walls were not load bearing and without the need to support a floor above them large windows could be incorporated. Here was a change in the basic design of houses that involved a change in structure and one that took advantage of the relatively new technology of joist hangers.

One can see a similar kind of change in the construction of some blocks of apartments in Britain in the 1930s, with a change from steel to concrete frames. From the end of World War I onwards, apartments in London had been built using steel frames, with floors of concrete. The common pattern was for the frames to span across the building with beams carrying a concrete floor. (Arrows on Figure 4.5 show the direction of span of the floor slabs.) Steel beams were also needed between the frames, partly to ensure overall stability, especially during construction, and partly to carry walls, especially those at the front and back, which would commonly be of brick masonry. Office buildings were constructed in much the same way. The main steel beams would not be able to span completely from front to back so that intermediate columns within the building were needed, resulting in a repeating rectangular grid of columns and beams.

With the use of reinforced concrete an alternative was possible in which the front and rear walls were treated as the frames with the floor now spanning across the building. An intermediate frame was needed because the floor still could not span all the way across. However, because reinforced concrete was not built as frames of standard sections joined together, there was no need to keep the same column spacing on these three longitudinal frames. The columns on the front, rear and intermediate frames could have a quite different

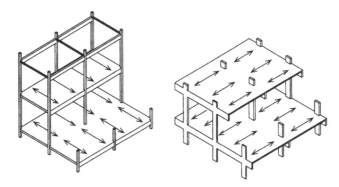

Figure 4.5 Possible floor spanning in steel and concrete frame buildings.

spacing if that suited the plan and the arrangement of openings, although few architects were to take advantage of this new freedom. Whether the habit of mind of using a rigid geometrical grid suited architects' approach to the planning of buildings or was simply a reflection of their lack of facility with structures, so that a grid seemed a safe approach, is an interesting question.

It was not just that the spanning arrangements of the floors could be turned round in this way. Reinforced concrete was a walling material as much as it was a framing material. In other words, it was just as suitable for load-bearing walls as it was for frames. This presented a number of structural possibilities, illustrated in a drawing by Ove Arup. Redrawn here as Figure 4.6, it shows four possible layouts for the construction of blocks of flats. In the first two the front and rear walls are shown as just that – walls. However, these would naturally be pierced by windows and so might take on much the same form as a frame. The

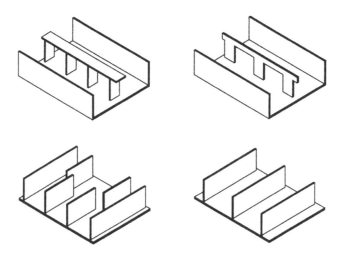

Figure 4.6 Ove Arup's suggested layouts for concrete frame of flats.

central row of columns and the spine beam might be constructed as short walls either set across the width of the building and carrying a broad shallow beam, or set along the length of the building with a deep narrow beam, The other two arrangements are for load-bearing transverse walls. The one on the right is the most basic 'cross-wall construction', but the other shows how walls might be at different spacings front and rear to accommodate different widths of rooms. Reinforced concrete offered different possibilities for those able to understand it sufficiently to take advantage of the flexibility in structural planning that it offered.

Nature of the loads

In all building structures there are two kinds of loads, those of the building itself, its self-weight, and those loads that are imposed upon it after the building has been completed – what engineers call superimposed loads, but which are often called live loads because they come and go. It is not the absolute magnitude of these loads that is of concern here, because this book is not about detailed structural analysis; what is of interest is the relative magnitude of these forces in any structure. As we have seen, a masonry arch bridge will carry quite large loads with no visible effect whereas a single person walking across a rope bridge will produce a very noticeable effect on the shape of the structure. The former weighs a great deal in itself and so the live loads will often be small in comparison, and have relatively little effect on the forces within the structure. In contrast, a rope bridge weighs very little so that anyone crossing it produces a large effect on the overall forces. These simple examples show that the relative magnitudes of the forces depend upon the kind of structure we are considering. At the same time it is important to be aware that loads in different directions can also be very different in magnitude.

Before we can deal with this we have to consider the units of measurement that we are using. What many people will be familiar with is the kilogram (symbol: kg) – but this is a unit of mass and not one of force. For the latter we use the newton (symbol: N). What Isaac Newton observed was that objects remain at rest unless they are acted on by a force, which will then accelerate them. We are largely concerned with objects that are acted on by the force of gravity. A newton is the force that will accelerate a mass of 1 kg by 1 m/s/s. That means that after 1 second from rest the body will be travelling at 1 m/s, after 2 seconds 2 m/s, and so on. But if I drop a kilogram weight it will accelerate downwards at 9.8 m/s/s. In fact in the absence of air resistance so will any object that is dropped on earth. This must mean that there is a downward force due to gravity of 9.8 N on the 1 kg weight. Thus 1 kg force = 9.8 N. Let us approximate this to 10 N. If I buy a kilogram of apples I will get about 10. This means that each apple exerts a downward force of about 1 N. This is the force in the stalk that held it to the tree, or the force that each apple in my fruit bowl exerts on the table that is now supporting it. Thus if an engineer gives you a figure in Newtons you might like to think of it as just so many apples.

Builders of medieval castles did not need to bother about the wind loads on their walls because they were of such massive construction that the wind forces were negligible compared with the walls' self-weight. At the same time carpenters building timber barns did need to consider wind loads because these were large compared with the building's self-weight. The design of the frame was determined as much by the need to resist wind loads as it was to carry the weight of the roof, something that those working with such buildings today need to be aware of. It is instructive to compare the dead loads and the wind loads on such a structure. The Wheat Barn at Cressing Temple, Essex, one of the major monastic barns of England, has bays about 6 m long, and with a height of about 10 m the area facing the wind is 60 m^2 (i.e. 60 square metres) on each bay (Figure 4.7). If the wind load is assumed to be 700 N/m^2 (newtons per square metre) then the wind force on each bay that the frames will have to resist is 60×700 N $= 42\,000$ N. To cut down the length of the numbers we commonly work in kilonewtons (1 kN $= 1000$ N), therefore this is 42 kN. The width of the barn is 12 m so the plan area of each bay is 72 m^2. However, the area of the roof must be greater as the roof slopes at 60°. In fact, at that slope the area of the roof is twice the ground plan area. Roof tiles weigh about 70 kg/m^2, producing a force of 0.7 kN/m^2. Thus one bay of roof exerts a downward force of $2 \times 0.7 \times 72$ kN $= 100.8$ kN. The wind load is approaching half of that and would be greater in proportion if a lighter roof covering had been used.

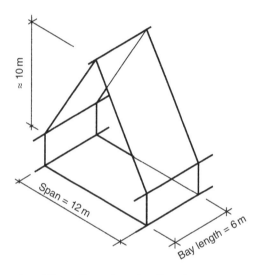

Figure 4.7 Dimensions of the Wheat Barn, Cressing Temple.

The weight of the tiles and the roof structure supporting them is something that can be calculated with a fair degree of precision but the wind load is determined statistically. 'In Hartford, Hereford and Hampshire, hurricanes hardly ever happen', but they do sometimes and it is well that we design for them. That is the basis of the wind load used. This statistical approach is also the basis of all the live loads that we use in designing buildings. The design load for a living room floor is not that for the normal arrangement of people and furniture but for the occasions when the furniture is pushed back and you have a crowded cocktail party.

In lightweight timber structures like the timber-framed barn that are not rooted in the ground it is friction forces between the sole plate and the plinth wall on which it stands that prevents a timber frame structure from being shifted sideways by the wind. Therefore the weight of the building has some advantages. Friction forces are dependent upon what is called the coefficient of friction between the two materials in contact and the magnitude of the force at right angles to the contact surface, in other words the weight of the building. It should be apparent that as the wind blows on the side of a building the vertical forces supporting it change and so too must the friction forces that can be developed. We can see this simply by taking moments of the forces; the force on the windward side is reduced and that on the leeward side increased. Whether or not this has a significant effect on the structure depends upon the extent to which it relies upon horizontal forces at the base, but clearly if the roof load is reduced so will the friction force that can be developed. If, as has so often happened, a farmer despairs of keeping a tiled roof on his timber framed barn in good repair and replaces it with corrugated iron, there is little more than the self weight of the timber frame itself to hold the building to the ground.

It is common for the self-weight of the building to change as dramatically as this but of course when buildings are being built not only is the weight on the structure changing, so is the nature of the structure itself. All buildings have to go through this phase and so all have to be capable of standing up during this process. Of course they may be assisted by temporary structures, sometimes referred to as *falsework*, but however it is done, understanding the process of building and the nature of the forces that are being carried at the time is a significant part of understanding the nature of some structures.

'Flow of forces', or action and reaction

Buildings are built from the ground upwards and it is the ground that provides the ultimate support. Loads, however, start at the roof and accumulate downwards, and so when a designer thinks about a structure it is from the top downwards. The roof timbers have to be carried by the wall plate, and the wall plate by the wall below it. Further down the wall has to carry all of this, the load of the floor and the weight of the wall between the roof and the floor. Loads add up as we work our way down the building and any horizontal forces they generate similarly increase. Moreover, each component has to be designed before its weight is known accurately. Sometimes, as we saw in the Quebec Bridge, we have to make an estimate (or if you prefer a guess – but then some guesses are more carefully made than others) but eventually this needs to be checked. Thus structural calculations work down from the top and that is also how one should think in qualitative terms.

Determining the forces in the structure is rather more than a simple accounting process. While the sum of the vertical forces at any point in the structure must equal the sum of the vertical loads that have been applied above that point, we have already seen that there may equally well be horizontal forces as a result of those vertical loads. Arches thrust outwards on their supports, as do vaults, domes and the rafters of a roof. Moreover, these horizontal forces can be larger than the vertical forces that have given rise to them. In the bracket with which we began, the horizontal force at the wall is commonly larger than the force applied at the end of the bracket, the ratio of the two depending of course on the geometry of the structure.

Having determined the structural scheme, the sequence and arrangement of members through which the loads are brought to the ground, this is best shown in a drawing (or drawings). Walls may be supporting the floors and the roof of a building but, as is clear from Figure 4.2, the question is to determine which walls. Nevertheless, it is not helpful to think in terms of the flow of forces, or at least not to draw forces as if they were flowing down the structure, all in the same direction, like some river gathering in size and strength as it goes. Structures are about resisting forces; the structure reacts to the applied loads and we are in fact dealing with Newton's third law – to every action there is an equal and opposite reaction – and this is how the forces are best shown.

If I place a bust of Newton on a stand, symbolised by an apple in the illustration (Figure 4.8), it presses down on the stand. The stand pushes upwards on the apple with an equal force but in the opposite direction. Therefore if I add together the two forces at the point of contact, taking into account their direction (positive for a downward force, negative for an upward force – or vice versa), the result is zero force. Neglecting for a moment the weight of the stand, it must push down on the ground with the same force as that produced by the weight of the apple, and so the ground will push upwards with an equal and opposite force.

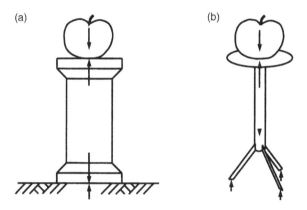

Figure 4.8 Forces supporting a weight on a stand.

For those concerned with the mathematics, this is another aspect of forces being vectors having both direction and magnitude. This applies even for forces acting in the same line; they may be positive or negative forces depending upon their direction. Here the downward direction has been chosen to be positive so that upwards is negative. It could have been the other way round; it is simply a sign convention. We choose these two directions because we are so frequently dealing with vertical forces. Similarly we would select a sign convention for horizontal forces, say left to right as positive and right to left as negative, although again it could be the other way round. Adding to this the requirement that all moments must sum to zero we have three simple equations of equilibrium:

$$\Sigma V = 0, \ \Sigma H = 0, \ \Sigma M = 0.$$

What we have are pairs of equal and opposite forces, the apple and the stand, the stand and the ground, and the apple and the ground. The last pair is important because these are the externally applied forces. No matter what the structure may be in between, the loads and the reactions from the ground must sum to zero. So too, of course, do the internal forces. The stand has equal and opposite forces at each end pushing outwards, so the stand is in compression. Of course this is complicated by adding in the weight of the stand but one can treat this as an additional external load acting at the centre of gravity of the stand.

Describing the structure

It does not matter how the stand supporting the bust of Newton is constructed, the forces at the base will be the same, or rather they will add up to the same. The reactions must equal the applied loads. That means that we can consider a structure as a whole. Instead of the simple stand of Figure 4.8a, assume our bust of Newton is placed upon a more modern looking stand comprising a disc at the top with a tube welded to three legs at the bottom (Figure 4.8b) (well, each to his own!). We still know that the three forces at the base must sum to the weight placed on the stand – there is no need to consider the forces in the welded joints to know that. Of course, these three forces need not be equal unless the whole thing is symmetrical about the central axis, including the placing of the load. If the load is not centrally placed we can still work out the distribution of forces in the three feet simply from the geometry and without reference to the construction in between.

In some circumstances it might be necessary to examine that intermediate structure. I might imagine another stand with three wooden feet, curved as shown (although only one is drawn – Figure 4.9) and fastened to the vertical member. Again the force at the foot can be worked out from the geometry, but suppose we are interested in the magnitude of the forces in the screws that hold a foot onto the upright of the stand. Here we are not looking at the overall forces but the forces on a part of the structure, in this case a single element;

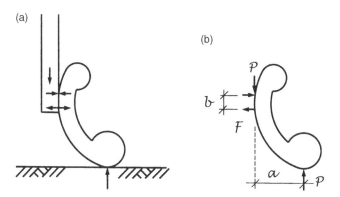

Figure 4.9 The forces on the foot of a stand.

but it might equally be a group of members that we wish to separate from the rest of the structure to examine. Of course, we have already done this in some of the earlier drawings, it is just that I did not draw attention to it. The purpose of doing so here is to introduce a technical term. If we separate the foot from the rest of the stand (Figure 4.9b) we can draw it with just the forces on the foot, i.e. the two vertical forces and the two horizontal forces. Such a drawing is called a *free body diagram*, drawn as if the part of the structure were float-ing in space, an abstraction that often helps one to think clearly about the nature of the forces on a part of the structure. These forces must of course be in equilibrium and, just as all the vertical forces on the stand must sum to zero, so too must the vertical forces on any part of it. Moreover, the horizontal forces and the moments of all these forces about any point must also sum to zero.

   A little thought shows that the bottom screw will be in tension. Looking just at the foot, the two vertical forces produce a moment that is the product of each force multiplied by the distance between them – distance measured as the distance between their lines of action, here shown dotted. The forces in the screws fixing the foot to the vertical leg of the stand also produce a moment, which is also the magnitude of each force multiplied by the distance between them – a distance that is a little more obvious in this case. These two moments must always be equal – hence $P.a = F.b$

For those wondering how to find the forces in each of the feet when the load is not placed symmetrically, first draw a plan with the positions of the load and the feet marked. Draw a line through two of the feet and take moments of the forces about that line. This will give the reaction provided by the third foot. Repeat the exercise for a second axis and second foot. The force in the third foot is found by arithmetic.

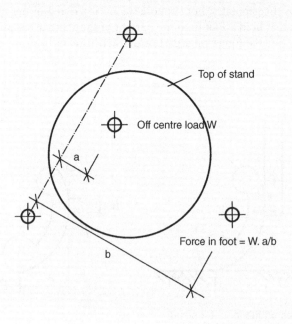

Top of stand

Off centre load W

a

Force in foot = W. a/b

b

Figure 4.10

Structures are three-dimensional

All structures are three-dimensional and we need to bear this in mind. In the roof of my house the slates are carried on battens laid from side to side over rafters that span from front to back. One might suppose therefore that all of the load is delivered to the front and rear walls, but in fact the rafters would be too small to do that. Instead they are in part supported by *purlins*, beams that span between the party walls; loads carried first by members spanning in one direction are transferred to members spanning in another (Figure 4.11). Nevertheless all the members of the roof are linear elements. These loads are then delivered to walls that are simple flat planes. Thus although the overall structure is three-dimensional it can be broken down into elements that can be fully represented in two dimensions. Although it is often very useful to draw the structure as a perspective or isometric so that one can see how the various elements relate to each other, once that is done we can then draw the structure as a series of two-dimensional planes: plans, elevations or sections. But we shall see the value of drawing the structure in three dimensions when we come to consider structures of walls in Chapter 5, when it will become apparent that they need the horizontal restraint of the floors and roofs, structures that act in a horizontal plane while the walls are acting in vertical planes. There are, of course, those structures that are inherently three-dimensional, those whose structural behaviour cannot be simply represented in one plane or another. These are left to Chapter 9.

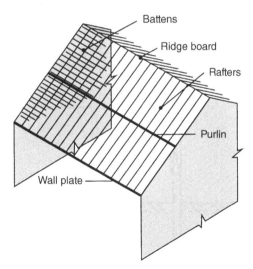

Figure 4.11 An arrangement of roof timbers.

We might reasonably distinguish between load-bearing wall structures and framed structures, and that is the implication of the division made in the next two chapters. However, this is not a rigid division, and not always helpful, nor does it necessarily depend upon the materials used. We think of steel and timber as materials from which frames are made, and while concrete can be formed into either frames or load-bearing walls, masonry is used for walls. Nevertheless the Gothic cathedral has such large openings in the masonry that it would perhaps be more useful to see it as a framed structure. At the same time there are timber frames where the vertical elements are so small and so close together that we choose to call them studs rather than posts and the whole assembly can be more sensibly thought of as a load-bearing wall. Today there are light steel frames that have been built in imitation of this timber stud construction. Thus, a division into types may be convenient in some respects, but beware of the boundaries.

This raises another point that we need to deal with here. The stand with three feet is called a statically determinate structure. That means that all the forces in it can be found from the simple laws of statics that we have been developing here – as clearly shown by the exercise above for those who cared to follow it. The same is not true if the stand has four legs. Then the forces in it cannot be found from this simple procedure. Such structures are called statically indeterminate. We have already seen such a structure in the Garabit Viaduct, the two-hinged arch. The detailed examination of such structures is beyond the scope of this book because they require more than the very elementary mathematics that I would assume of the reader – and, truth to tell, more than I now care to bother with most of the time. But some qualitative appreciation of such structures is useful and possible. The simple rule is that the stiffer members of a structure attract the most load. Imagine two fence posts of different sizes planted in the ground but connected together with a rope (Figure 4.12). If we pull on the rope both will deflect by the same amount. But we know that it will take a larger force to deflect the larger and therefore stiffer post than the smaller more flexible one. We can turn this into a general principle that when a load is applied to a structure with components of different stiffness those with the greater stiffness 'pick up' the larger proportion of the load. In a simple arrangement of two members like this it will simply be in direct proportion to their relative stiffness. Of course, this is not true of statically determinate structures where the forces remain unchanged by any change in stiffness.

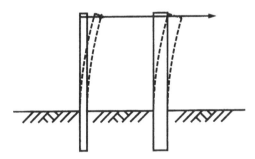

Figure 4.12 Two structures of unequal stiffness connected together will deflect equally.

There is a cautionary tale associated with this that illustrates the point. I had been asked to design the structure for a large timber building on the shores of the Bosporus. It was the reconstruction of an historic yalı. The client was unsure of the structural soundness of timber, which he thought might rot or catch fire, and our meeting largely involved my attempts to reassure him. I clearly had not succeeded because after the outline design was completed he wanted some steel incorporated into the structure. The architect, at a design meeting with the other consultants present, presented me with a drawing that showed two steel beams that the client wanted. I could see this was going to be a problem. 'What I suggest that we do is put in the steel beams that the client wants but not connect them to anything.' Much laughter. But that was the most sensible thing to do with them. The Bosporus is an earthquake-prone area. With other steel put in to support the beams that the client wanted the resulting steel structure, being much stiffer than the timber structure around it, picked up the majority of the earthquake loads, concentrating them at a few stiff points whereas they had previously been shared over a much larger number of members. It proved impossible to accommodate the forces on the steel.

The designer of a structure is dealing with stiffness as much as strength, and in many cases relative stiffness. In Figure 4.12 the relative stiffness is the relative ability of the two posts to resist bending, but it might involve other kinds of load resistance. A wall taking loads in its own plane would be very stiff; we might even consider it to be rigid. This sometimes means that something that has not been considered as part of the structure will pick up loads in an unexpected way. While you are designing the structure to act in the way that you think it will, it will eventually behave in the way that it chooses to do so, and it is as well to look to see where the forces might go just as much as where you want them to go.

Finally, while this chapter has been about what forces come onto what members, the route by which the loads are transmitted to the ground and those parts of the construction that are brought into play, we should note that forces need to be transmitted from one member to another. There will therefore be forces between the members that have to be transmitted across the junction. This might be as simple as a timber beam or joist resting on a masonry wall. The question would then be simply whether there was enough bearing area between the two so that the timber, the weaker of the two materials, did not crush under the load. This is a very simple example, but similar issues are raised with all structures. Moreover, much of the design effort on the part of the engineer, perhaps the majority of the effort, may well be in the design of the connections between members.

5 Safe as Houses? – Walls

Something there is that does not love a wall,
That sends the frozen-ground-swell under it,
And spills the upper boulders in the sun;

Robert Frost – *Mending Wall*

Putting up a building means either first constructing some form of frame or building walls, and the latter seems to be the simpler structure to understand. All that is necessary is to pile up the stone, brick, or perhaps even earth, except that, as Robert Frost's poem shows, it has at least to have a good foundation. He points out something that is clear to all who live in northern climates. Ground water near the surface can freeze in winter producing small movements that will eventually disrupt the masonry of a simple dry-stone wall that has no proper foundations. For a cheaply built boundary wall, making a good foundation is too much trouble and it is simpler to repair the wall from time to time in the way that Frost describes, the neighbours working either side of it. Making sure the wall is well founded means taking it down to below the frost line but also to a soil that is capable of bearing the load; Biblical authority says that it is no use building on sand.

In spite of that there are plenty of examples of structures built on foundations that are clearly inadequate. The leaning tower of Pisa is not the only tower to lean in such a dramatic way, even if it is the most famous. The lean on the campanile of the church of Santa Martino on the island of Burano can be clearly seen across the lagoon from Venice about 10 km away. Walls also lean, but whether because of inadequate foundations or because they are being pushed into that position is a moot point. The walls of ancient churches may lean but this might well be because without gutters water dripping off a roof has softened the soil on the outside of the building and allowed the wall to settle more on that side than on the inside. Walls sometimes show some differential settlement along their length because the nature of the soil varies.

If we build on rock, which will bear as much load as the masonry, the question is whether there are any limits to the height of wall that can be built. This depends upon whether it is a thin wall or a thick wall, which in turn involves defining what we mean by those terms. Try building a wall of toy bricks to see how high you can make it. As the wall gets higher it becomes more and more wobbly until eventually, no matter how carefully you place the bricks, the wall falls over. No horizontal force has been applied; the wall has simply become unstable. Of course, if the wall were outside and had to resist wind forces it would collapse much sooner. If the wall were made thicker one could build it higher before this happens, but that is not the most efficient solution for a higher wall, and what thicker and higher walls would show when they too fell over is that the height limit for all of them was some multiple of their thickness; a wall falls over because it becomes too slender.

Given whatever height is required, making the wall thick enough to stand would seem to be the simplest approach but, as we shall see, there are other ways of improving a wall's stability. The question is then whether there are any other limits to the height of a wall; would it be practicable to build a brick skyscraper? The limit here is the compressive strength of the mortar. Building higher means carrying more load, both of the floors and the wall itself, and the wall thickness at the bottom has to be increased to cope with that. Eventually a height is reached where the area of the floor added is no more than the reduction in floor area produced by the increased thickness of brickwork lower down. The effect can be seen in the construction of the first Monadnock building in Chicago, which reached this point of diminishing returns. When the second Monadnock building was built next to it a steel frame was used instead, with a consequent increase in lettable floor area. But other tall structures have demonstrated the practical limits of masonry. In Renaissance Italy rich families competed in building towers as symbols of wealth, power and prestige: Bologna had a number of such towers and is still famous for them. Like walls they were built by piling masonry units one on the other. Many have collapsed, some quite recently, so that the condition of some of those remaining is a cause for concern, even though they are not particularly slender. In 1902 the sixteenth century campanile in the piazza at St Mark's, Venice, collapsed suddenly so that the structure that we have today is a reproduction of the original. Although it had survived hundreds of years it was presumably built close to the limits for such a structure. Small ground movements, the vibrations produced by the ringing of bells or damage from lightning strikes are all factors that might weaken such a structure and result in a catastrophic failure. But why should such structures be so vulnerable? What kinds of stresses are they under that they cannot withstand? While the behaviour of these tower structures has only recently attracted the attention of structural engineers[1] the behaviour of thick walls is fairly well understood.

The stability of a wall is therefore something that needs to be considered as carefully as the soundness of its foundations. A minority of walls are simply a solid sheet of masonry; the majority have openings for doors or windows so that their design and construction also has to address that issue. And while today we are used to brick masonry or concrete block walls, in the past builders made do with other materials, perhaps the poor quality stone of Robert Frost's wall, or even mud and straw. We might not be building with those materials today but conservators might well have to repair such structures and so need to understand how they work. Therefore it is necessary to look at a range of walling materials and also, bearing in mind Robert Frost's description, consider something of the foundations on which they stand.

Bricks and mortar

Mortar is used to overcome the problem of bedding the bricks or stones. While one might suppose that because modern cement mortar adheres to the bricks its purpose is to stick

---

[1]See for example Bartoli, Gianni and Paolo Spinelli, 'The "Torre Grossa" in San Gimignano: Experimental and numerical analysis', *Proceedings of the First International Congress on Construction History*, Madrid 2003, 341–51.

them together, in fact it is there to keep them apart, providing a bedding at the top of each course on which the next one is laid. Lime mortar has been the most commonly used material for this, comprising lime (calcium hydroxide) and sand mixed with water. More recently cement has been added to the mortar because it produces a mix that is quick-setting, allowing more rapid construction, but lime mortars have some advantages, particularly in allowing some movement to occur in the wall without cracks developing. Lime mortars first dry out as the water in the mix evaporates and then eventually harden as a result of a chemical reaction between the lime and atmospheric carbon dioxide, but this is a slow process that can take decades in a thick wall.

Chemistry of lime

The lime is made by heating calcium carbonate in a kiln, the calcium carbonate being obtained from limestone or chalk deposits or even seashells. This produces calcium oxide, or quick lime, which is then slaked with water to give calcium hydroxide, sometimes called slaked lime. This is the material that is used for lime mortar, mixed with sand and sufficient water to make it workable. There is no chemical reaction between these constituents but the reaction between the calcium hydroxide and atmospheric carbon dioxide produces calcium carbonate, the material that we started with.

In some places, where either the lime or the fuel to burn it has not been available, clay has been used as a mortar. This dries out naturally to form a rather more brittle filling material, susceptible to disturbance by vibrations, and also one that can easily be washed out from the joints if there is heavy wind-driven rain. In the Kathmandu Valley of Nepal clay mortar is used with tapered bricks for the outside face of the wall. These produce a tight joint in the face of the wall, a sensible defence against monsoon rains, but sufficient width behind for the mortar bedding.

Mortar even allows what might seem to be rather unsuitable materials, such as flint or beach cobbles, to be used for the walling. The rounded or irregular shapes of these prevent them from being stacked up dry to form a wall, but they can be used if there is sufficient mortar between them, although walls of these materials require some bricks or stone to provide a little discipline at the corners and at the sides of openings. Such walls make abundantly clear what might not be so obvious with brick walls, that the properties of the mortar are as important to the wall's behaviour as the bricks or stone. While bricks or stone will withstand very high stresses without noticeable strain the mortar will not and is subject to *creep*, i.e. gradual movement under load that can continue for several years. This might seem to be a disadvantage but in fact it allows some relative movement between parts of the wall. Many early brick walls were built on poor foundations that have settled under load. Either the more heavily loaded parts have settled more than relatively lightly loaded parts or the same effect has occurred because some areas of soil were simply less able than others to carry the load. In either case the result is some uneven settlement of the wall. If this took place slowly enough, creep in the mortar might have absorbed the movement as it occurred so that no visible cracking developed. The amount of movement that can be absorbed in this way naturally depends upon the proportion of mortar used. Buildings of large stone blocks with little mortar in the joints will allow very little movement without cracks appearing while buildings of brick or small stones and relatively large amounts of mortar can accommodate large movements without showing signs of distress because the movement occurs within the mortar joints.[2]

Thin walls

Consider first building a simple garden wall. As the toy brick experiment shows, as it is built higher it will eventually become unstable and fall over. The simplest solution would seem to be to make it thicker, and the standard size of bricks that are twice as long as they are wide means they can be laid so that they form a thicker solid wall. This is done by having bricks laid across the wall, called *headers*. The bricks laid along the wall are called *stretchers*. Various patterns are possible, the two basic standard methods being English bond and Flemish bond (Figure 5.1a,b), alternate courses of headers and stretchers or alternate headers and stretchers along each course. Whether there is anything particularly English or particularly Flemish about these is questionable; there is plenty of English bond brickwork in Flanders. More commonly in cheap construction there are several courses of stretchers to a course of headers, sometimes as many as five. These are various forms of 'garden wall bond' but the original English garden wall bond derives from the occasional practice of building garden walls with two courses of bricks turned on edge at the back of the wall to the three courses at the front laid normally, so saving bricks (Figure 5.1c). The face shows three courses of stretchers to each course of headers. It is of course possible to build thicker walls if one wants to go higher, multiples of the brick width, but the bonding becomes more complex.

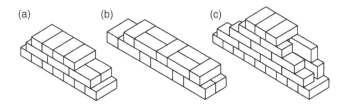

Figure 5.1 Brick bonding: **(a)** English, **(b)** Flemish and **(c)** English garden wall.

Other methods for ensuring a stable wall are possible. Jefferson's campus at the University of Virginia has thin walls between the gardens of the tutors' houses that are built in a serpentine form. Curving the walls in this way stiffens them in their out of plane direction so that they can be built very thin. The more common alternative is to incorporate piers into the wall that form strong points at intervals to stiffen it. The piers need to be large enough

---

[2]Creep in the mortar will result in changes in the overall geometry of the structure that can be used to indicate the direction of the forces acting. See the note on Hagia Sophia in Chapter 9 on vaults and domes.

to be effective and sufficiently close together so that there is no out of plane failure of the wall between them. If the wall is tall enough these piers will need to be large enough to act as buttresses to resist wind loads.

While we will need to consider the behaviour of buttresses we might wonder what happens to the wall between them when the wind blows against it. If the wall is fairly thin, what prevents strong wind forces from blowing out a panel of brickwork between the buttresses? The answer to that is that a panel of brickwork will behave horizontally just as the coping stones on the dry-stone wall (Figure 3.4) behaved vertically. There will be arching action in the horizontal plane providing that the piers are not too far apart.

Eighteenth and nineteenth century houses tended to have 9-inch (225-mm) thick walls and 9 ft (2.7 m) ceiling heights and one can see that the *slenderness ratio* for a two-storey brick house, simply measured as the ratio of thickness to height, appears to be 1 : 24. It would be very difficult to build our wall of toy bricks as high as that and it would be equally difficult with a real brick wall. Therefore there must be something preventing such slender brick walls from falling over. Two factors are at play here. If the building is relatively small then the party walls between the houses, at right angles to the front and rear walls, will provide some resistance to out of plane movement. By the same token, the front and rear walls resist out of plane movement of the party walls. Thus the walls give each other mutual support. But we can hardly rely on that; the other, and more important factor is that the floors and roof act to stiffen the walls.

One might suppose that the function of the wall was to support the floors and roof but it is these that are ensuring the stability of the walls. In a brick building, it is not simply a matter of the walls supporting the timbers, the two are mutually dependent. A brick masonry

---

Effective height

One might suppose that the ratio of thickness to height is the measure of the slenderness ratio of the wall, 1 : 12 perhaps for the 9-inch wall standing 9 feet high as the floor-to-floor height of the early houses described here. However, in design what needs to be considered is the effective height of the wall, and this depends upon the degree of restraint provided. In fact the same is true for all components in compression. The garden canes of Figure 1.6 are assumed to be free to rotate at either end and so bend into a simple curve between these points. Their effective length is their actual length. When a garden wall fails because it has become too slender nothing prevents the top from moving horizontally but at the base it remains vertical and so the curve that it adopts during the process of collapse will look like half of the curves shown in Figure 1.6. The effective length is found by completing the curve so that the effective height of such a wall is actually twice the actual height. If the wall, or any other kind of structural member, can be prevented from rotating about its ends, when it eventually buckles under load the shape will be more complex. Its effective length is then the length of the simple curve of Figure 1.6 that can be identified between what are called the *points of contraflexure*, i.e. the points where the curve changes from one direction to another.

house is a brick shell with timber structures within; take away all the timber and the brick-work will fall down. Indeed, there have been cases where exactly that has happened. In more than one instance, contractors working on the rehabilitation of eighteenth century houses in London have removed timber floors and partitions only to have the remaining part of the building collapse. Present-day contractors seem not to understand the way in which these buildings work. When the houses were built, the walls were brought up to each floor level and the beams and joists of the floor were put in place. At the time this was called 'naked flooring', unclothed as it was by the floorboards. This had the convenience of providing a working platform for the bricklayers to start the next lift of brickwork, but because the timbers were attached to the wall they ensured the stability of the latter. The very process of construction that was used ensured that the building would stand.

The box structure

The four walls of a building can be likened to the walls of a cardboard box; each of the walls is prevented from falling over by being attached to two other walls at the corners. The walls are mutually supporting. If forces act against one of the walls, compression forces will be mobilized in the two adjacent walls to prevent it from moving (Figure 5.2a). This assumes that the wall is able to resist such forces in the manner suggested earlier, but there is the possibility that if the forces are acting against a long top edge, as shown, then this edge might easily bend inwards. To prevent that from happening the lid of the box needs to be in place so that forces can be mobilized in its surface.

(a) 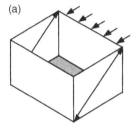   (b)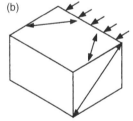

Figure 5.2 The structure of a cardboard box.

In a building it is the roof that holds the tops of the walls in place just as the lid of a box holds the top and sides in place (Figure 5.2b). This is possible because the ceiling joists are part of the roof structure. They are fastened to the wall plates, which in turn rest on the tops of the walls, and in modern construction the wall plates will be strapped down to the walls. Not only this, but the floors too are attached to the walls and so restrain them. The effective height of the wall is not the height from floor to roof but will be no more than the height between floors, thereby halving the slenderness ratio of our two-storey building to something more like 1:12.

Of course a building is not quite the same as a cardboard box because the roof normally slopes and the gable rises above the ceiling level. Between the upper floor and the eaves level the gable wall will at least be bonded into the front and rear walls, and possibly to an internal wall, but above the eaves level the gable becomes a relatively tall triangle of masonry which might not be attached to anything. While the interconnectivity between the roof and the walls is something that we will need to return to in the chapter on roofs, it is something that is essential to recognise. If the roof has purlins supported on the gable walls then they will help to ensure its stability. But some roofs simply span between front and rear walls so that the gable wall has nothing to stabilise it unless special provision is made to connect it via the roof to the other walls. Moreover, there is also the problem of resisting wind loads on a tall gable.

The point is well made by Figure 5.3a, which I have taken from an advisory document produced by Fairfax County, Virginia – doubtless other US authorities issue similar documents. This shows the tendency of the roof to move in the direction of the wind and the way in which the walls must be holding back the roof, but it does not show clearly the forces within the roof. This is redrawn as Figure 5.3b with the arrows for the wind forces left as they are showing a positive pressure on the windward gable and a negative pressure (suction in common parlance) on the leeward gable. Between the windward gable and the flank walls there must be some compressive forces but between the leeward gable and those walls there must be tension forces; the gable has to be held back against the wind.

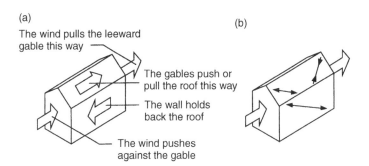

(a)

The wind pulls the leeward gable this way

The gables push or pull the roof this way

The wall holds back the roof

The wind pushes against the gable

(b)

Figure 5.3 Wind forces on a roof and wall.

Point loads and openings

Walls are not simple planes of masonry with a uniform loading. Such a wall would have a uniform stress along any course, but in practice window and door openings will both weaken the wall and serve to concentrate loads in the piers between them, while the floors and roof might well impose concentrated loads from roof trusses or large beams. The resulting variations in stress within the wall can sometimes be clearly seen in practice. In Nepalese construction, where the clay mortar provides little adhesion, bricks can sometimes be removed from the wall where there is no compressive stress between them. In contrast, a short distance away in the same wall bricks show spalling of the faces where the edges of the tapered bricks have been pressed against each other. There is clearly considerable variation in the compressive stress in various parts of the wall – from zero in some places to rather more than the brick (or at least the edges in contact) can comfortably carry in other places.

Openings have some structure across their tops, either arches or lintels that carry load from the masonry above to the sides of the opening. But exactly how much load is this? And are we then to assume that there is a panel of masonry as wide as the opening and extending down to the ground that carries no load? Common sense suggests that this is unlikely to be so but the designer needs some method of knowing just how loads might be distributed. The place to start is to consider how a point load is carried by the masonry below it.

Imagine a beam resting on a single bearing block set into a wall and which is in turn resting on two other blocks below it (Figure 5.4). The load on the top block will clearly be distributed to the pair below. If these two were then supported by three blocks in the course below, we would hardly assume that the central stone picked up the entire load; it would be distributed over all three. Thus at progressively lower courses the point load produces a lower stress over a wider area of wall. By continuing the distribution of load from each masonry block to those in the course below one can see that the tendency is for a gradual outward spread of forces with point loads on the wall producing a distributed load lower down and so eventually on the foundations. This is what is wanted because the soil will compress under load and if it were not fairly uniform there would be different settlements under different parts of the wall that could lead to cracking in the masonry. In practice a 45° spread from a point load is assumed.

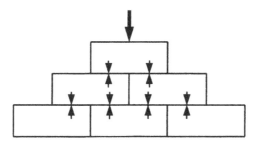

Figure 5.4 Load distribution in brickwork.

The two shaded areas in Figure 5.5 have the same area and represent the stresses in the wall both immediately under the beam and at the foundations (ignoring the effect of the wall's self-weight). Their depths 'a' and 'b' represent the stresses and their widths the area over which it is distributed. As force = stress × area, $W = a.x.t = b.y.t$. For the total stress at the foundations the effect of the wall's own weight has to be added to this.

Openings

The simple way to span an opening is to put a beam across it, called a *lintel* (or lintol – both spellings will be found), and this is what is commonly done. But supposing one does not have the material for such a beam, nor the components to build an arch. This is the common

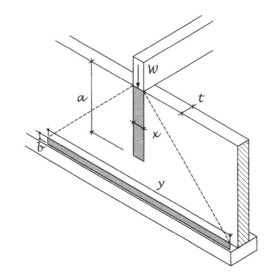

Figure 5.5 Stresses in a wall from a point load.

problem confronted by a child with a box of wooden bricks. Anyone who has played with toy bricks as a child will surely recognise the situation. Given a gap to span and no long blocks with which to do it a child discovers that it is possible to project a brick from the side of the opening providing that at least half of the brick remains over the support (Figure 5.6a). A second brick cannot be placed in the same way without toppling the first (Figure 5.6b) unless it is counterweighted with another brick at the back of it (Figure 5.6c).

Figure 5.6 Balancing a corbel.

Continuing this balancing act, the gap might eventually be spanned by erecting an upside-down triangle of bricks on either side. Of course what children actually build is a complete wall (Figure 5.7); the balancing act simply shows the part that is active in forming what are called the *corbels* on either side. Pre-Columbian architects in Central and South America practised this method of corbelling to bridge across openings, but corbels can also be found in European construction associated with large slabs of stone to bridge openings or to form a ceiling. Where the slabs available are not long enough for the required span, corbels are used on either side to reduce the span until it is small enough for the slabs.

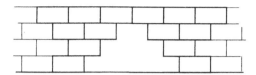

Figure 5.7 Spanning an opening with toy bricks.

Once complete a pair of corbels across an opening produces another mode of behaviour. If a load is added that unbalances the corbels so that they try to collapse, to do so they would have to rotate about the inside edges of the supports (Figure 5.8). The central blocks, in moving downwards in this way, would also have to move inwards and so some compressive force would be generated between them. In this way the corbels produce a primitive arch action that prevents collapse.

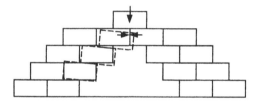

Figure 5.8 Arching action within a corbelled opening.

This triangular pattern in the masonry over an opening can sometimes be seen where a lintel has failed or perhaps where a timber lintel has gradually deflected under load. The masonry above will move down leaving a triangular pattern of cracking in the wall. This demonstrates rather graphically how loads are transmitted in the masonry above. Clearly no compressive forces are being transmitted across the cracks that appear so the lintel is only supporting the triangle of masonry they define. This means that there is no need to design a lintel to carry the whole height of the wall above the opening, it just has to support this triangle of masonry, and of course the load of anything fixed to the wall within that triangle – floor joists perhaps.

Having added window or door openings the nature of the wall has changed. As the purpose of windows is to provide light it follows that the deeper the room the higher the windows need to be to ensure that there is sufficient light at the back. Thus, apart from the desire to have well-proportioned rooms with a height appropriate to the width, deep rooms need high windows with fairly narrow gaps between them. The result is that the wall becomes not so much a sheet of masonry with holes in it but more a series of openings framed by the masonry; tall, thin panels of masonry that do not have the advantage of being bonded into anything except the spandrels above and below the windows but which must carry the load of the whole wall. Clearly it is the stability of these that governs the stability of the whole.

Cavity walls

The relatively thin walls of solid brickwork used up to the end of the nineteenth century were gradually superseded by cavity walls and then by walls of more than one material. It was realised around the turn of the twentieth century that building a wall of two leaves of masonry (wythes is the American term) with a cavity between produced a more weather-tight construction because rainwater soaking the outer leaf would not penetrate to the inner one. As long as the two leaves were tied together in some way – and small metal ties are commonly used – the two would act together in ensuring the stability of the wall.[3] Once this separation was made it was possible to build the inner leaf of cheaper concrete block, reserving the brick for the visible outer leaf. (Of course, if the wall were to be rendered (stuccoed) both leaves could be of a cheaper material.) Today we take advantage of this by using insulating blocks on the inner leaf.

Even solid walls need not be all of the same material. The outside of the wall has to be of something that will withstand the weather and, because the walling will absorb some water when it rains, in cold climates it must be tough enough to resist frost action. Behind this, much cheaper materials could be used, especially as the inner surface was finished with a coat of plaster. To save on expensive materials, brick walls were made with facing bricks on the outside face and poorer quality 'place bricks' on the inner face. Headers would be of facing bricks set across the wall thickness but some builders cheated by breaking facing bricks in half to use both ends as headers in the outer face. Of course such 'snap headers' provided no bond between the two leaves so that such walls are much less stable than properly bonded ones. Also, if builders cheated in this way it was equally likely that the front walls of a terrace of houses might not be properly bonded to the party wall that was supposed to ensure the walls' stability.

In cavity walls each leaf will be carrying different loads. Floor beams and joists are carried by the inside leaf, while the wall plate to which the roof rafters are fixed may well be on the outer leaf. Even in solid walls the loads will be applied to one side or the other but more important is that the floor construction may interrupt the continuity of the wall. It was once common to rest floor joists on a timber plate set into the wall (Figure 5.9). These not only support the floor timbers but in thin walls also have a significant effect on the behaviour of the wall itself, simply because they are a large proportion of the wall's cross-section.

Apart from being useful in that such timbers provided grounds for nailing on internal finishes, the intention seems also to have been as a precaution against cracking of the brickwork should there be any uneven settlement. Long continuous timbers set into the wall were called *bond timbers* and provided some horizontal continuity within the wall.[4] The problem with such timbers is that they eventually decay leaving voids in the masonry that threaten its stability. In the nineteenth century 'hoop iron' was used in the *bed joints* instead of bond timbers but the eventual corrosion of the iron presented its own problems. Today bed reinforcement, when used, is of galvanised steel.

---

[3] There have been failures simply because bricklayers have been too idle to include these ties.
[4] Lawrance Hurst, 'The rise and fall of the use of bond timbers in brick building in England', *Proceedings of the Second International Congress on Construction History*, 2006.

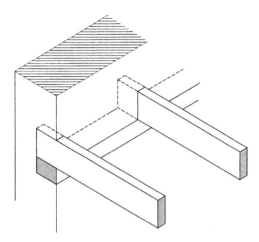

Figure 5.9 Floor joists resting on a timber plate.

Thick walls

While thick walls do not raise the same problem of overall stability as thin walls, because they are generally less slender, they usually have a more complex construction and that leads to a more complex behaviour. They generally have facings of a good material with a core made of much poorer material. How such walls carry loads and behave depends upon the relationship between the facings and the core.

A few thick walls are just a solid mass of the same material through and through, usually those of the most basic walling materials such as earth and sun-dried bricks. These have been used from the earliest times, but even today some people still use this material because it can make a perfectly satisfactory wall as long as it is kept dry. Of course its compressive stress is limited so it cannot be used to support beams carrying heavy floors unless some precautions are taken to spread their load. Cobb walls were used in parts of England where both building timber and good building stone were in short supply. Comprising a mixture of clay and straw binding these were constructed in short 'lifts' or layers. The rather wet material was pitch-forked onto the top of the wall and trodden down to consolidate it, and it was then necessary to allow each layer to become dry and firm enough to support the weight of the material to be placed above. These walls need to be protected from the weather by plastering, but if the plastering falls off the separate lifts of the construction can often be seen in the material underneath. This is not the only earth-based construction; *pisé de terre* consists of earth rammed between timber forms, and another method that has been used in some areas is clay lump – essentially blocks of dried clay.

Roman concrete walls can also be treated as a single homogeneous mass. The concrete was a mixture of Roman cement and stones that was placed between brick tile facings. Roman cement incorporated a volcanic material mixed with the lime that hardened rapidly. Unlike modern concrete, which uses small stones to form the aggregate with just sufficient cement to glue them together, Roman concrete used rather large stones with a much greater mass of concrete. If the facings were well bonded to the fill, the whole would act together but at intervals there were also layers of brick tiles right across the wall.

Scaffolding

The construction of all walls is dependent upon the reach of the masons so that scaffolding must be provided from which they can work. This has to be built up at intervals and tied into the wall for its stability. One sometimes sees horizontal rows of holes in the masonry. These are *putlogs* holes, putlogs being the horizontal members of the scaffolding that are set in the wall itself to hold the relatively slender scaffold in place. If these are left unfilled when the scaffold is taken down they remain as a permanent record of the height of each lift of scaffolding. For Roman brick and concrete construction, Adam shows these to be a little under 2 m high.[5]

Dry-stone walls

The complexity of other thick walls is illustrated by dry-stone walls, i.e. walls built without mortar, which are often used as boundary walls, exactly the kind being described by Robert Frost. The stones have irregular surfaces that do not sit well on each other making a dry wall difficult to build. They are built with two facings of large stones and an infill of smaller material in order to use the variety of stone sizes available. The trick in building such walls is to keep the centre filled with small stones as the faces are brought up (Figure 5.10). This is so that the larger facing stones are always well bedded, both on their fellows below and to

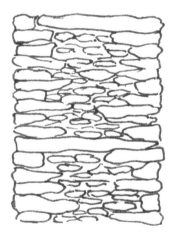

Figure 5.10 The section of a dry-stone wall.

---

[5] Jen-Piere Adam, *Roman Building*, Indiana University Press, Bloomington, IN, 1994.

those either side of them but also on the infill material in the core of the wall. It is also useful to include occasional through stones to bond the two faces together. It is these through stones that enable the wall to act as a single unit rather than as two separate walls. For this to be possible the wall has to be relatively thin so that there can be stones long enough to connect the two faces together. If it is too thick for that to be possible the best that can be done is to tie the two faces into the core material, perhaps overlapping long stones from each face.

Even when built with mortar a thick wall will comprise well-laid facings with a core of poorer material. Problems arise because the latter tends to settle with time. Water penetration, daily thermal movements in the wall or seasonal movement in the ground below it, and nowadays traffic vibration, all have the effect of loosening small particles of the mortar of the core, which then drift downwards in the wall. The result is that the loads on the wall tend to be carried by the faces. The faces effectively become thin walls, which can buckle outwards and fail, a problem that can be exacerbated by the loosened mortar. Any tendency for the facings to move outwards, because of vibrations or thermal movements, allows these small particles to move into the space created, preventing the facings from returning to their original positions. The result is a ratchet effect, a gradual change in the wall with increasing outward pressure from the loosened mortar, which can eventually cause a partial collapse. Such collapses of the face commonly occur near the base of the wall where loosened material accumulates, but this does not usually result in immediate collapse of the whole wall because the core has become sufficiently compact there to take up the load. This is also where natural arches can form in the wall's facing, referred to at the beginning of Chapter 3.

One normally finds floors supported entirely by the inner face of the wall but there can be exceptions. In Nepalese construction there are timber plates at each floor set along the tops of both the facings, with the floor joists taken through the wall and resting on them (Figure 5.11). One might still suppose that this would result in the inner face carrying most of the load but at the top deep overhanging roofs rest on a plate on the top of the outer leaf.

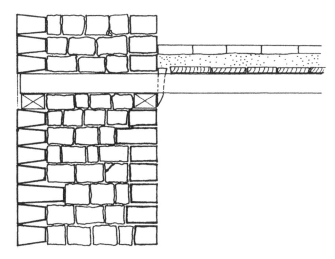

Figure 5.11 Nepalese construction of floor and wall.

Moreover, with fairly closely spaced floor joists taken through the wall they are likely to distribute its weight across the two facings, especially if there is any settlement of the core material below.

We can see that with the load coming onto the facing bricks and these not very effectively bonded into the core, then effectively the load is carried by two slender brick walls. Although the storey height might be only a little over 2 m (7 ft), with a brick only 125 mm (5 in) thick the slenderness of the unbonded facings would be 1 : 17 and behave more like tall, thin walls. The method of supporting the floors might not be typical of other construction types that use thick walls with facings and cores but it does present some fairly typical problems; the core is unlikely to be load-bearing, and just as in cavity walls, the load on the two facings may be different. Moreover, the clay mortar presents a more severe problem of downward drift of material within the core with corresponding outward pressure developing towards the bottom of the facings.

The present-day conservator is in a position to improve the bonding between the two faces of masonry walls by introducing modern ties, either metal or fibreglass ties, set in drilled holes and bonded in with resin. A number of products have been developed for this purpose.

Foundation loads

The task in designing foundations is to limit the amount of settlement that will occur and certainly to prevent differential settlement between one part of the structure and another. Unless the wall is built on rock there will be some movement of the soil under the foundations of a wall, the amount of such ground movement depending upon the pressure exerted on the soil and the nature of the soil itself; the greater the pressure the greater the movement. If the pressure on a foundation is significantly different in different parts of the building, or if the soil is different even if the pressure is the same, there will be different amounts of movement, and this differential settlement will have to be absorbed within the masonry.

The ideal foundation condition is a uniform soil with a uniform distribution of load, the latter achieved by careful design. For example, while piers of Figure 5.12 carry a concentrated load they may be built with comparatively large bases to ensure that the foundation pressure is similar to that under the more lightly and uniformly loaded sections of wall in between. Another way of dealing with a number of concentrated loads produced by piers or columns within the building was to have a series of inverted arches spanning between their bases. Just as the arch of a bridge brings a distributed load down to the supports as concentrated loads on the bridge foundations, so concentrated loads could be spread by inverted arches into a distributed load on the soil below.

Walls may also have horizontal loads on them as well as vertical loads and we need to consider how those loads affect the foundations. Simple observation shows that there are many walls that are leaning, a common phenomenon in medieval churches. Obviously if they are no longer vertical, as they were when built, they might have been pushed into their present position by some horizontal force or have moved because an eccentric load has

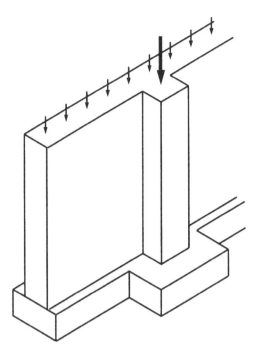

Figure 5.12 Foundations for a wall and pier.

produced an uneven distribution of stresses across the foundation. The simplest way to consider such foundation loads is to begin with walls that are designed to carry horizontal loads, such as a gravity dam.

A dam wall

Civilisation depends upon water, and providing an adequate supply has always been a major concern for civic authorities. Where the source of the water was sufficiently regular, it could be tapped fairly simply, but in other cases some impounding was necessary to regulate the supply, with dams built to form a reservoir; water held back in times of high flow provided a reserve during the dry season. Because of this, all civilisations have left a legacy of dams, aqueducts and cisterns. Sadly, in spite of their historic importance, these are not well known and appreciated, partly perhaps because they are in rural areas and so not easily visited by tourists, and partly because many water-carrying or storage structures are underground. Dams are visible and fall into three basic categories: (i) earth dams that rely upon the mass of soil to retain the pressure of the water; (ii) arch dams that have been built in reinforced concrete, and are the most dramatic structures; and (iii) masonry gravity dams.

A dam has to be able to withstand the pressure of the water and gravity dams are so called because they rely upon the weight of the masonry to resist the horizontal thrust of the water behind them. The higher the dam the thicker the masonry has to be. If the dam is thought of as a simple rectangular wall then the pressure of the water will be trying to overturn it. If this happened it would rotate about its toe, the point marked 'a' in Figure 5.13a, and it is a relatively simple matter to find how thick the dam has to be to prevent such a disaster by taking moments about that point. The pressure of the water increases with depth and if the dam is completely full, then the pressure is shown as the shaded triangle acting against the upstream face.

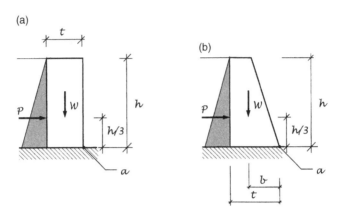

Figure 5.13 Resistance of a dam to overturning.

If the pressure at the base of the dam is p and the height h the total force P is p.h/2. This either comes from knowing that the area of a triangle is half the base multiplied by the height or by realising that the force will be the average pressure multiplied by the height. The centre of pressure of the water acts at the 'centre of gravity' of the triangle, which is at 1/3 of its height, so that the triangle of pressure can be simplified to the single force P at that depth. Multiplying the force P by the height above the base at which it acts, h/3, gives the overturning moment P.h/3 = p.h²/6. The weight of the dam is resisting this by producing a moment in the opposite direction about the point a. This moment is W.t/2, where W depends upon the height and thickness of the dam, and also upon the density of the masonry, typically 20 times the density of water.

> We can do better than this. The horizontal pressure at any depth is the same as the vertical pressure and that is simply the weight of water down to that depth, which we can calculate fairly simply. 1 cubic centimetre of water weighs 1 gram. A cubic metre of water will therefore weigh $100 \times 100 \times 100$ grams, i.e. 1000 kg. Assuming the acceleration of gravity is 10 m/s/s, this is 10 000 N, or 10 kN. Thus the pressure at any depth in kN/m² is the height in metres to that depth multiplied by 10.
>
> Draw a graph of pressure against depth and the result is the triangle similar to that in Figure 5.13. Given that p = 10.h, therefore P = 10.h²/2 and the overturning moment produced is 10.h³/6. If we go through the same exercise for the weight of the dam, assuming the density of the masonry is n times that of water, we can work out the ratio of t to h.

The Romans built simple rectangular dams like this but anyone who troubles with the calculation suggested above can see that it is not very efficient. It is much better to make the dam thicker at the bottom than it is at the top, which explains the sloping downstream face of most gravity dams. In Figure 5.13b the overturning moment has remained the same but the distance of the dam's centre of gravity from the toe, i.e. the distance 'b', is no longer halfway along the base as it was before. In fact it has shifted towards the back of the dam so that b is greater than t/2 (b > t/2) and the same retaining job can be done with a smaller mass of masonry.

Another way of dealing with the same problem is to back the dam with an earth embankment, but this produces its own problems. As the water presses on one side of the dam it has to overcome the pressure of the soil on the other side, but the soil itself exerts some pressure and an empty dam must be able to resist that. Unfortunately the Roman dam at Alcantarilla, near Toledo, fell backwards into the reservoir when the water was drawn down and the earth pressure on the downstream face became too large. One might wonder how the dam was built in the first place if that could happen. Two explanations are possible; either the earth fill on the downstream side was added as the water filled the upstream side or the earth pressures increased over time. The latter might occur with gradual consolidation of the soil as a result of weathering and particularly the saturation of the soil with rainwater.

With no water in the dam the structure had become a retaining wall, the other kind of wall with horizontal forces on it other than the wind. Walls like this might be wanted either to contain soil or to retain some stored material. Granular soils, such as sands or gravels, flow in a manner something like liquids although not to the same extent.[6] They will flow until they take up some angle of slope (called the *angle of repose*). The result is that the horizontal pressure against a retaining wall is only a proportion of the vertical pressure at any level – the proportion being related to the angle of repose. Clearly some experiment is needed to find out what it is for any particular material but, given the pressure against it, the stability of a simple retaining wall working by gravity would involve a similar exercise to that of the dam. While masonry walls might have been built in the past to behave in this way, modern retaining walls are normally built of reinforced concrete relying upon the bending strength of the concrete to contain the soil or other material. Nevertheless similar considerations of overall stability still apply.

The wall shown in Figure 5.14 will again rotate about the point 'a' if the soil pressure is too great but what is preventing rotation is the weight of soil behind the wall that will have to be lifted by the structure for any rotation to occur. While a large toe increases the lever arm distance between the weight of the soil and the assumed point of rotation, it is clearly necessary to have sufficient holding down weight at the back of the wall.

Horizontal loads

In buildings horizontal loads occur where roof rafters rest on the top of the wall. This is simpler than the dam because we know that the wall is normally rectangular and the load is applied at the top. The complication is that there is also a vertical load being applied at the

---

[6]Cohesive soils, such as clay, behave in a quite different way.

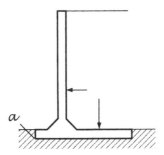

Figure 5.14 Resistance to overturning of a modern retaining wall.

same time because the wall is carrying the weight of the roof as a vertical load on the wall plate. Ignoring this vertical load for the moment simplifies the situation to that shown in Figure 5.15. The force P is trying to rotate the wall about the point a, the moment being P.h. The weight of the wall is acting to prevent this with a moment W.t/2. All will be well if the restraining moment provided by the weight of the wall is greater than the overturning moment produced by the applied force, i.e. W.t/2 > P.h.

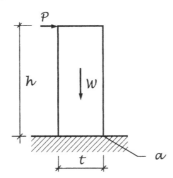

Figure 5.15 Resistance of a wall to a horizontal load.

Of course the weight of the wall is proportional to its height and thickness. If the density of the wall is given the symbol r/unit of volume then W = r.h.t and the moment = r.h.t²/2. If we now equate the two moments then P.h = r.h.t²/2, h can be cancelled from both sides leaving the perhaps rather surprising result that P = r.t²/2. The force required to push the wall over is independent of its height even though one might imagine that the taller the wall the easier it would be to push it over. Of course if it is the wind that is pushing the wall over then, like the dam, the higher the wall the greater will be the force. Moreover, in a building part of the restoring moment is provided by the load on the wall, and that does not increase with height.

There is then the question of how the horizontal thrust from the roof gets into the wall because this is by no means obvious. Why does the wall plate, to which the timbers will normally be fixed, simply not slide off the top of the wall? The answer in much early construction is friction (Figure 5.16a). The friction force F that can be generated is proportional to the force W between the two surfaces so that F = k.W. The constant k is called the

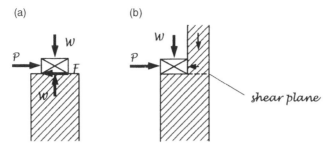

Figure 5.16 Restraining a wall plate against horizontal load.

coefficient of friction and will be different for different pairs of materials. Note that it does not matter what the area of contact is. Having a wider wall plate gives no advantage over a narrow one.

Finding friction forces

Friction forces can be found from a simple experiment. If a block of wood or a brick is placed on a flat surface and a cord attached to it via a spring balance, the force required to move the block can be measured. This is of course the force required to overcome the friction between the surfaces. Place a second block on top of the first and the force required will be doubled. But what about the effect of contact area? If the first block is cut in half and the pieces placed one on top of the other the contact area will have been halved. Of course the pressure between the surfaces will have doubled because the weight remains the same. It will be found that the friction force remains the same.

An alternative experiment requires a little more mathematics but less apparatus. If the block is placed on a surface that can be tilted, then at any given angle there will be a component of the weight of the block perpendicular to the surface and a component parallel to the surface (Figure 5.17). Increasing the angle reduces the former and increases the latter until the block begins to slide down the surface. The angle provides a measure of the coefficient of friction. In this experiment N = W. cos Ø while F = W.sin Ø. When the block begins to slide, F/N = the coefficient of friction, k = W.sin Ø/W.cos Ø = tan Ø.

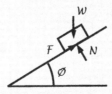

Figure 5.17

It will be apparent from what has already been said that it is easier for the wall to carry a steeply pitched roof rather than a shallow roof because the former exerts a smaller horizontal thrust. However, the ability of the wall to resist horizontal thrusts at the top can be increased by increasing the weight above the point where the thrusts are applied – by adding a parapet for example. In Figure 5.16b the wall plate is restrained by the parapet wall and failure, if it occurs, will take place across the shear plane shown. This means that the critical factor in this construction is the ability of the masonry to resist shear. If a simple lime mortar is used that does not adhere to the bricks or stone we are again relying upon friction but now it is the weight of the parapet that is crucial to the forces that can be generated.

This brings us back to the flying buttress problem of Chapter 3. At their lower ends the flying buttresses are carried high above the ground on piers and as they are still thrusting outwards the piers need to be broad enough to resist this thrust, but what happens at the top is also critical. It is often suggested that the pinnacles at the top of the buttresses are there to add weight in order to produce a steeper line of thrust within the buttresses and so reduce their depth. That is possible, but it is difficult to see how the designers at the time would have planned for it. A more satisfactory explanation is that while the pinnacles are there to add weight the purpose is to increase sliding resistance in the bed joints of the masonry. The piers are preventing the flying buttress thrust from pushing the top courses of masonry off the top of the buttress.

We might now bring together a number of ideas developed so far and consider the behaviour of a buttressed wall where the purpose of the buttresses is to resist outward thrust at the top of the wall. This is a common situation in masonry-built medieval barns where large roof trusses pick up the roof loads and concentrate them at specific points (see Chapter 8). The roof frames will be delivering concentrated vertical load and horizontal load to the wall. The problem for the builders at the time was to prevent the wall from being pushed over by the horizontal force and for that buttresses were added at those points. Figure 5.18 shows the situation, but note that the forces from the common rafters onto the wall plate have been ignored. For the buttress to fail it would have to rotate about the axis a, but in doing so the part of the buttress that is against the wall would tend to lift up. We may assume that the

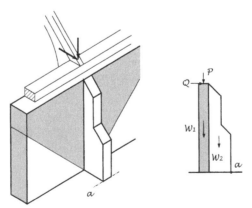

Figure 5.18 Areas of the wall resisting rotation of a buttress.

buttress is keyed into the masonry of the wall so that if the inside face of the buttress were to lift it would have to take some of the wall with it.

Any attempt by the buttress to lift part of the wall implies a concentrated upward force at the base of the wall. The effect of this on the wall will be the inverse of the situation shown in Figures 5.4 and 5.5, where a point load was applied to the top of the wall; now it is being applied at the bottom. Therefore the area of wall that is resisting rotation of the buttress is the area indicated by the shading in Figure 5.18. Stability is ensured if the clockwise moment of the outward force Q about 'a' is less than the combined anticlockwise moments of the three forces: P, the load from the roof; W_2, the weight of the buttress itself; and W_1, the weight of the shaded area of masonry. W_1 will be the most significant of these three.

Foundation stresses

The effect on the foundations that might be produced by a horizontal force can be seen from a simple demonstration. Place a block on a foam rubber pad to represent the foundation under a wall and the pad will be compressed under the weight (Figure 5.19a). If a horizontal force is applied to one side of the block it will tilt with an upward movement on the side that the load is applied and a downward movement on the other side. This means that the

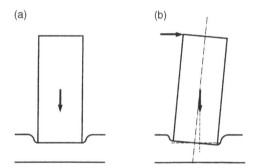

Figure 5.19 The response of foundations to loads.

stress under one side has been reduced while that under the other has increased (Figure 5.19b). The horizontal dotted line shows the level to which the foundation material was originally compressed before the horizontal load was applied. (If the applied force were a wind force we would refer to the windward and leeward sides of the wall – a handy short-hand.) If the applied force is gradually increased it will eventually become large enough for there to be no stress under that side of the wall. Increase it still further and the bock will partially lift off the pad at that edge with a smaller and smaller contact area subject to larger and larger stresses.

What is happening can be shown in simple diagrams. With the wall acting alone on the soil there is a simple uniform stress at the base of the wall represented by the grey shaded

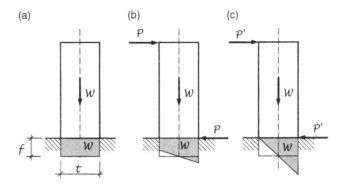

Figure 5.20 Stresses under a wall with varying horizontal load.

area (Figure 5.20a). The area of this stress block is proportional to the weight of the wall, W, = f.t. When the horizontal force, P, is applied, apart from the horizontal force that must occur at the base of the wall to resist it, the stresses at the base of the wall will change, as seen in Figure 5.20b. The shaded area of the diagram is now a trapezium and as this area is proportional to the weight of the block, which has not changed, the area must be the same as before. The upward force now acts through the *centroid* (or centre of gravity) of this trapezium but at this stage the stress under the centre of the wall will have remained the same as before. The simplest condition is that where the horizontal force is such that the stress on one side of the wall has become zero so that the stress diagram is a triangle (Figure 5.20c). Let this force be P^1.

Instead of looking at the stresses under the wall we can reduce the stress block to a single force just as we did for the pressure of water against the back of the dam. In that case the force when $P = P^1$ acts at 1/3 of the distance from the leeward edge of the wall. If that is so, then in Figure 5.21 the distance b = t/6, and taking moments about the point a, the moment of the overturning force P.h = the moment of the restoring force W.t/6. Of course the forces

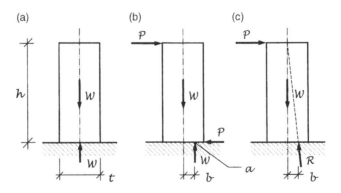

Figure 5.21 The horizontal force resisted by a separate or a single force.

P and W at the base of the wall can be combined into a single force R. There are then three forces acting on the wall and these must pass through a single point in the middle of the top of the wall. Note that the force we have just found is not the overturning force. Compare Figure 5.21 with Figure 5.15. As larger forces are applied the dimension b will increase until the force R acts through the 'leeward' edge of the wall.

6 Frames – A Problem of Stability

A frame can be thought of in two ways: as a number of members connected together by joints, or as a number of joints connected together by members.

The alternative to load-bearing walls is to construct some form of frame to support the floors and roof, an assembly of posts and beams. There are two aspects of such assemblies to consider, the nature of the joints between the members and ensuring overall stability. For many frameworks, the joints may take most of the design effort. There are two kinds of joints to consider: pin joints, where all of the members are free to rotate relative to each other, and fixed joints. As we shall see, timber structures have relied upon pin joints and such structures require bracing to ensure their stability. Thus to complete the list of members comprising a frame we need to add bracing. However, with the coming of iron, and then steel, it became possible to form fixed joints between members, i.e. joints in which the members were not free to rotate, and because of this at least some, and possibly all of the bracing could be dispensed with. Fixity at the joints depended upon the careful design of first riveted or bolted connections, and then eventually the use of welded connections between members. And so it was until the advent of so-called Hi-Tec architecture, when a number of architects interested in exposing the structure as a form of architectural expression chose to return to pin-jointed frames. If Hi-Tec seems to you to be a curious term for what might technically be regarded as a retrograde step it is not for me to comment.

Where timber was available it was often a simpler form of construction than masonry and was the construction of choice in medieval England. The change to brick masonry was a response to the danger of fire in towns but we should be careful not to try to attempt to divide buildings into two distinct categories – timber frame and masonry walls. Apart from the extensive use of timber-framed walls within masonry buildings, referred to in the last chapter, the factories and warehouses of the industrial revolution, and even large agricultural buildings of the parallel agricultural revolution, used timber frames set within a masonry box. The posts and beams of the frame supported floors, providing an open space within, while the masonry formed the weather-tight skin and at the same time ensured the overall stability of the building. These later frames were therefore simpler than the braced frames of medieval buildings. Eventually the timber posts and beams were superseded by cast-iron posts and beams in so-called fire-proof construction, but the masonry wall remained. When the frame eventually 'expanded' to include the external walls and the masonry wall became just a weather cladding supported by the frame, designers again had to turn their attention to methods of bracing frames to ensure their stability. Moreover, as heights have increased, the need for bracing to resist wind loads has come to dominate the design of some modern buildings. Of course, in many parts of the world bracing is also needed to resist earthquake loading.

The distinction between braced frames and frames that rely upon fixed joints can be seen most clearly in the contrast between timber-framed buildings and some simple timber furniture. The buildings rely upon bracing while the furniture relies most often upon fixed joints. And yet both use essentially the same basic jointing method. The fact that in one case the joint can be made rigid while in the other it is a pinned joint is a matter of scale. The difference between these seems to be a useful place to begin.

Timber framing

In many countries in medieval Europe timber framing was the basic form of construction – called half-timbering in England, fachwerk in Germany and colombage in France – using substantial timbers for the main frames and often exposed for decorative reasons. Of course the framing might be plastered over or covered with tile or even brickwork, so that examples may be more numerous than at first appears. It seems curious that people worry about removing walls from a masonry building because they might be load-bearing, but they do not seem to be so concerned about removing the bracing from timber frames if they are in the way. What is critical about any frame is its stability, so discarding the bracing sometimes has unfortunate results. Take away the braces from a timber-framed building and it will sway sideways. Perhaps people show such little concern about stability because they have had little experience of building a timber frame, when the issue of stability would have made itself immediately apparent. Or perhaps they see few examples of failures that have occurred because of lack of stability. That would not be surprising because while structures that are too weak often show signs of distress before they actually fail, structures that fail because they become unstable can collapse with distressing suddenness. Sometimes we are fortunate in that a frame that lacks sufficient stability will sway sideways and in doing so mobilise some other forces within the structure that prevent complete collapse. In those cases remedial action might be taken, but this occurs rarely.

The problem of ensuring overall stability of a framed structure can be demonstrated fairly simply. Make a simple frame of four uprights and four beams loosely joined at the corners (Figure 6.1a) and it will be completely unstable – floppy might be the commonly used term. Short of embedding the posts in the ground, the simple way to solve this is to fasten braces across the corners, providing at least one brace for each side (Figure 6.1b). Now, with the braces added, one of the angles in each of the faces is fixed as a right angle by the brace that creates a triangle at that corner. The other way of preventing the frame from collapsing is if the joints between the members could be made rigid. A piece of furniture, such as a stool or a table can be made with tight joints between the members so that large *racking* forces can be applied to it without causing noticeable distress. Slide a wooden table across the floor and there will be friction forces at the feet of the legs resisting its movement but the joints at the top will cope with this. It manages this because the joints resist the turning moment at the top of the leg produced by the friction forces from the floor at the foot of the leg. Joinery joints are so stiff that it is even possible to rock onto two legs of a wooden chair or stool without having it collapse.

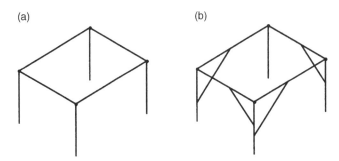

Figure 6.1 Bracing a simple frame.

Torsional instability

A common exercise given to architectural students is to construct a framework to support a given load, or perhaps to carry the largest possible load with the minimum amount of material. While the students appreciate the need for bracing to prevent sidesway of the framework the structures that they build most often fail because of torsional instability. This is when the top rotates relative to the base. This is possible in the frame of Figure 6.1b if the faces twist so that the members are no longer all in the same plane. We need not concern ourselves with this type of failure because it is not generally a problem for building structures. However, you might want to think about it if you are building a tower.

Stiff joints might seem to be the answer to the instability of the frame, the only difficulty about that being that it was simply not possible to make stiff joints in a timber building frame. The basic joint in both the piece of furniture and the building is the mortice and tenon (Figure 6.2). In making a piece of furniture the tenon is a tight fit in the mortice, the joint often incorporating a wedge to tighten a split tenon into a dovetailed mortice. However the joint is made, it should be sufficiently well-fitting that the tenon has to be driven into the mortice with a mallet. It is inconceivable that adequate forces could be applied to the members of a building frame to make such tight joints. Certainly the joints have to be made reasonably tight, and means were used to ensure that they were, but they could not be tight enough to withstand the racking loads produced by wind forces on the building.

The method adopted was to use timber pegs to hold the joint together and these ensured that the joints were tight by so called draw-boring. Briefly, the hole in the tenon to take the peg was made slightly off centre from the hole in the morticed timber (sometimes called the foundation member). The joint would be fairly loose when first assembled but driving a tapered peg through the holes in the two members drew the tenon down into the mortice so tightening the shoulders of the tenon against the surface of the foundation member, the contact surface shown shaded in Figure 6.2a. The pegs must be able to distort to accommodate the offset in the holes and so the forces between the peg and the tenon pull it down into the mortice and then hold the joint together. While a joint in a piece of furniture can

(a)

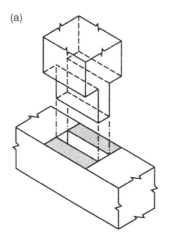

(b)

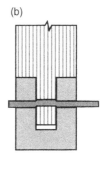

Figure 6.2 Mortice and tenon joint.

rely upon the close contact between the sides of the tenon and the ends of the mortice to resist racking loads, there is no such close contact in the joints of a building frame, where the first line of defence against racking is the tortured peg, bent in its passage through the timbers and already stressed by its duty in drawing the joint together (Figure 6.2b). Any tension force on the joint and the peg might break.

There has been recent research to determine the loads that pegged joints can take in tension. However, pegs have been known to break, and the condition of the peg within the joint must remain a mystery. It is partly a matter of workmanship both in making the pegs and in making the joint.

Note also that this method is less satisfactory in softwood, where there would be a tendency, in such straight-grained timber, for the timber between the peg and the end of the tenon to shear along the grain.

Early buildings did use earth fast posts, posts set into the ground like fence posts, but they would eventually rot at the ground. The solution for ensuring both durability and stability of a frame was to raise the frame off the ground and use some form of bracing (Figure 6.3). Posts were brought down onto a timber cill, which was itself raised above the ground on a low masonry wall (not shown in the sketch) to keep it from the wet.

The frame required two other types of mortice and tenon joint. One was used for connecting beams into posts, the other at the ends of the braces. As a beam carries load at right-angles to the joint there would not be enough timber on the side of the tenon to provide enough bearing. Therefore the posts were notched slightly to give the beam more bearing (Figure 6.4a) – again the shaded area on the drawing shows the area in bearing. Where the joining member is a brace the joint will be cut as in Figure 6.4b. The compression force in the brace will have a component at right angles to the foundation member and a component

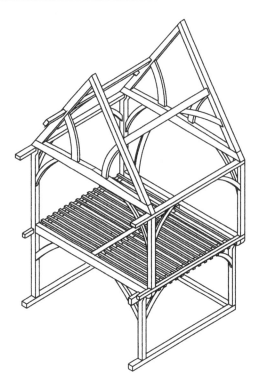

Figure 6.3 A basic timber-framed building.

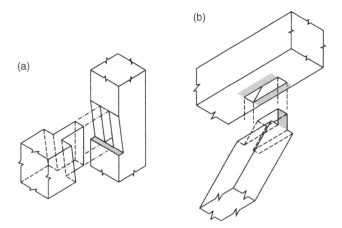

Figure 6.4 Bearing areas in mortice and tenon joints for **(a)** a post and beam, and **(b)** a brace.

in the direction of the foundation member. The first will be carried across the shoulders of the joint, the second transmitted between the end of the tenon and the end of the mortice. Note that the brace is commonly narrower than the post and beam into which it is framed and will be aligned so that one of its faces is flush with a face of the foundation member.

It might seem that the obvious step would be to brace between the cill and the posts to keep them upright while the rest of the frame was built except that the walls were prefabricated on the ground and raised into place when complete. This allowed considerable freedom in the design and arrangement of the bracing, with different countries and different regions within those countries adopting a variety of traditional methods. So much so that the different patterns of framing have attracted some antiquarian interest with scholars cataloguing the different types and their geographical distribution. But structurally this misses the point; it is not the wall bracing that is significant but the internal, or lateral bracing that is most important.

This should be clear from Figure 6.3. The area of the gable may be larger than the area of a single *bay* of the building, as shown here. However, there can be braces in every bay of both the front and rear walls to resist the wind load on the gables. Moreover, the infill in the walls will also provide some resistance to wind loads. In contrast the bracing within a single cross-frame has to resist the wind loads on each bay of the front and rear walls. Clearly, providing adequate longitudinal bracing is a comparatively trivial issue compared with providing sufficient lateral bracing. Nevertheless the lateral braces in the cross-frames are the very ones that some building owners have been tempted to cut away, concerned for convenient planning but ignorant of structural requirements.

The larger timber-framed barns are a slightly different problem. Like houses, these need longitudinal as well as transverse bracing of the frame, but while they also have bracing between posts and beams, aisled barns are effectively buttressed by the aisle framing. Perhaps this is just as well because monastic barns, built in many parts of England and also in parts of continental Europe, were gigantic structures of their day.[1] They are not very different in structural form from the barns found on some farms but they are considerably different in scale. Their size can sometimes be explained because some monasteries farmed their lands on a commercial basis,[2] but even without such commercial ventures, monasteries were large households that had to produce food for their own needs and those of their horses. The barns that were a part of this process were often of such a scale that they dwarfed nearby parish churches. Many of course had masonry walls, so that stability of the carpentry was ensured by this enveloping structure, but when the barn was completely timber framed, adequate bracing had to be provided within the timber framing.

Construction of a barn

Aisled barns were based on longitudinal framing just like houses. Two rows of posts were connected by arcade plates (Figure 6.5). There would be longitudinal bracing between the

[1] There are also a number of large timber-framed market halls in northern France that are of a similar size.
[2] Farringdon, the town near Great Coxwell barn, gave its name to Farringdon Market in London to where the produce of the lands around the barn were sent.

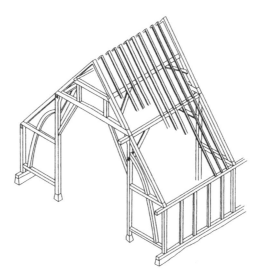

Figure 6.5 A timber-framed aisled barn.

posts and the plates that ensured longitudinal stability as the frames were lifted up, and they would then be connected together with the tie beams and knee braces to give lateral stability. The aisle framing would then be added, so providing additional buttressing. These were long, high structures so that they attracted very large wind loads. The simple solution using knee braces between the posts and the tie beams was necessary for assembly but perhaps thought insufficient for the completed structure. Therefore the aisle structures contain additional braces, bracing between the arcade posts and the wall posts rather like the buttresses in the walls of masonry barns. The outstanding examples of such buildings are the pair of barns at Cressing Temple in Essex, the so-called Barley Barn and Wheat Barn, and the barn at Harmondsworth, now next to London's Heathrow Airport, which is the largest timber-framed building in England. Although the bracing arrangements developed by the medieval carpenters have proved satisfactory it would be difficult to determine how the loads are shared between the various braces in the complex arrangements that they often used.

The form of the barn naturally responds to the patterns of farming. In Holland and Germany the barn and farmhouse were combined, with the dwelling at one end of the building. This led to a quite different construction with a transverse beam, which has been called an *anchor beam*, set well below the arcade or wall plate and connected to the posts with a through tenon. This then supported an upper floor. Longitudinal bracing was provided between the arcade or wall plates and the posts. Transverse bracing was provided between the posts and the anchor beam although some resistance against racking of the frame is probably ensured by the wedging of the through tenons against the posts. If aisled there was no bracing across the aisles. This was also the form of construction that was transmitted to the early American colonies and became the basis for American barns.[3] The construction implies a quite different erection sequence from that used in English barns. For these struc-

---

[3] See John Fitchen (1968), *The New World Dutch Barn*, Syracuse University Press, Syracuse, NY.

tures cross-frames must have been made, reared and then connected together by the arcade or wall plates. Here I shall restrict analysis of the structures to English barns.

Given that there are two kinds of frame, the diagrams of Figure 6.6 show how these must react to horizontal loads applied at wall plate or arcade plate level. (Only the structurally active members of the frame have been shown.) As the frames try to sway over, as suggested by the dotted lines, braces on the leeward side go into compression. Although there are braces on the windward side, shown by the feint lines, and these might be thought of as also helping to resist racking, they can only do so by going into tension. At the ends of the braces tension forces can only be produced by the pegs preventing the tenons from pulling out of their mortices, and, as already argued, one cannot rely upon the already highly stressed pegs to provide the force required. There must be vertical forces at the ground to resist the tendency of the wind to simply roll the building over and these are also shown. Note that in the frame on the left the brace will be trying to lift the tie beam up, a tendency resisted by the weight of the roof, and it will also be producing some bending in the post.

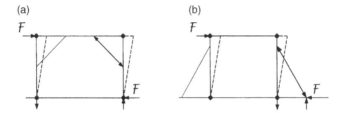

Figure 6.6 Two kinds of frame reacting to horizontal loads.

Lap dovetails and dovetail tenons

Those who want to look at timber framing in more detail should note that early carpenters devised two joints that were specifically designed to take tension forces: one was the lap dovetail, the other the dovetail tenon. Lap dovetails were used at the ends of tie beams and between wind braces and roof purlins where one timber could be dropped over another. Dovetail tenons were commonly used in aisle ties, the wedge being driven in to hold the tenon in place (Figure 6.7). The use of this last device suggests that the carpenters at the time were not happy to rely upon pegs to carry tension forces.

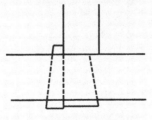

Figure 6.7

Bracing forces

We have already seen from Chapter 4 how large the wind forces on a barn might be compared with its own self-weight. The time has now come to see how this translates into forces within the structure. A house, or a barn without aisles, is simply a four bar chain braced across the corners, while an aisled barn is effectively buttressed by the aisle structure, which will almost certainly be stiffer than the knee braces. Therefore we might ignore the knee braces when considering the forces in the aisled structure. This leads to the two diagrams of Figure 6.6. The basic principles for both structures are the same but we might start with the simpler knee braced arrangement of Figure 6.6a. If a frame were assumed to have a single brace on the leeward side, then the wind tries to push the frame over, as indicated by the dotted lines, but to do this the angle where the brace is would have to become smaller, and the brace shorter in length. The brace therefore goes into compression and it is the leg that it is attached to that will be transmitting the horizontal wind force to the ground. The other leg cannot provide any horizontal restraint because, with no brace, it is free to rotate at both ends.

But why the vertical forces? They have to be added in to prevent the whole frame from being rolled over, i.e. from rotating about the foot of the leeward post. Imagining this shows that there has to be a hold-down force at the foot of the windward post, although, as the frame will be carrying the weight of the roof, this will normally be far larger than any hold-down force that would be needed, but we might, as suggested earlier, be concerned about a barn roofed with corrugated iron.

If we look at the forces on the post we can easily find the relationship between the wind force on the frame and the resulting force in a brace. This is where the free body diagram comes into its own. Looking first at the lefthand diagram, the force F in Figure 6.6, produced by the wind, will be transmitted to the top of the post and must be resisted by an equal force at the ground. We need not be concerned about the vertical force because we will be taking moments about the post along which this force acts. Imagine first the post pivoting about the end of the inclined brace. The force F at the bottom produces a clockwise moment F.a about this point (Figure 6.8a) and so the tie beam must be producing an anticlockwise

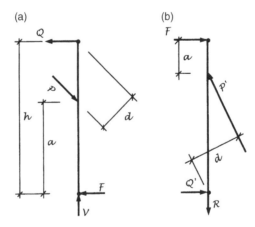

Figure 6.8 Forces on a braced post (see Figure 6.6).

moment to prevent rotation. This accounts for the force Q in the tie beam. In other words, all of the wind load is transmitted to the leeward post via the brace. Now consider moments about the top of the post, where F is producing a clockwise moment of F.h. This is resisted by an opposite moment P.d produced by the brace. If this is turned into a simple equation F.h = P.d then P = F.h/d. As d is made larger the force P in the brace will be reduced and simple geometry shows that for d to be larger the brace must be longer.

The forces in the buttressing arrangement of the aisle framing are a little different (Figure 6.8b). If we ignore any possible force in the knee brace and assume all of the wind resistance is produced by the aisle brace, then the wind load is transmitted to the top of the post by the tie beam. The aisle brace is pushing upwards against the post and in the absence of any roof load we would require a hold-down force. But again we are not concerned with this. Now taking moments about the end of the brace we require a force Q′ at the foot of the post. If we then take moments about the foot of the post we equate the racking moment F.h to the bracing moment P′.d.

Bending in the post

As well as looking at the forces in the brace we need to consider the bending produced in both the post and the beam. In the knee braced structure the brace pushes upwards against the beam tending to lift it off the tops of the post, and this upward force must be resisted by downward forces at the ends of the beam. At its other end the brace produces a force on the post tending to bend it outwards (Figure 6.9a). This is more serious because the tie beams tend to be large, and so have considerable bending resistance, while posts are much smaller. It should be apparent that the magnitude of the bending in the post is given by the product of the horizontal force at the foot multiplied by the height to the brace, i.e. F.a in Figure 6.8. Therefore the shorter the brace the larger will be the bending in the post – and the force in the brace.

If it were possible for both braces to be acting, one brace being in tension and the other in compression, the forces and the bending in the posts and beam would look rather like the frame shown in Figure 6.9b, where F = P$_1$ + P$_2$. We do not know how the forces at the ground that resist the wind load are distributed but we might assume them to be equal, unless there is a good reason to think otherwise. The tie beam now has an upward force on it from one of the braces and a downward force from the other, so is bent accordingly. Although we have

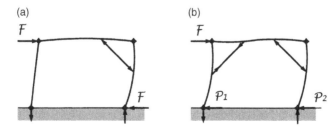

Figure 6.9 Deflections in a braced frame.

assumed that this does not happen in a timber frame this pattern of bending is significant in iron and steel frames, discussed below.

Light frame construction

The kind of carpentry used for the timber-framed buildings of medieval Europe required timbers large enough to be jointed and the carpentry skills to make the joints. The alternative was to use small scantling timbers joined together with nails. This was the approach used in Ottoman construction, still to be seen in surviving timber houses in Greece and Turkey. It was also the approach used in America when the balloon frame was devised to use readily available machine-sawn *lumber* and semi-skilled labour.

The framing of Ottoman houses used light stud construction with bracing much as that shown in Figure 6.10. Carpenters would use large posts with short spreaders to carry the plates. These formed the basic layout of the building and were braced with long diagonal braces across each panel of the frame. With this basic frame in place short studs would be cut to fit between the plates and the diagonal braces. This fairly simple carpentry used fewer large-section timbers and the small studs could be cut roughly to length because the diagonal brace allowed them to be fitted in easily and simply nailed top and bottom.

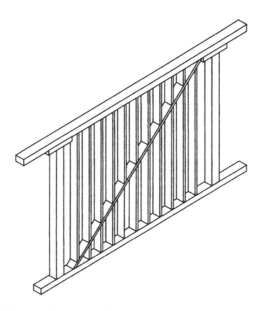

Figure 6.10 Bracing of light stud construction.

As these countries are prone to earthquakes one might wonder how such construction provides adequate racking resistance when subjected to the violent horizontal shaking during such events. The answer is that the framing is not the only thing called into play under such conditions. In some areas the wall between the studs was built up with small stones so that this primitive masonry provides the resistance required. The masonry helps the timber frame and the timber keeps the crude masonry together in a symbiotic relationship. Such walls would simply be plastered over to provide a weathering surface. In other places there is no masonry infill but the walls are boarded on the outside to form the external finish. The boarding, being nailed to all the studs, acts as a *diaphragm* to give in-plane stiffness to the wall. Traditional buildings in Cyprus use the first of these methods but, as the masonry and timber frame are plastered over, the construction is not always apparent. Boarded timber frames were used in Istanbul and the towns along the Bosporus. In both cases the feature that they have in common with timber framing in Western Europe is that they all use platform framing, i.e. the walls are only one storey high and the joists at each floor form a platform on which the walls of the next floor stand.

Carpenters in the early American settlements naturally used framing methods that were similar to those they were familiar with in Europe, and this can be seen in the forms of the structures used. Roofs, for example, might be distinctly English or distinctly Dutch or German. There were clearly adaptations to suit the different circumstances and differences in jointing details might well be the result of the different kinds of timbers available to the carpenters, but one major structural difference should be noted. The much harsher winter climate of New England encouraged the building of large central chimney stacks. These could therefore act as a buttress against wind loading so that bracing was only needed for the construction of the frames. This resulted in much lighter bracing to be found in some New England houses.

Eventually a new form of framing was developed. Circumstances in America were naturally very different from those in Europe. The country was expanding rapidly but skilled carpenters might be in short supply. A method of using sawn lumber was needed that could be nailed together into frames to meet the demand for housing. The result was the so-called balloon frame, different from earlier frames in its whole concept. Pairs of long studs, which would have been easy to obtain in a timber-rich country, had a floor joist and roof rafters nailed to them. These frames were then assembled together at close centres to form the skeleton of the house (Figure 6.11). It was an ideal form of construction where demand was high and skilled labour in short supply. Although both use small studs the distinction between this and the light framing of Ottoman construction is that there was no platform. Neither was there any bracing, which begs the questions how did it actually work, and what kept the frame stable?

We can see from Figure 6.11 that the structure is built up from a set of repeated frames, each comprising a pair of studs rising from wall plate to eaves, floor joists and collar-braced rafters. The joists appear to be carried on ledges although the nailing to the studs would have transmitted the load. The frames have no lateral stiffness, except what little might be provided by the nailing, and the whole thing has no longitudinal bracing. Some drawings of this form of construction show a pair of braces across a bottom corner, which would have served to keep the frame stable during construction, but once complete more than that would have been required to resist wind loads. This type of framing must have relied upon the cladding for stiffness as the frames have little lateral stiffness. Presumably the upper floor and possibly the roof, if it had *sarking* boards, acted as a diaphragm to transmit loads to the end walls. Seen like this a balloon frame house might be thought of as acting something like a big cardboard box. In the twentieth century the availability of plywood, and then other sheet

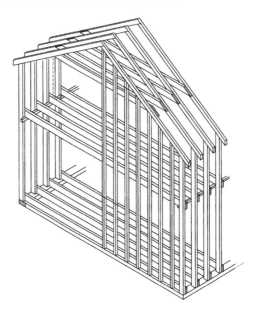

Figure 6.11 Balloon framing.

materials, has made timber framing using light studding a popular form of construction. This can take the form of either platform framing or balloon framing, each having its own advantages.

The coming of iron

When iron castings became readily available they were often used in conjunction with timber structures. A simple change that might be adopted was to replace the transverse bracing in a large barn or mill structure with cast-iron brackets. This would be especially valuable in those with an upper floor because the bracket bolted to floor beams and posts would help to carry the floor load rather than the mortice and tenon joint. It also had the advantage that it produced less obstruction in the space. It is useful to imagine the effect of such brackets with either relatively flexible beams or relatively flexible posts. The brackets ensure that the angles between the posts and beams remain right-angles if the frame sways sideways as a result of wind loads. In the first case (Figure 6.12a), which assumes stiff posts and a flexible beam, the beam bends down at one end and up at the other to accommodate the distorted shape of the frame. In the second (Figure 6.12b), where the beam is very stiff, it is the columns that have to bend. In practice there will be some bending in both the beam and the columns.

This is the principle upon which wooden tables resist the forces if they are slid across the floor. The legs of a table are connected into the horizontal timbers that carry the top in such a way that they cannot rotate. This is, of course, a statically indeterminate structure. Providing both columns are of equal stiffness we can assume that the horizontal forces at their feet

(a)   (b)

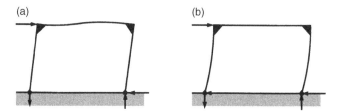

Figure 6.12 Deflection of a frame with rigid corners depending upon the relative stiffness of the members.

are equal. However, if one is stiffer than the other it is this one that will attract the larger force at the ground.

It might seem to be a simple progression to copy something like this in iron but it did not happen quite like that. When the first completely framed iron buildings were built, cast iron was already a well-established material for buildings, but as their designers had relied upon the external masonry walls to ensure their stability something new had to be devised. Brackets, similar to those used in the timber barns, were not used because it was simpler to support iron beams directly onto lugs formed in the column castings. Fixing was wanted within the depth of the beam. This was the approach used in two significant buildings, both presenting similar problems but differing in construction details. The first, the Crystal Palace, seems to have survived as much by luck as engineering skill. It was one of the earliest essays in iron framing and it would hardly be exaggerating to say that it only just survived the summer of 1851 and might well have become one of the world's more famous disasters. What was significant about the Crystal Palace was not simply its gigantic scale, but the fact that its walls were lightweight timber panels relying upon the support of the frame rather than giving support to it. Somehow the frame itself had to have adequate stiffness and simple methods, such as cross bracing or knee bracing, could not be used because these would interrupt the spaces. It was not clear how to combine the need to prefabricate the frame with the need to produce rigid connections between beams and columns, but the designers were well aware that the latter was essential.

Paxton's design for this great building needs to be placed in context. In the summer of 1850, the competition for the building's design failed to attract any entries that met with the building committee's approval. Then, with the support of the railway engineer Robert Stephenson, Paxton's late entry was accepted and approved. Paxton was a gardener and designer of glass houses and the overall form of the Crystal Palace was simple and utilitarian. His famous blotting paper sketch for it, drawn during a committee meeting that did not have his full attention, simply showed a basic rectangular frame stepping up to three storeys at the centre. The much-illustrated 'vaulted' central transept, which relieved the monotony of this, was in fact an afterthought, included to avoid cutting down some mature elm trees. Paxton's major contribution to the detailed design of the building was in the glazing system that covered the acres of roof. To Paxton this was simply a huge greenhouse.

The detailed design of the ironwork was left to the contractors who were to make it, and Paxton's box-like layout with repeated columns and beams certainly suited simple manufacture and assembly as it comprised a series of identical elements. What presented difficulties was that previous designs of iron buildings of this scale had relied upon the shape of the building to provide lateral stability. These included a large foundry at Bendorf, Germany, Richard Turner's design for the palm house at Kew, only recently completed, his Crystal Palace competition entry, and also an entry by Hector Horeau.[4] These designs had something in common with the medieval aisled barns, aisles buttressing the central nave, and while Paxton's design stepped down from the high central nave to lower storeyed galleries on either side, there was no provision for bracing within these aisles. The whole thing comprised nothing more than beams and columns, and if anything was to prevent racking of the structure it had to be the stiffness of the connections between them.

Naturally the design of an important public building on this scale attracted a certain amount of attention and exercised some important minds. It was essential that the structure would be safe and in part people were naturally concerned about the strength of the cast iron structure that was to support the exhibits and the throng of people that would crowd the galleries. Tests, reported in the *Illustrated London News* (1 March 1851), were carried out, first with a static load and then with various dynamic loads of workmen walking, running and jumping on a test section of the floor (supported just above the ground in case of failure). But what of its stability? X bracing would clearly have been inconvenient as it would have interfered with the circulation. It was used in some places, notably along the sides of the transept, where it is clearly visible in the illustrations of that part of the building, and it was also used in the end walls, but more bracing was required than this could provide. Ensuring stability of the rest of the frames exercised the minds of the engineers at the time and the method used was to produce a rigid joint between the columns and the deep floor girders.

The idea was that it should work as shown in Figure 6.13a. This is similar to a diagram produced at the time by Digby Wyatt to explain it.[5] The deep girders were fixed top and

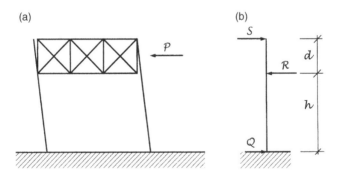

Figure 6.13 Wind resistance of the Crystal Palace.

[4]These designs are all discussed by Tom Peters (1996), *Building the Nineteenth Century*, MIT Press.
[5]Digby Wyatt, 'On the construction of the building for the exhibition of the works of industry of all nations in 1851', *Minutes of the Proceedings of the Institution of Civil Engineers*, 10 (1850–51), 127–91. But see also Downes, Charles (1852), *The Building Erected in Hyde Park for the Great Exhibition* ..., John Weale.

bottom to the columns. Any tendency of the frame to sway as a result of wind forces would produce forces between the beam fixings and the columns. If we look at the lefthand column of the diagram, then there are three forces on it seen in Figure 6.13b. The applied force on the frame will be transmitted at the lower fixing where the post and the girder are in contact, i.e. there will be compression between the two. This horizontal force on the frame is resisted by a force at the ground. Where the post and the girder are shown separated there will be a tension force. (Readers might draw for themselves the forces on the other column. Assume that Q = P/2.)

The basic principle seems fairly simple but the problem was to produce a structure that worked like this in practice. Like all structures, its design had to achieve two things, be stable when completed but be simple in manufacture and construction. In this case what was needed was something that could be assembled rapidly, simply because so much building was wanted in so short a time. The method of construction can be seen from the contemporary illustration in the *Illustrated London News* (Figure 6.14). With the posts erected the girders could be lifted up using *gin poles* and connected to the columns.

Figure 6.14 The Crystal Palace under construction.

But if one looks closely at the detailed illustration (Figure 6.15) it is clear that the girders were not connected directly to the columns. Instead a cast-iron connector was first bolted to a flange on the top of the column and the girders fixed into this connector. The connector

(a)

(b)

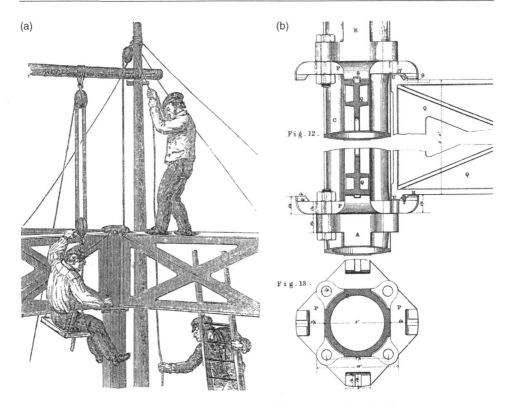

Figure 6.15 (a) Lifting a girder with a gin pole and **(b)** the connection detail.

had flanges top and bottom so that it could be bolted to the column below and to the column placed on top of it. Both the connector and the girders had lugs cast onto them in such a position that the girders must have been brought up and moved sideways so that the lugs engaged – or almost so. Wedges were driven in between the opposing lugs on the connector and girder so making a tight connection.

The wedges must be in compression to keep the whole thing tight. As the bottom wedges were driven in they pressed against the upward projecting lugs on the connectors and the downward projecting lugs on the girders; similarly for the top wedge. This has the effect of driving the ends of the girders back against the body of the connectors. Iron wedges were used in the transverse direction; this is where the racking forces on each joint would be greatest. Wooden wedges were used in the longitudinal direction to provide some allowance for expansion. Presumably there was supposed to be sufficient resilience in the timber to enable it to take up the movement without crushing. The whole structure relied upon the soundness of two connections, the wedged connection between girders and connectors and the bolted flanges between the connectors and the columns. With columns one above the other it was as if tables were stood upon each other but connected together so that the legs were continuous.

If rotation between the connecting piece and the column was prevented by the bolting between the two, the columns had to be capable of taking bending. Cast iron is a rather brittle material and cannot resist much bending. But this was not the only problem: the other was the effect of temperature changes on the building, which the contractor's design using wooden wedges was supposed to take care of. Metal expands and contracts considerably with changes in temperature and under all that glass large temperature changes were to be expected. But the problem was not simply the expansion of a single bay, which presumably each set of oak wedges was supposed to accommodate, there was a cumulative effect on the building. Multiply the length of the building by the possible rise in temperature and by the coefficient of expansion of iron and you have the change in length that has to be accommodated.

The coefficient of expansion of iron is $1.1 \times 10^{-5}/°C$. The length from the central transept was 278 m and if we assume a temperature rise of 20 °C there would be a change in length of 60 mm – a little over two inches in the units of the day.

At the time some regarded this method of bracing as insufficient and it seems that they might have been right. So often failure can be attributed to more than one thing going wrong at the same time rather than to a single cause. Here it was a combination of inadequate bracing and inadequate provision for thermal movement that put the building at risk. One of the most famous buildings of the nineteenth century might have turned out to be the most famous disaster. Having visited the building in use Robert Mallet later wrote that:

We … had an opportunity, during the early afternoon of one of the hottest days of the summer of 1851, of examining with some accuracy the effects of expansion by solar heat upon the frame of the building; and we can testify to this as a fact, that the extreme western end, and at the fronts of the nave galleries, where they had been here the longest and the most heated, the columns were actually about two inches out of plumb in the first range in height only. Unaided by measurements, we could not perceive that any change in the plumbness of the coupled columns at the corners of the intersection of the nave and transept had taken place. Their rigidity and other causes appeared to have resisted the whole thrust, and visited it upon the extreme outer ends of the building.
    As we gazed up at these west end galleries densely crowded with people, and over the ample spread of the nave equally thronged, and thought of the prodigeous cross-strains that were at that moment in unseen play in the brittle stilting of the cast iron fabric, we certainly felt that 'ignorance was bliss'[6]

Mallet's observation and the calculations above give the same result, and note that he makes the same assumption about the rigidity of the central transept so that expansion

---

[6] Robert Mallet, *The Record of the International Exhibition*, 1862.

occurs outwards from that. He was only thinking of the stresses on the columns produced by expansion, but what if a sudden wind load had added to them? A sudden summer storm perhaps.

A problem raised by his observation is to explain how this was happening. For the column to be inclined in the way that he described there would either have to be some rotation between the components – just what the design was supposed to prevent – or there would have to be some bending. It seems unlikely that there could have been much bending deflection in the members but it is bending stresses that Robert Mallet meant when he referred to cross strains. (At that time the word 'strain' was used where we now speak of stress.)

The deep girders could not possibly have deflected to allow the columns to lean but it is difficult to imagine cast-iron posts being sufficiently flexible to accommodate the amount of movement that Mallet reported. Therefore there must have been some rotation at the joint, which was possible because of the wooden wedges in the connectors; with large forces on them the wedges would crush. Of course we can never know for certain because no forensic examination was made of the structure when it was taken down. When the structural components were reused at Sydenham it was for a rather different building. It had more transepts with shorter sections between them, which would have mitigated the expansion problem. Also additional bracing was incorporated to improve its resistance to wind loads. Nevertheless there was a collapse of part of the structure between the time of its re-erection and Mallet's essay on the building. He noted that 'a very large wing has been actually blown down', the part that 'probably more accurately represented the structure of the building as it stood in 1851'. It seems that a greater disaster in the original building was only narrowly avoided.

Things were managed rather better at the Sheerness boat store. This was not the only boat store that the military had built at that time; there was one at Woolwich, built of a combination of timber and iron, but for which only measured drawings survive. These stores had to provide 'shelves' or racks on which the boats were stored and were little more than large boxes with a simple rectangular cross-section. The Sheerness store has an open 'nave' at the centre with four-storey aisles either side (Figure 6.16). Both the central nave and the aisles either side are 45 ft (13.5 m) wide, and the whole building is 210 ft (63 m) long. Floor heights vary, diminishing towards the top, being 12 ft 6 in, 11 ft, 9 ft and 7 ft 6 in (3.75 m, 3.3 m, 2.7 m and 2.25 m).

Boats brought into the 'nave' were lifted to the required height then moved onto a floor of one of the aisles. Like the Crystal Palace there were no dividing walls and the external walls were of light construction, in this case corrugated iron below the windows, a new material of the nineteenth century. The floors comprised longitudinal wrought iron beams 18 in (457 mm) deep and spanning 30 ft (9 m) between columns. These carried timber joists, shown dotted on the plan of Figure 6.16a. Between the columns were cast-iron transverse beams 12 in (300 mm) deep. In this structure the fixing between the beams and columns was much more positive. The columns were cast H or I sections two storeys high with projecting lugs on which sat both the cast-iron transverse beams and the deeper wrought iron longitudinal beams. Holes in the flanges of the column corresponded with holes in the ends of the cast-iron beams so that the two could be bolted together top and bottom (see sketch – Figure 16b).

Bolts were capable of transmitting the tensile forces either at the top or the bottom of the connection so that this joint would easily be able to prevent rotation between the beams and

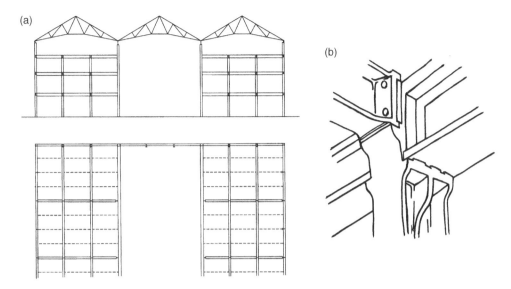

Figure 6.16 (a) Section and **(b)** detail of the Sheerness Boat Store.

columns. Moreover, the column section used is a much better shape for resisting bending than the circular columns of the Crystal Palace. This was a much better structure because the beams were bolted directly to the columns with no separate connecting piece. Of course, with much shallower beams the forces on the joints must be much larger for the same racking force, but these bolted joints provided a much surer connection. If we make the assumption that the applied load is shared equally between a pair of columns we can work out the forces within the connections; it is the familiar balance equation. The moment at the top of each column is the height of the column multiplied by the racking load carried at its base – Q.h of Figure 6.13. This is resisted by a pair of forces within the connection, the equivalent of the bracing distance for the braced timber frame, being the distance between the two fixings, i.e. d. Thus if we take moments about the bottom fixing, S.d = Q.h. Just as the bracing force in a timber frame increased with a reduction in the length of the brace, so in an iron frame the shallower the beam the larger the forces have to be. However, a difference between the iron frame and the timber frame is that we can have every confidence in the ability of the fasteners in the joint to transmit the tension forces generated. This is clearly not a complete analysis because we do not know how the wind loads will be distributed between the connections at each floor of the boat store's frame, for which we would need more knowledge of the properties of the sections and the construction of the building than we have here.

The two structures of the Crystal Palace and the boat store show clearly the change that was necessary from the frames of the early mill and warehouse buildings to the independent iron frame and eventually steel frames. Building up the frames storey by storey presented no problems. But with no stabilising masonry walls, preventing racking was a serious design issue for these buildings, and one can see that it eventually became a mater of joint design. At the Crystal Palace, the racking of the frames had to be resisted in more than one step, by the connection between the girder and the column connector and then by the connection between the connector and the rest of the column. The two-stage transfer was far from satisfactory but in the boat store there was a direct connection between columns and beams. Naturally one cannot have columns in one length as high as the building and it has often proved convenient to make the columns two storeys high with the connection between the lengths just above each floor. (In fact at the boat store the connections are just above the floor on the external columns and just below the floor on the internal columns.) The effect of this is that the frames are like two-storey portal frames.

The frame today

Avoidance of bracing within the building is the ideal and this is possible even if all the joints in the frame have to be considered as pinned. But with steel, reinforced concrete, or even in timber today, it is possible to have frames with stiff joints at the knee between posts and either a beam or inclined rafters. Steel structures may be welded or rely on bolting, much as in the boat store, while reinforced concrete structures provide natural continuity with appropriate placement of the reinforcement (for which see Chapter 7). Timber frames have been made continuous at the knee joint by using plywood *gussets* nailed to posts and rafters. The resulting structures are called either *portal frames* or pitched portal frames, depending upon whether the roof is flat or pitched. Assuming that the feet of the posts are hinged, if the apex of a pitched roof is a pinned joint the structure is a three-hinged arch, a common arrangement where factory-made components comprising post and rafter are joined together on site.

A building then comprises a series of such frames joined together with purlins and rails, the cladding often being some kind of profiled metal. Longitudinal stability relying upon stiff joints is seldom possible because, while the joints for the transverse frames might be factory made, joints on the long wall of the building would have to be made on site. With steel, site welding is always possible but is more expensive and possibly disruptive of the construction process. However, simple X bracing can be put between the columns of the end bays to carry the wind loads on the gable walls. Bracing is normally by tension members that are simple to use with today's materials and jointing methods, and again one of the bracing members is active whichever way the wind blows.

If a stiff transverse frame is not possible then it is possible to brace a pin-jointed frame to form a box-like structure. This is done by treating the roof or the ceiling plane as a beam or girder transmitting the wind loads to the end walls where they can be carried by X bracing. Figure 6.17 assumes a completely pin-jointed frame. With the wind blowing on the gable, the wall plate has to be stiff enough to transmit load to the corner posts, but longitudinal racking is prevented by the tension members in the end bays. The inactive brace members are shown as dotted lines. With wind blowing on the side of the building racking resistance is ultimately provided by the bracing in the gable walls. To prevent racking of the intermediate frames the ceiling plane has been turned into a truss, abcd. The tie beams of the roof form the internal compression members of the truss while the different diagonals come into play to serve as the tension members, depending upon the direction of the wind. With the wind in the direction shown the section of the wall plate ab must be in tension while the

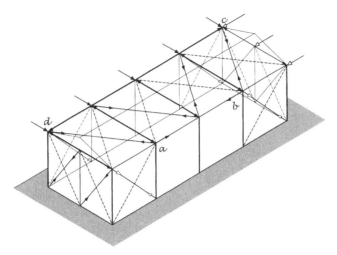

Figure 6.17 Bracing of a pin-jointed frame.

whole length of the other wall plate is acting as the compression chord of the truss. This kind of structure has been successfully built in timber, where moment-resisting joints are difficult to make, but with steel tie rods to form the bracing.

This is the kind of scheme referred to in Chapter 4, where the side walls carry the weight of the roof and the end walls carry the wind loading. It is obviously not necessary for the bracing in the gable ends to be divided into two as shown but the proportions of end walls will probably make it convenient to have the bracing across more than one panel or possibly in only part of the gable wall. It is equally possible to truss within the plane of the roof instead of in the ceiling plane.

In frames where the structure has been exposed architects have tended to put bracing in all the bays to give a uniform appearance. Richard Rogers did this in his Reliance Control Factory, Swindon (1967). However, he not only put bracing along all the bays in the longitudinal direction of this external frame but also along the other wall. There, with the I beam that serves the function of the wall plate welded to the columns, the end frames were effectively five welded portal frames that would have had some stiffness without the bracing.

The development in materials that affected architecture in the latter part of the twentieth century was the availability of structural hollow sections – tubes – although these could be square and rectangular as well as round. Lattice girders formed by joining these together produced a structure that was far more elegant than the same thing formed of angles, and if assembled into a triangular cross-section the compression chord of the truss was braced against buckling. Figure 6.18 shows what a short section of such a truss might look like. It takes the form of a series of upside down pyramids with the tension chord joining their apices. As with the bridge trusses of Figures 2.19 and 2.22, the diagonals will be alternately in compression and tension. Although joints could be formed by welding one tube directly to another, a simpler technique is to flatten the tubes at the ends, when the flattened tube can be bolted to lugs welded to the other tube.

Such lattices could be used for columns as well as beams and the two combined to form a portal frame. This is what Richard Rogers did for offices for B & B Italia in Como, Italy

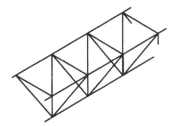

Figure 6.18 A triangular-section truss.

(1973), with the offices hung inside this exposed structure. For the Sainsbury Centre at the University of East Anglia (1978), Norman Foster used this kind of truss for the modern equivalent of earth-fast posts. Deep trusses form a thick wall within which services are run. Of course they do not actually go into the earth but are cantilevered from the ground slab to support trusses that span between them. There is a clear separation between the structure of the wall and that of the girders across the roof, although both have a similar depth. The structure is therefore a series of vertical cantilevers to resist wind loads and simply supported trusses spanning between the tops of these. We will return to the distinction between these two kinds of structure at the end of the next chapter.

The most extensive example of cross bracing is the Centre Pompidou, Paris, where it is not only in all 12 bays of the frame but is also carried up through all five levels. However, it is set outside the frame proper and is not directly connected to the main columns. This exercise in structural gymnastics is full of indirect methods of load transfer where everything is made visible but nothing is straightforward. The girders supporting the floor are not connected directly to the columns but are supported on the short ends of stocky double cantilevers, the so-called gerberettes. These are pivoted at the columns and held down by tension members on the outside of the building. Taken alone these have the force diagram of our seesaw, although one might note that with two downward forces on the gerberettes the columns are actually carrying a load that is larger than the weight of the building. It is the outer ends of the gerberettes that are braced rather than the main columns so that any wind forces on the end walls of the building need to be transmitted across the zone between the edge of the floor and the plane of the vertical bracing. There are horizontal braces incorporated at intervals within this zone, although they are not easy to see with so much else going on.

The general cross-section on the left of the centreline in Figure 6.19 shows the floors to be open and without any cross bracing, so transverse loads must be transmitted back to the end walls just as in the simple structure shown in Figure 6.17. This can be done through the concrete floor plates. The transverse bracing is in the less frequently photographed ends, seen on the right of Figure 6.19, where there are three triangles formed (here only 1½ can be shown) between the top of one truss and the bottom of the one above. This turns the end wall into a rigid structure above the first floor level. At the ground floor a stiff X-shaped bracing is introduced at both sides of the building, the sections used for these being far heavier than the others in the end frame and so speaking of the forces that they have to carry.

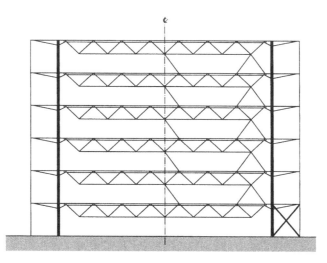

Figure 6.19 Centre Pompidou, Paris, typical section (left) and end framing (right).

The multi-storey frame

While the Crystal Palace and the boat store are useful examples in that they show different ways of ensuring stability in a completely framed building they lie outside the mainstream of structural development of the time. That is because their use of lightweight walls, which made it necessary for the frame to be stiffened in some way, was not to come into general use until the widespread adoption of curtain walling a century later. Instead the most common use of framed construction in nineteenth century buildings was that used extensively for mills and warehouses. The main requirement for such buildings was the provision of open floor spaces with enclosing roof and masonry walls, enough windows to provide adequate light and, in mills, a plan that accommodated the machinery and the drive shafts. No subdividing walls were required so that only columns were wanted to carry the floor beams. What developed was a simple grid of columns and beams supporting a fireproof floor, but in which external walls also supported the beams. In America this form of construction was initially adopted for commercial buildings of increasing height, where it was called cage construction. Skeleton construction came later and referred to building where the external walls did not serve to carry loads from the floors. Instead the frame carried all the floor loads and the external walls were eventually to be supported by the frame.[7]

Bracing of such frames became much more of an issue as buildings increased in height. For a while as buildings went higher the external walls continued to be self-supporting until

---

[7] For an account of this development see Donald Friedman, *Historical Building Construction*, Norton, New York, 1995.

eventually they were carried at each floor on the frame. Some means was then needed to stiffen the frame against wind loads but it was by no means clear what methods were best. The first building that might reasonably claim skyscraper status was Tower Building in New York, a long thin building 11 storeys high and completed in 1889. The only drawing of this that survives is the one showing the wind bracing (Figure 6.20), but this is hardly very informative and raises some questions. A single diagonal was used on each floor so they must have served as both compression and tension members, depending upon the direction of the wind. That the diagonals did not extend the full width of the building was to allow for a passage on one side. The puzzle is what was happening on the two street level floors. (The site sloped by a complete floor level between Broadway and New Street.) No diagonals are shown there and one might wonder if they were simply omitted from the drawing? Here our structural knowledge can be used for some historical detective work.

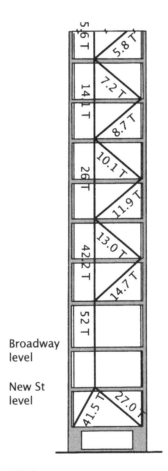

Figure 6.20 Tower Building, New York.

If we assume that the drawing is accurate so that the angles of the diagonals in the basement are correct, then using the figures provided by Bradford Lee Gilbert, the building's architect, a triangle of forces can be attempted for the three forces meeting at the New Street level. Try this and you will find that it almost closes. In other words the vertical components of the two inclined forces add up to the value of the force in the vertical member and their horizontal components are equal. Therefore the horizontal wind force, the horizontal component of the 14.7 ton diagonal force at the floor above the Broadway level, must have been accommodated in some other way not shown on this drawing, possibly by treating internal walls as shear walls. Landau and Condit, writing about the development of the skyscraper, report the disquiet among other architects and engineers at the time and have suggested that the building relied upon the mass of its masonry walls to ensure its stability.[8]

When Freitag was writing his book on framed buildings, around the turn of the twentieth century, engineers were still using a variety of methods for bracing the buildings.[9] There was simple diagonal X bracing, deep girders working much like the deep beams of the Crystal Palace, and even the substantial portal frame used in the Old Colony Building in Chicago, although that seemed to be the only building of note to use such a method. Freitag pointed out that where bracing rods were used in connection with cast-iron columns the rods were often far stronger than the lugs to which they were attached, a comment that takes us back to the design of connections. This had become a matter of some concern to engineers in late nineteenth century America, where buildings were going to greater heights and being subjected to much larger wind loads than in Europe. We can see from the discussion of the timber frame that simple knee bracing would not be a satisfactory method for tall framed buildings because of the large bending moments that would be induced in the floor beams and columns. Whatever bracing method was used the forces naturally accumulated towards the bottom of the building so that it is the ground floor that has to take the largest load; bracing naturally increased towards the bottom of the building.

Resisting wind loads became easier with the development and extensive use of reinforced concrete because, although tall buildings often continued to rely upon steel frames, the lift shafts and particularly the associated escape stairs were built in concrete to provide fire resistance. Add to that the lavatories, because the plumbing has to be grouped together vertically, and the result is effectively a stiff concrete tube, the service core, extending the whole height of the building, and this could be made stiff enough to resist the wind loads. All this could be grouped in a service tower placed either inside or outside the main floor plan of the building. An example of the latter is the CWS building in Manchester, while the towers of the World Trade Centre, New York, were devised as 'tubes' of steel columns on the outside to carry vertical loads only with a central service core both picking up floor loads and resisting the wind loads. Nervi, for his Pirelli Tower in Milan, the first Italian skyscraper, placed 'service cores' at either end so that wind loads are transmitted to these by the floors acting as horizontal beams, or diaphragms between these two, just as we have seen done in the simple single-storey building of Figure 6.17 and in the Centre Pompidou.

---

[8] Landau, S.B. and Condit, C.W. (1996), *Rise of the New York Skyscraper, 1865–1913*, Yale University Press, New Haven & London.
[9] Freitag, J.K., *Architectural Engineering with Special Reference to High Building Construction*, 2nd edn, John Wiley, New York & London, 1902.

A quite different approach to handling wind loading on tall buildings is to use diagonal bracing and expose it. This has the advantage that the bracing does not affect the planning of the building while at the same time it can be arranged over several floors. Each floor does not have to be braced separately and the walls can be turned into vertical girders whose effective 'depth' is the width of the building. Here a range of different patterns has been used. The most direct is the diagonal bracing on all four faces of the John Hancock Centre, Chicago, the bracing clearly apparent as a feature of the elevations (Figure 6.21b). I.M. Pei's Bank of China building, Hong Kong, which is much the same height, incorporates an apparently much simpler bracing arrangement into the façade of the building (Figure 6.21a). This is despite the three-dimensional form of the building being much more complex. However, all is not quite what it seems. The steel frames on the different façades were built separately and then knitted together with reinforced concrete at the corners.[10] The ability to use the full width of the building in this way to incorporate bracing seems likely to continue. It has been used by Richard Rogers in a variety of ways in his recent development at Paddington Basin, London.

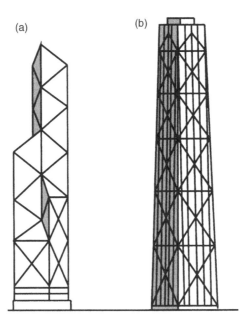

(a)   (b)

Figure 6.21 Wind bracing of **(a)** Bank of China, Hong Kong, and **(b)** John Hancock Centre, Chicago.

We can hardly discuss the Bank of China without noticing Norman Foster's nearby Hongkong and Shanghai Bank Building. This is a building that wears its structure outside so that all seems to be visible, although this is only true in one direction. In the other direction there is bracing across the building that is less easy to see. This is a particular type of structure

[10] Leslie E. Robertson, 'A Life in Structural Engineering' in Guy Nordenson (ed.), *Seven Structural Engineers: The Felix Candela Lectures*. Museum of Modern Art, New York, 2008.

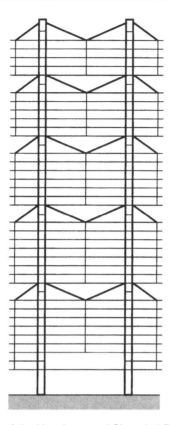

Figure 6.22 Structural scheme of the Hongkong and Shanghai Bank Building.

where floors are hung from cantilevers at intervals up the building. Here all is not quite what it seems, or at least not as logical as one might suppose. The cantilevers are of unequal length and if we compare the double cantilevers of this building with our seesaw of Chapter 1 we would expect the longer cantilever to be carrying the smaller load. But here it cannot be so – the longer cantilever must be carrying the greater load as it supports a larger area of floor (Figure 6.22). In a tower crane the load can rarely be balanced against the counterweight. Out of balance is catered for by bending in the tower – and so it is here. While the structure is exposed for all to see, it is not the most obvious means of supporting the floors.[11]

Columns

The bulk of this chapter has been about the stability of frames, but the essence of a frame structure is the column, whose principal behaviour as a compression member, with the

---

[11]For a critique of this building see the article by Frank Newby and Tom Schollar in *Architectural Review*, p. 179, No 1070 (April 1986). The structure itself is described in G.J. Zunz et al., 'The structure of the new headquarters for the Hongkong and Shanghai Banking Corporation, Hong Kong', *The Structural Engineer*, 1985; 63A, No. 9 (September).

attendant likelihood of buckling under excessive loading, was dealt with in Chapter 1. There are, however, two aspects of the column that are worth dealing with here. One, of architectural significance, is that columns are generally thought of as vertical elements but are not necessarily so, and this is illustrated in one particular building. The second aspect is literally a matter of life and death and concerns the earthquake resistance of buildings. As that particularly concerns the behaviour of reinforced concrete columns, readers might like to leave the reading of this section until after reading the next chapter, which deals *inter alia* with the behaviour of reinforced concrete beams.

It is quite possible for columns to be inclined and in this way the load path can be shifted horizontally. The requirement for this is simply that some means is provided for taking out the horizontal component of the column force to avoid having large bending loads in the columns. Louis Kahn produced a rather fanciful design for a structure in Philadelphia that had nothing but inclined columns, but this was hardly a practical proposition. However, practical use of inclined columns is seen in James Stirling's Engineering Laboratory, Leicester. The tower of this is a rectangle with the corners clipped off so that pairs of columns were needed to frame out these corners. However, Frank Newby, the engineer, showed how just above the lecture theatre each of those pairs of columns could be brought to a single point using inclined columns so that the frame below was a simple rectangle. A tiny sketch for this (redrawn here as Figure 6.23) shows Newby making an estimate of the horizontal forces at the top and bottom of the inclined columns – the horizontal components of the forces in them – that must be resisted in the beams. The inclined column needs to have a force in it such that its vertical component is equal to the force from the column above. Thus the force in the inclined column must be larger than the load from the columns above. Once this is worked out the horizontal components of that force can be calculated. What this sketch shows is the kind of 'back of envelope' calculations that an engineer will so often be carrying out to get some measure of the forces that he will be dealing with.

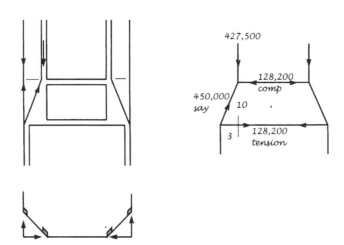

Figure 6.23 Estimated horizontal forces at the top and bottom of inclined columns.

For those who want to work through this calculation, the floor-to-floor height is 10 ft – in the units of the time – and the offset 3 ft. This produces an angle $\emptyset$ = arctan 3/10 = 16.7°. The vertical load coming onto the inclined column was 427 500 lb so that the force in the columns must be 427 500/cos $\emptyset$, approximately 450 000 lb. Actually it is slightly smaller than that but Newby was rounding up here. The horizontal component of this force, 450 000.sin $\emptyset$, = 128 200 lb.

The matter of life and death brings us back to more humble structures, but vitally important ones nevertheless. Horizontal forces from the wind are greatest toward the bottom of the building and this is also true of earthquake loading, and a problem for fairly humble frame buildings. For the tall building the problems are clearly recognised and engineers have even devised shock-absorbing foundations to alleviate the problem of earthquake loading. Unfortunately builders of humbler buildings may not be aware of this issue and fail to take account of it. In many countries where recent earthquakes have occurred, there have been disastrous failures of concrete-framed buildings while traditional buildings have survived, simply because a reinforced concrete frame seems to be a simple and reliable way to build. But this has not simply happened in countries where reinforced concrete frames have been used instead of a more robust traditional construction, either masonry or timber. Failures also occurred in a Californian earthquake because of the use of what has been called soft storeys at the ground floor level.

We need not concern ourselves with the construction of the upper floors of what might be an apartment building, which, subdivided by internal walls, will have some stiffness. The problem comes with ground floors that are open for car parking. As the ground moves horizontally (Figure 6.24) the building above tends to get left behind, as suggested by the dotted lines of the ground floor columns. Because ground movement involves a horizontal acceleration that has to be transmitted to the building, it is as if a large horizontal force has been applied to the building in the opposite direction to the movement. From Newton's law, which states that force is equal to mass times acceleration, the magnitude of this force depends upon the mass of the building and the severity of the earthquake; and it is the ground floor columns that have to transmit this force from the ground to the first floor depending upon the degree of seismic activity in that location. The horizontal force on each column might be as much as a quarter of the vertical load.

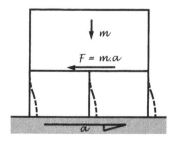

Figure 6.24 Bending of columns of a 'soft storey' under earthquake loads.

As the diagram clearly shows, there will be some bending in the columns but there will also be considerable shear force at each end of the columns. In reinforced concrete it is the shear resistance that has proved to be the Achilles heel of many reinforced concrete buildings. It may not be obvious to builders that columns need to be designed to resist shear forces. The reinforcement in a column comprises vertical bars held together with horizontal loops of steel to form a cage. The loops, or binders, are rectangular in a rectangular column. It may appear that they are only there to keep the vertical bars in place – 'So why put in more than I need for that?' In fact it is the binders that are providing the shear resistance and because that is greatest at the top and bottom of the column one would expect to see the binders much closer together in those areas to give greater strength. If the builder does not understand what they are there for the tendency will be to leave some of them out – less cost to him and less time and trouble in making up the reinforcing. Of course, under normal conditions the shear forces generated by wind loads are comparatively small and so if the builder has skimped on the amount of shear reinforcement in the columns it will not be a problem – not until there is an earthquake, and then the high shear forces at the top and bottom of the columns causes them to break at these points with disastrous consequences.

7 Floors and Beams – Deflections and Bending Moments

Walls or frames are there to support the floors and roof, and in dry climates where the roof can be flat both of these are made in the same way, by having timbers span across between the walls carrying either the flooring or the roof surface. The task for the builders was always to select an appropriately sized floor joist or beam but at the same time using the material available. Floors that can still be seen in surviving medieval buildings in England use fairly small timbers slightly broader than they are deep and set fairly close together. This might seem curious because common experience tells us that a timber is stronger in bending if it is laid 'on edge' rather than on its broader side, and the carpenters would certainly have known that. But at that time both floor joists and roof rafters were obtained from coppiced timber, which limited their size and shape. When a tree was felled a stool was left that would then sprout and the limbs growing out of it would grow up towards the light producing long, fairly straight timbers with few if any branches. When these were harvested, squared and sawn down the centre the sawn face was the one straight face and would become the upper surface of a floor joist or rafter, resulting in members that were shallower than their width. To obtain straight timbers that were deeper than their width would have involved more effort in sawing and much more wastage. It was not efficiency of the structure that was sought but efficiency of the whole process. Only the larger members were obtained from the trunks of mature trees.

The joists in timber-framed houses are often visible externally because at the front of the house they rest upon the plate at the head of the ground-floor wall and carry the sole plate of the first-floor wall, called the bressummer. In parts of Europe where softwood was used to build frame houses, and where the joists are also visible, one can see that much larger sections were used and hence placed wider apart. This is because softwood cannot be coppiced like hardwood and floor beams were simply sawn out of larger diameter trunks. With the joist size limited by the method of conversion their span was also limited. If their span was too great, joists would deflect more than was acceptable and it was not possible to span the full width of a room. Therefore this had to be divided in half with a central spine beam carried by the cross beams of each frame. This method of framing floors persisted into the seventeenth century even though houses were by then built with masonry walls (Figure 7.1).

Finding the loads that the beams are carrying is a matter of simple arithmetic. If the loads are distributed uniformly across the floor, half the load on each joist is transmitted to each end and the floor can be divided into panels with the loads taking the paths shown in Figure 7.2. Ignoring the openings for chimneys and stairs, the spine beams are carrying half the total load on the floor, with the walls carrying the other half. The area A of Figure 7.2 is

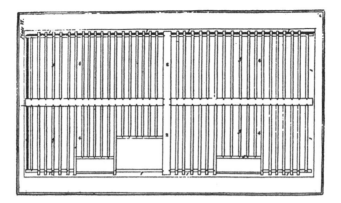

Figure 7.1 Early floor layout.

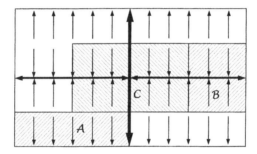

Figure 7.2 Load tracing for the floor in Figure 7.1.

supported by the walls whereas each spine beam carries twice that area. Each spine beam delivers half its load to the end walls, area B. The cross beam then carries half the load on each of the spine beams, the area marked C. This means that each spine beam is carrying the same load as the cross beam although the former is distributed along the length of the beams whereas the latter is a point load at mid-span. We shall see below that such a central point load is a more severe loading.

In Britain the first attempt to regulate the sizes of structural timbers came in the Act of Parliament passed after the Fire of London in 1666 to ensure proper standards of construction in the rebuilding of the city. The principal concern of the authorities was to prevent such a disaster from recurring, and so much of the Act was designed both to make buildings less likely to catch fire and, in the event of such a fire, to make it less likely that it would spread to adjacent buildings. It was this Act that transformed London from a city of timber-framed buildings to one of brickwork. But within these regulations was a table setting out the required sizes for structural timbers including those for the floors.

The commissioners appointed to draw up this Act were Sir Roger Pratt, an amateur architect, Christopher Wren, who had designed significant buildings at Oxford and Cambridge, and who was to become the leading architect of the day, and Robert Hooke, principally a scientist but who also designed a few buildings. Although Robert Hooke was the experimental scientist of the Royal Society there was clearly no time to carry out experiments to determine the appropriate sizes, perhaps by loading a number of timbers and observing the effect. Something was wanted immediately, and for that the commissioners simply drew upon the experience of carpenters who would already know what sizes were appropriate for what spans. In the Commissioners' own words they were 'well consulted by able workmen before they were reduced into an Act', and such workmen would have had the experience to know what sizes were necessary. Timber bends a good deal before it breaks, so much so that it is the deflection of a floor that determines its serviceability rather than its ultimate strength, i.e. it is the stiffness of a floor that we are principally concerned with. If a floor is not stiff enough then it will be too 'lively' when we walk across it. If there is a plaster ceiling below a floor that deflects too much there will be cracking of the plaster. That being so carpenters would have immediately appreciated when floor joists were inadequate, and some well-understood rules of thumb would have developed for selecting appropriate sizes. It must have been such informal rules that informed the table in the Act.

Because rooms had generally been larger than could be spanned by joists alone, the tables had also to specify the scantlings of the girders that supported the joists. This is not the end of the story because the carpenters' manuals that were published throughout the following century or so included such tables of sizes but they did not stick to those specified by the Act. Whatever the reasons for this, one thing that the manuals had to deal with was the change in the material used. Until the Fire of London, oak was the preferred building timber in England (although elm is common in some places). After the Fire the demand for timber for rebuilding, and the navy's competing requirement for oak for shipbuilding, caused

---

'Hardwood' and 'softwood'

The distinction between the terms softwood and hardwood in English today has nothing to do with the hardness of the timber, although this is the origin of the term. Hardwood refers to wood from any deciduous tree (which includes balsa wood) while softwood refers to wood from coniferous trees. The term 'fir' used in the late seventeenth and into the eighteenth century is taken from a Norwegian word, thus beginning a confusion over timber terms that has lasted to this day. In fact the timbers imported at the time would have been Scots pine, *Pinus sylvestris*, and Norwegian spruce, *Picea abies* (these timbers are also called redwood and whitewood by timber merchants today). However, because the properties of Scots pine vary considerably with growing conditions, builders became familiar with the differences between timbers from different ports of origin and called them by these names even though the species was the same. Thus fir was from Christiania (Oslo), Riga, Danzig or Memel.

Table 7.1 Sizes of timbers from Francis Price, *The Britsh Carpenter*, 1733.

A TABLE *for the Scantlings of Timber.*

A Proportion for Timbers for ſmall Buildings.				*A Proportion for Timbers of large Buildings.*			
Bearing Poſts of Fir		Bearing Poſts of Oak		Bearing Poſts of Fir		Bearing Poſts of Oak	
Height	Scantling	Height	Scantling	Height	Scantling	Height	Scantling
if 8 Feet	4 Inch.Sq.	if 10 Feet	6 Inch.Sq.	if 8 Feet	5 Inch.Sq	if 8 Feet	8 Inch.Sq.
10	5	12	8	12	8	12	12
12	6	14	10	16	10	16	16
Girders of Fir		Girders of Oak		Girders of Fir		Girders of Oak	
Bearing	Scantling	Bearing	Scantling	Bearing	Scantling	Bearing	Scantling
if 16 Feet	8 I. by 11	if 16 Feet	10 I. by 13	if 16 Feet	9½ I. by 13	if 16 Feet	12 I. by 14
20	10 12½	20	12 14	20	12 14	20	15 15
24	12 14	24	14 15	24	13½ 15	24	18 16
Joiſts of Fir		Joiſts of Oak		Joiſts of Fir		Joiſts of Oak	
Bearing	Scantling	Bearing	Scantling	Bearing	Scantling	Bearing	Scantling
if 6 Feet	5 I. by 2½	if 6 Feet	5 I. by 3	if 6 Feet	5 I. by 3	if 6 Feet	6 I. by 3
9	6½ 2½	9	7½ 3	9	7½ 3	9	9 3
12	8 2½	12	10 3	12	10 3	12	12 3
Bridgings of Fir		Bridgings of Oak		Bridgings of Fir		Bridgings of Oak	
Bearing	Scantling	Bearing	Scantling	Bearing	Scantling	Bearing	Scantling
if 6 Feet	4 I. by 2½	if 6 Feet	4 I. by 3	if 6 Feet	4 I. by 3	if 6 Feet	5 I. by 3½
8	5 2¼	8	5½ 3	8	5½ 3	8	6½ 3½
10	6 3	10	7 3	10	7 3	10	8 3½
Small Rafters of Fir		Small Rafters of Oak		Small Rafters of Fir		Small Rafters of Oak	
Bearing	Scantling	Bearing	Scantling	Bearing	Scantling	Bearing	Scantling
if 8 Feet	3½ I. by 2½	if 8 Feet	4½ I. by 3	if 8 Feet	4½ I. by 3	if 8 Feet	5½ I. by 3
10	4½ 2½	10	5½ 3	10	5½ 3	10	7 3
12	5½ 2½	12	6½ 3	12	6½ 3	12	9 3
Beams of Fir, or Tyes		Beams of Oak, or Tyes		Beams of Fir, or Tyes		Beams of Oak, or Tyes	
Length	Scantling	Length	Scantling	Length	Scantling	Length	Scantling
if 30 Feet	6 I. by 7	if 30 Feet	7 I. by 8	if 30 Feet	7 I. by 8	if 30 Feet	8 I. by 9
45	9 8½	45	10 11½	45	10 11½	45	11 12½
60	12 11	60	13 15	60	13 15	60	14 16

Principal Rafters of Fir, ſcantling			Principal Rafters of Oak, ſcantling			Principal Rafters of Fir, ſcantling			Principal Rafters of Oak, ſcantling		
Lgth	Top	Botm.	Lgth.	Top	Botm.	Lgth.	Top	Botm.	Lgth.	Top	Botm.
if 24ft	5 I. & 6	6 I. & 7	if 24ft	7 I. & 8	8 I. & 9	if 24ft.	7 I. & 8	8 I. & 9	if 24ft.	8 I. & 9	9 I. & 10
36	6½ 8	8 10	36	8 9	9 10½	36	8 9	9 10½	36	9 10	10 12
48	8 10	10 12	48	9 10	10 12	48	9 10	10 12	48	10 12	12 14

builders to turn to imported *softwood* instead. It was said that the Norwegians, who exported this, warmed themselves on the Fire of London. As softwood has different structural properties from oak one would naturally expect the sizes for the two timbers to be different. And so it was that the carpenters' manuals included both timbers (Table 7.1).

The curious thing about the table of sizes is that those given for oak are larger than those for fir when we know (and surely the carpenters of the time would have known) that oak is both stronger and stiffer than fir. That being so the sizes for fir should have been the larger and not the other way round. The explanation for this can only be that oak is denser than fir, and carpenters made allowance for that. Even that might seem strange by today's standards because the weight of a floor is very small compared with the live load that we design for it to carry. Today we design for very large loads compared with those that commonly occur – a living room with the crowded cocktail party referred to in Chapter 4. That is the kind of thing that modern design codes allow for, while the eighteenth century carpenters would have been thinking more of the common loads on a floor. Looked at like that, the weight of the floor was significant compared with the live load and the difference between the weights of oak and fir was noticeable; that is until one takes account of the superior structural properties of oak. This must eventually have been realised because later manuals reversed this difference in size.

The other thing to note about the table is that it refers to bridgings as well as joists and beams, and to understand this means looking at contemporary floor construction. The arrangement shown in Figure 7.1 was that used in timber-framed houses, but with masonry walls girders did not have to be aligned with posts, and central summer beams were no longer used. A plan by Francis Price[1] (Figure 7.3) shows that girders placed across rooms to carry the floor joists might not be orthogonal to the room because it was important (and required by the 1666 Act) to keep their ends out of the chimney breasts. However, there are two kinds of floor shown in Price's illustration, single floors and double floors.

Single floors are what one naturally assumes, an arrangement in which joists simply span onto the girders (Figure 7.4a). Clearly the girder would often be deeper than the joists so that in good quality work there would be separate ceiling joists (not shown here) to allow the ceiling to be flush with the bottom of the girder. Price does this by having every fourth joist deeper than the rest (Figure 7.3 – his detail V). So-called double floors were also used in some of the better quality houses (Figure 7.4b). In these floors the boards rested on small 'bridging joists' that spanned across between larger 'binding joists'. It was the latter that were carried by the girders that spanned between the walls. Separate ceiling joists would again be used.

These then are the bridgings referred to in Price's table. Their effect was to produce a stiffer floor, but that might not have been the only reason for their use. In a large room, too wide for joists alone, the use of girders spanning across the room would, with single joists, result in the boards also running across the room. A double floor would have the boards running the length of the room, which would look more elegant at a time when there was no such thing as fitted carpets. This seems a likely explanation for those houses that have double floors in some rooms and single floors in others.

This approach to the design of domestic floors using a simple rule of thumb to determine their sizes continued into the twentieth century. At one time one might size the joists for a house by the rule that the depth of a floor joist should be half the span in inches plus two. That meant that if a room was 10 ft (3 m) wide then the joists should be 5 + 2, i.e. 7 in (175 mm) deep. As joists of that depth were a standard 2 in (50 mm) wide, this fixed the size as 7 in by 2 in (or for Americans 2 × 7). Such a simple and useful rule was abandoned once

---

[1] Francis Price, *The British Carpenter*, 1733.

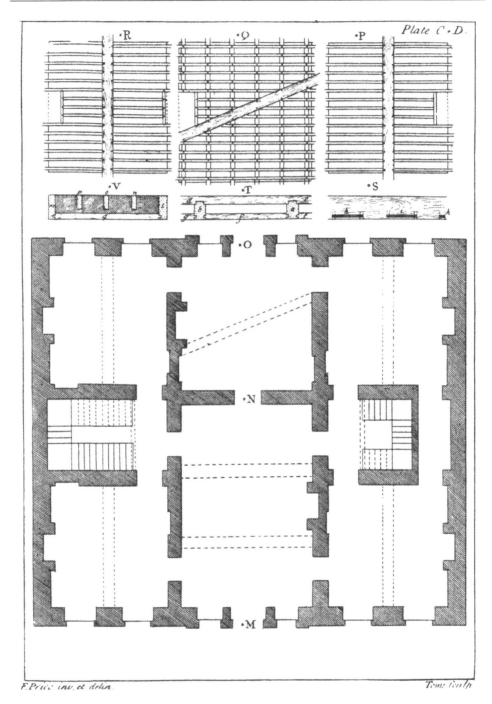

Figure 7.3 Floor plan by Francis Price.

(a)   (b)

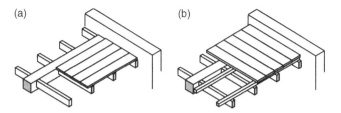

Figure 7.4 (a) Single and **(b)** double floors.

Britain adopted the metric system, but I understand that Norwegian carpenters, in a country that adopted the metric system in the nineteenth century, still have rules based on inches. Today, tables for the sizes of joists (and some roof timbers) are still found in building regulations.

The need for science

When iron came into use as a building material such a simple approach based on observation and experience was no longer adequate as a method of design, partly because there was no previous experience to draw upon for this new material. But it was also because of a profound difference in its behaviour. Designing timber beams to limit their deflection meant that even if one had been under-designed it would give some warning of its impending failure. The same was not true of cast-iron beams, which were very stiff and so deflected very little before failure; deflection was no longer the critical factor in design. Moreover, because the material is brittle as well as stiff it would give no warning before it failed. In such circumstances something more than experience and rules of thumb was required and one approach was to require beams to be proof loaded, i.e. tested before use, with a larger load than was expected in service. But that was largely to ensure there were no defects in the castings, and before getting to that stage, some science was needed to enable designers to decide upon the size and shape to specify. After all, as iron did not come in rectangular sections, it was sensible to cast it into the most structurally efficient shape as well as the right size.

Continental scientists had considered beam behaviour, and the result that the strength of a beam increased with the square of its depth (twice as deep, four times as strong) was published in England in the *Builder's Dictionary* (1736). But this was of little use in design, partly because it could not be related to the properties of the materials. Also it was hardly helpful when timber beams were sized for deflections. When iron was adopted as a structural material it was of no use because iron beams were not cast into simple rectangular shapes. However, it is not important to follow the development of structural theory but rather to develop our own ideas about beam strength, and we can do that in quite a different way.[2]

---

[2]For those interested in the history of structural ideas see: Jacques Heyman in *Structural Analysis A Historical Approach*, Cambridge, 1998.

Floors and deflections

If we use a plank between a couple of supports to stand on to paint a ceiling, we know its deflection becomes greater as we approach the centre and will also be larger if the distance between the supports is increased (Figure 7.5). We also know that if the load on the plank is increased it will deflect more.

Figure 7.5 Deflections under load.

Longer spans and heavier loads clearly require larger beam sections and there was a natural limitation on the scale of building that could be put up. Was there some way of combining timbers to produce still larger beams? The answer perhaps was to place two beams one on top of the other, but try that and see what happens. Place two planks on top of each other across the trestles to paint the ceiling and the deflection will be halved but look closely and one will see that as they deflect the two planks slide relative to each other at their contact surfaces (Figure 7.6).

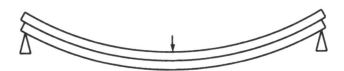

Figure 7.6 Deflection of two planks.

In Italy it was realised that if the two beams were keyed together to prevent this sliding between the two contact surfaces the combination would be much stiffer. Clearly, if the two surfaces are trying to move relative to each other, whatever we do to prevent that from happening must involve some forces that will act on whatever is holding the two surfaces together. The trick was to join them together in such a way that these forces would be transmitted effectively between the upper and lower parts of the beam with a joint that was simple to make. Square keys in notches in the opposing faces might be satisfactory, but while they would prevent any relative movement they would be troublesome to make. The simpler solution was some form of zigzag, or saw-tooth cut between the two (Figure 7.7). This would be easier to make and still provide vertical bearing surfaces that prevent relative movement.

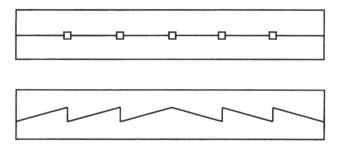

Figure 7.7 Methods for keying two beams together.

The forces in the beam

One can see from the two planks of Figure 7.6 that, unrestrained, the lower surface of the upper timber moves outwards from the centre relative to the upper surface of the lower beam. Therefore in the saw-tooth joint the vertical surfaces of the lower beam have to face inwards to prevent this movement. The saw-tooth pattern will only work one way round and this tells us something about the forces within the beam. There are clearly compressive forces across the vertical faces of the saw-tooth cuts. Drawing these forces on the 'teeth' shows that they are pushing inwards on the top member and outwards on the lower member. This must mean that the top member is in compression while the bottom member is in tension (Figure 7.8).

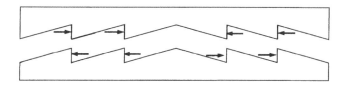

Figure 7.8 Forces on the 'teeth' of two beams keyed together.

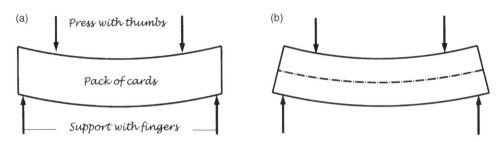

Figure 7.9 Bending a pack of cards.

A simple experiment with a pack of cards will provide a better understanding of what is happening. Take a pack of cards and bend it between your fingers. It is fairly easy to do this because the cards slide over each other taking the shape shown Figure 7.9a. Now imagine glueing the cards together first and then trying to bend them. The cards would still want to slide over each other but the glue would prevent this and the pack would be much more difficult to bend. If it could bend it would take the shape shown in Figure 7.9b. (One might produce something like this shape by bending a soft eraser.) As we have seen, the tendency for sliding is called shear, and this experiment shows that as well as the compression and tension forces, there are horizontal shear forces in the beam, the force resisted by the glue.

Strain

It should be clear from the geometry of Figure 7.6 that for each of the planks the top surface is shorter than the bottom surface, although the two must have been the same length before bending. In Figure 7.9b all of the material above the central dotted line has become shorter to some degree, while the material below it has become longer. Bending has produced some changes in the lengths. This change in length in a material under load, its *strain*, needs to be examined in a little more detail.

Strain was first understood only in the nineteenth century when scientists began to explore this phenomenon; it is the measure of the distortion of a material when it is loaded.[3] The stretch in a rubber band is an example of strain. This is *elastic material*, which means that it returns to its original length when the force stretching it is removed. (In plastic materials there is a permanent deformation when a load is applied.) As materials strain internal forces are generated that resist the forces that have been applied to them. The more they strain the more internal force is generated so that they will strain just sufficiently to resist

---

[3] During much of the nineteenth century the word 'strain' was used for what we today call stress, which might cause confusion when reading nineteenth century accounts of the behaviour of structures.

the applied load. Walk across a floor and it deflects, or strains, under our feet as we walk; even granite paving does this, although so little that we cannot see it. All materials under our feet deflect because of our weight, just as the springs in a mattress would deflect if we walked across the mattress. Just as different materials have different strengths they also strain by different amounts when loaded. It is easier to bend a piece of wood than a steel bar of the same size. The measure of this is called the *modulus of elasticity* of the material, sometimes called Young's modulus after the physicist Thomas Young who first measured the effect. The important aspect of this is that for the structural materials we are considering here the strain is directly proportional to the stress in the material.

Measuring strain

For those with a mathematical bent strain is measured as the ratio of the change in length to the original length. Thus if a column of length l is loaded and shortens by an amount ∂l, the strain is $\partial l/l$. One can see that this will usually be a very small number, but much larger for an elastic rope than for a steel cable.

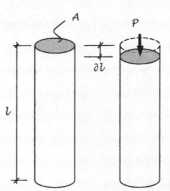

Figure 7.10

If the force producing this strain is P and the cross-section of the column is of area A then the stress in the material must be P/A. Young's modulus for any material is the stress divided by the strain that is produced, i.e. $(P/A)/(\partial l/l)$. As the strain in most materials is a very small number, much smaller than unity, the result of this division will be a very large stress. Theoretically it is the stress required to either double, or halve, the length of a piece of the material depending upon whether it is put into tension or compression, but few materials could sustain that amount of strain. Rubber bands can and the stress in them is very low.

It should be clear from the geometry of Figure 7.9b that if we were to draw horizontal lines on the side of a beam before bending, then after bending the change in length of the lines would vary with the distance from the dotted line down the middle. This line is called the *neutral axis* and does not change in length. The further from the neutral axis, the greater is the change in length. In fact the change in length can be assumed to be proportional to the distance from the neutral axis. As the stress in timber and steel is generally proportional to the strain then the stress in the beam is also proportional to the distance from the neutral axis. To be able to design a beam we need to relate the stresses developed in the material to the externally applied load and the span of the beam.

> Materials have an elastic limit, a stress beyond which the strain is no longer proportional to the stress. Present-day design methods take this into account but for simplicity we may restrict ourselves to materials working within their elastic limits.

Galileo's cantilever

It was Galileo who first tackled the problem of finding the forces in a member in bending by considering the effect of a load on the end of a cantilever (seen in Figure 7.11). This is

Figure 7.11 Galileo's cantilever.

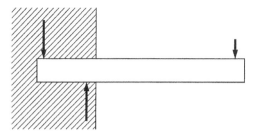

Figure 7.12 Forces on the cantilever.

similar to the bracket that we have dealt with previously except that the timber is embedded in the wall and held in place by vertical support forces. The downward force on the end of the cantilever is trying to rotate it about the wall, i.e. the force creates a moment about the wall, which must be resisted by forces both within the beam and within the wall. Common knowledge of the way things work tells us that by applying a large enough load to the end of the cantilever, and providing the cantilever itself does not break, it is possible to lever stones out of the wall. The wall must be providing an upward force to support the load but it must also provide a downward force at the back of the cantilever beam to prevent rotation. For the latter there must be sufficient weight of wall above the embedded end of the cantilever to provide this hold-down force (Figure 7.12).

As the embedded length of the cantilever is normally much shorter than its projection, the hold-down force will normally have to be much larger than the applied load. The calculation of the required load is exactly the same as that for the seesaw except that it is not clear exactly where either the support or hold-down forces are applied. Although the diagram suggests a single force at the back of the cantilever there is in fact continuous contact between the wall and the embedded length. The cantilever is not held down by a point force but by the whole mass of masonry over the whole of the length within the wall. This is a clear example of where an engineer might make some simplification in his calculations. Figure 7.12 might represent the situation just before failure where there has been some downward deflection of the cantilever and corresponding upward movement of the embedded end. Then the forces may well act close to both the end of the embedded part of the cantilever and to the surface of the wall.

The problem of supporting forces in the wall does not seem to have concerned Galileo because the wall into which his cantilever was built seems rather narrow for the size of the weight hung on its end. Galileo's problem was to find the forces within the cantilever itself. The nature of these can be seen by imagining a cut through the beam and then providing forces to replace those disrupted by the cut (Figure 7.14). This reduces the cantilever beam to a diagram, rather like that of the bracket attached to wall. The cantilever is very shallow compared with the bracket and so the forces must be correspondingly larger.

As with the bracket of Figure 1.9 there has to be a vertical supporting force and this acts across the imagined cut equal to the force on the end, so stopping the beam sliding down the wall. This force is a vertical shear force. To prevent the beam from rotating there must be two equal and opposite horizontal forces that provide a turning moment in the opposite direction to that produced by the load. When considering the bracket we assumed that the

Distributed force

We might instead imagine the forces to be as shown in Figure 7.13, where the single force at the back of the cantilever has been replaced by a distributed force. In this case the centre of the hold-down forces will be a little way from the back of the cantilever and the total force that much greater. We do not know exactly what the distribution of forces might be in any given situation so some assumptions have to be made. In this case the arrows representing the hold-down force have been drawn so that their length, and by implication the magnitude of the force, varies with the distance from the bearing under the cantilever. Of course, a distribution such as this can only happen if the walling above the cantilever is built to be in contact with it, and is well built. We cannot know that and calculations of the forces on a structure are often dependent on such assumptions about the nature of the construction. There always has to be a certain amount of guesswork in analysing a structure – only always be sure to call it engineering judgement.

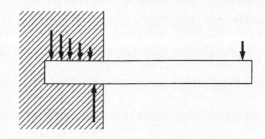

Figure 7.13

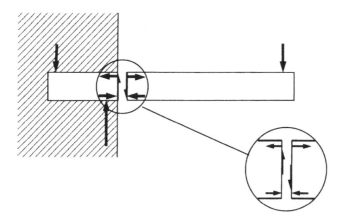

Figure 7.14 Forces across an imagined cut in the beam.

applied load was trying to rotate it about the wall and so made the moments of the two fixing forces at the wall equal to that produced by the load. The same must hold here, but instead of having discrete forces at the top and bottom there are forces distributed throughout the depth of the beam.

Finding the stresses

Galileo's problem was that he did not know how the stresses in the timber were distributed. He assumed correctly that there were tension stresses in the top of the beam but thought that the whole of the beam was uniformly stressed in tension with the whole of the compression concentrated at the bottom. This assumption still gives the result that the strength of a beam is proportional to the square of the depth because as one increases the depth of the beam the force that can be developed for a given stress and the lever arm of that force about the bottom edge of the beam both increase. But from our understanding of strain and the geometry of a deflected beam we can see how the stresses are distributed. As the strain, and hence the stress is directly proportional to the distance from the neutral axis, the stresses can be represented as a pair of triangular blocks. The neutral axis, N-A, is a plane through the centre of the beam (Figure 7.15).

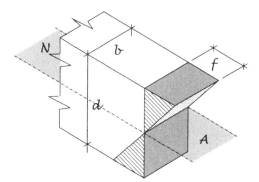

Figure 7.15 Distribution of stresses in a beam.

The same graphic technique is being used here as that for the foundation stresses under a wall with a horizontal load on it. In that case the whole of the wall thickness was in compression whereas here half is in compression and half in tension.

From cantilever to beam

We seem not to have progressed much beyond the bracket, and it was beams that we set out to understand, but we can go from cantilevers to beams by a simple trick of the imagination.

Calculating the stresses

With a little mathematics it is possible to go from Figure 7.15 to calculate the stresses in the beam. The two triangular blocks representing the stresses can be reduced to two forces, the forces being equal to the volume of each of the blocks, i.e. ½.f.b.d/2. These forces will act at the centroid of each block, which being triangular in shape will be ⅓ of the height of each triangle or from the edge of the beam, making the distance between them ⅔ of the depth of the beam.

The moment of this pair of forces about the centre of the beam will be the magnitude of each force multiplied by the distance between them, i.e. ½.f.b.d/2.2d/3 = f.b.d²/6. This will equal the externally applied moment at that point in the beam.

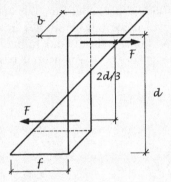

Figure 7.16

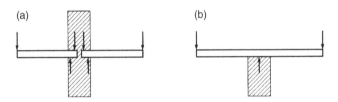

Figure 7.17 Combining two cantilevers.

First imagine two cantilevers back to back (Figure 7.17a) in which the wall is providing restraint for both. If these are the same length and each carries the same load at its end then the stresses in both cantilevers at the wall will also be the same while the wall will be providing forces to restrain both against rotation. If the two cantilevers are now joined together the wall will no longer have to provide any restraining forces against their levering action, each cantilever will provide the forces the other one requires to prevent its rotation. The wall simply has to provide a vertical force to support the two (Figure 7.17b) and the material above the cantilevers that was providing the restraint against their rotation can be removed. We have a beam seesawing over a wall, and like the seesaw the loads can be different providing the lengths of the cantilevers are different. Turn this assembly upside down and the result is the diagram for a beam on two supports carrying a point load (Figure 7.18). The support has become a load and the two loads have become supports, but as far as the beam is concerned they are just forces, one way or the other. For a load that is not at the centre of the beam the trick of turning a pair of cantilevers upside down still works and it is the support forces that are now different (see Figure 2.23).

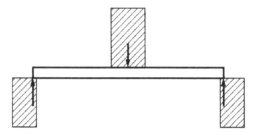

Figure 7.18 A beam on two supports carrying a point load.

While the strength of a rectangular beam is proportional to the square of its depth, just as Galileo believed, what is important for the design of iron and steel is that the material towards the top and bottom of the beam is doing most of the work. It is at a higher stress, and so produces a greater force for the same area as material nearer to the neutral axis, but it also has the greatest lever arm about the neutral axis. If one had any choice in the matter it would be better to shape a beam so that most of the material in it was concentrated towards the top and the bottom rather than close to the middle. That would result in a stronger beam for the given amount of material, and is exactly what was done with iron and steel beams.

Iron and steel beams

In the nineteenth century iron was widely adopted for mill construction because it facilitated the construction of fireproof floors. Iron was also used for railway bridges where, apart from its greater strength and of course its greater durability, it had the obvious advantage that it could be cast into larger and longer sections than any timber sections available. Unfortunately in both uses there were failures. Not only was there the collapse of the Dee Railway Bridge, already referred to in Chapter 1, there were also collapses of iron-framed mills. What designers were finding about cast iron was that this stiff, brittle material could fail without warning. Because of this, they needed to develop a method of design based on knowing the stresses in beams. In some ways understanding the internal stresses in an iron beam is simpler than for a timber beam because they can be more easily reduced to two discrete forces.

As the material at the top and bottom is doing the most work, beams were cast with large top and bottom flanges and a thin web of material in between. The beam was shaped like an upper case I, hence the name commonly given to it. Most of the material in an I-shaped beam is concentrated in the top and bottom flanges, and it is these that provide the bending resistance. The vertical part of the beam joining these flanges together, the *web*, resists the shear force but can be largely ignored as far as bending is concerned. If in a beam of depth d, the two equal flanges have an area A and an average stress f, the two flange forces F will be f.A and the moment of resistance of the beam f.A.d (Figure 7.19).

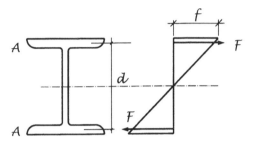

Figure 7.19 Forces in a steel beam.

Cast iron

As it happened the problem was more complex for cast iron beams because, as was soon realised, cast iron is rather weak in tension compared with its strength in compression. The force in the two flanges must be the same so that the problem faced by those making cast-iron beams was to cope with the smaller tensile strength of the material compared with its compressive strength. If it could only resist a lower tensile stress, but the forces were necessarily the same, the cross-sectional area in tension would have to be larger, i.e. the beams had to be cast with an asymmetrical shape. The problem was to proportion the sizes of the flanges to make economic use of the iron, and for that the relative strengths had to be known. All of this led to a developing science of materials and materials testing in the nineteenth century, with important work carried out by Hodgkinson, who devised a formula for the proportions of cast iron beams.[4] The beam shown in Figure 7.20 has the proportions recommended by Hodgkinson.

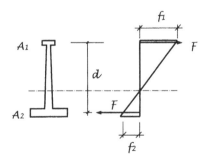

Figure 7.20 Forces and stresses in a beam cast with unequal flanges.

---

[4]Sir Alfred Pugsley, *The Safety of Structures*, Edward Arnold, London, 1966, provides an account of this.

With the beam cast with unequal flanges as shown, there will be different stresses in the two flanges but the forces in them must be the same. The result of having different stresses at the top and the bottom is that the neutral axis will no longer be at the mid-height of the beam. However, we need not be concerned about where it will be. For our purpose it is sufficient to note that in the diagram $F = f_1.A_1 = f_2.A_2$. The resistance moment provided by the beam is still the magnitude of the two equal forces multiplied by the distance between them, F.d.

As it happened this was not a great disadvantage because in the mills and warehouses of the nineteenth century the floors between these beams were formed of brick jack-arches, short span arches between the lower flanges of the beams on which a concrete floor could be formed. The larger bottom flanges thus formed convenient springings for these brick arches. It is not only the cross-section of these beams that deserves comment but also the fact that they were often made deeper towards the middle, but understanding why this was useful requires a little more abstraction. This is something well worth grasping because it helps to understand reinforced concrete.

The mathematics involved, such as it is, is simply that of the graph, which most people will be used to. In the simple diagram of the cantilever with a load on the end, we know that the load is attempting to bend the cantilever at the support. Thus the rotational effort being exerted by the load has been called the *bending moment*. But it is also trying to bend it about any other point along the cantilever. The bending moment increases the further away from the load because the lever arm distance increases. Therefore we can simply draw a graph showing this moment at any point along the cantilever (Figure 7.21a). If we plot this graph it is simply a straight line starting at zero at the loaded end and becoming W.l at the wall. As this is a graph of the bending moments at any point along the cantilever produced by the weight, the graph is called a bending moment diagram.

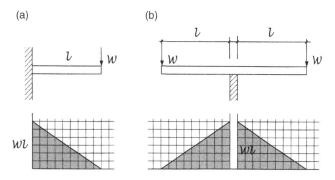

Figure 7.21 Graphs of bending moments on cantilevers.

Note how the shape of the diagram is the shape of a bracket. A bracket is a structure in which the member forces remain constant but in which the depth increases towards the support. In a cantilever beam the depth remains constant but the forces, and hence the stresses, increase towards the support, and the graph provides a simple indication of how those forces increase. Putting two cantilevers back to back and joining them together as before produces two graphs back to back. There will be some bending where the two cantilevers cross the wall but we need not be concerned about that. As before, turn the whole thing upside down reducing the wall load to a single point load and the two graphs become a single graph, the bending moment diagram for the beam. Note that in the beam diagram (Figure 7.22) both the value of W and the value of l are different from those of the cantilever diagram of Figure 7.21, and the central bending moment for the beam with a point load is W.l/4

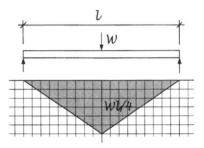

Figure 7.22 Graph of bending moments on a beam.

The sequence adopted in this explanation has resulted in the graph being on the tension side of both the cantilever and the beam. This is the normal convention adopted by structural engineers in Britain. In the USA the convention is to draw these diagrams the other way up. Whether or not the diagram is drawn on the tension side of the beam, as here, or the compression side is simply a 'sign convention', i.e. of whether we call the bending positive or negative. As it happens the beam-like bending, which is more normal, is regarded as positive, while the cantilever like bending is called negative bending, so there is perhaps some logic in the American drawing convention.

This might not seem particularly useful because most loads on beams are not point loads but distributed loads. Without going into the mathematics of why it is so, the bending moment diagram for a beam carrying a uniformly distributed load across it is a parabolic curve. The load is indicated by the shaded area in Figure 7.23. For the same span and the same total load the bending moment at the centre of the beam is half that for the point load.

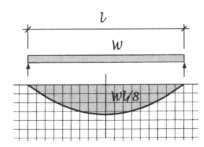

Figure 7.23 Bending moments for a beam carrying a uniformly distributed load.

The simple relationships to remember are that if the load is W and the span length is l then the point load bending moment is W.l/4 and the distributed load bending moment W.l/8. Unfortunately it is not possible to use the trick of turning a pair of cantilevers upside down to find the bending on a uniformly loaded beam.

As the forces in the flanges of a beam are determined by dividing the bending moment by the depth, and the stress by dividing the force by the area of the flange, if the flange area is the same all the way along the beam the stress could be kept constant by varying the depth according to the bending moment. Thus a beam carrying a uniformly distributed load (commonly written as UDL) might ideally be shaped the same as the bending moment diagram. If the beam only had to carry bending it would be theoretically possible to reduce the depth to zero at the supports, but the beam also has to carry the shear forces. These are carried by the web of the beam and this determines the minimum size of a beam at the ends. While iron beams could be cast with varying depth, steel beams are rolled at a constant depth and for many decades it was not possible to adjust their size. Engineers simply had to accept the fact that the material in the flanges nearer the supports was working at well below its maximum stress. However, improvements in welding methods have meant that it is now a practical proposition to cut out part of the webs of steel beams, bending the flanges and welding them back to form beams that are shallower at the ends, somewhat like cast-iron beams.

Reinforced and prestressed concrete

Reinforced concrete was an invention of the late nineteenth century and was used by some architects as a substitute for masonry or for steel frames, but there were others who saw its wider potential and it became the significant material of the Modern Movement. Prestressed concrete, an invention of the 1930s, was extensively used during World War II but came into its own in the post-war period, contributing to some significant modern buildings.

The idea of reinforcing is fairly simple. If the concrete is unable to take tension then steel bars may be embedded in the material where tension would occur. Load a plain concrete beam and it will break suddenly at fairly low stresses. The failure is obviously a tension failure because concrete will take much higher compressive stresses. Embed steel bars in the bottom of a concrete beam and as the beam deflects the steel strains in tension and carries the tensile forces while the concrete in the top of the beam is able to handle the compressive forces. For this to be a practical method it is important that the steel is bonded to the concrete so that both strain together, that the steel does not corrode and that temperature changes do not have any adverse effect. The first condition is satisfied because the concrete adheres to the steel and special deformed bars can be used if greater adhesion is required. Concrete is alkaline and the steel will not oxidize in this alkaline environment. The third condition is satisfied because steel and concrete have very similar coefficients of thermal expansion.

One might wonder what is happening to the concrete in the bottom of the beam if it is unable to cope with tensile strains, and the answer is that it develops small cracks. This is important because it affects the protection that the concrete provides for the steel. Corrosion may eventually occur because atmospheric carbon dioxide gradually reduces the alkalinity of the concrete until it is unable to protect the steel. How quickly this occurs depends upon the amount of cover provided to the steel and the ability of the carbon dioxide to penetrate the material. But these are details, and what we are concerned with here are the basic structural principles.

Essential properties of reinforced concrete

This is not the place to go into the details of reinforced concrete but a brief outline of the differences between this material and timber and steel is useful. Unlike these materials the stress is not directly proportional to the strain. Instead for simplicity it is assumed that the concrete in compression has a uniform stress whose value is adjusted to below the ultimate stress at which concrete fails to give the same failure load for the calculations as for an actual beam. The effective depth of a reinforced concrete beam is not its full depth but the depth to the reinforcement, and the neutral axis is taken to be at half of that depth (Figure 7.24). This gives a safe estimate of a beam's capacity. Note that the lever arm between the centre of compression and the level of the steel is ¾ of the effective depth of the beam.

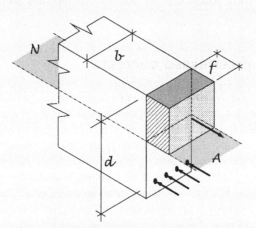

Figure 7.24 Stress in a reinforced concrete beam.

Just as a cast-iron beam was complicated by the fact that the stresses it would carry in tension and compression were different, so in a reinforced concrete beam we need to recognize that we are dealing with different materials that can fail independently. Put in a large amount of steel and the concrete will fail first by crushing. This is called an over-reinforced section. Put in a small amount of steel and that will yield first. This is called an under-reinforced section. In a so-called *balanced section* the steel and the concrete will both reach their maximum capacity at the same time. Note that the terms under-reinforced and over-reinforced relate to the theoretical capacity of the beam rather than to the job that it has to do in practice. Many beams are sized such that they are under-reinforced. This is because one frequently sizes a number of beams for the one that carries the largest load. The others are made to the same size but with only sufficient steel to carry the required load. If an under-reinforced beam is loaded to failure it would be found that the neutral axis was not at the centre of the beam. Only as much concrete would go into compression as was necessary so that the lever arm between the centre of compression and the steel would be greater than ¾ of the effective depth. To avoid using more steel than is necessary an adjustment has to be made to the lever arm depending upon the ratio of the actual moment applied to the beam and the ultimate moment for a balanced section. Beyond that the reader needs to look at the design codes.

Reinforced concrete differed from steel and timber in one very important aspect. While steel and timber came in discrete elements, assembled together, concrete was poured on site and was continuous. The beams and the floors they supported were no longer separate elements – and possibly made of separate materials – they were cast as one. Moreover, a number of beams supported over a row of columns were not separate beams, they too would act as one so that deflections of one beam would have an effect on the beams either side. All this had to be taken into account in design, but presented new opportunities. The absence of a need for a rigid grid of columns and beams has already been noted (Figures 4.5 and 4.6) but here we must consider the implications for structural behaviour.

Reinforced concrete beams

So far the beams we have considered have all been simply supported, i.e. resting on simple supports only at each end. That was how steel beams were designed, but it was not possible to treat reinforced concrete beams in the same way. This was something that led to an important change in methods of design and analysis.[5] The problem can be simply demonstrated. Two beams placed end to end will deflect separately, as shown by the dotted lines in Figure 7.25a, with the result that at the central support there will be some relative rotation between the two beams as shown by the inset sketch. But if the beams are connected together such rotation is impossible. In fact, if both the loads and the spans are the same the whole thing is symmetrical and one would expect there to be no rotation at the support. For that to be so the beams would have to take up a quite different shape, as suggested by the dotted lines in Figure 7.25b, and the deflection of the beams would actually be smaller.

The other effect is that if only one of the spans of Figure 7.25a is loaded it will deflect and the other span will not. If the beams are continuous and one of the spans is loaded it will affect the other span, as in Figure 7.25c. Because there is some rotation at the central support that is imposed upon the unloaded span it must lift up and the force at the lefthand

---

[5] Hardy Cross developed a method of analysis called moment distribution that was particularly useful in the analysis of reinforced concrete.

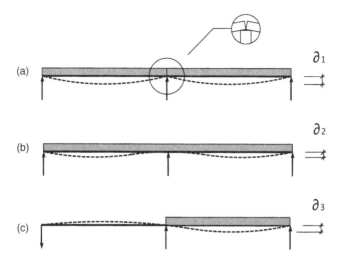

Figure 7.25 Deflections of simply supported and continuous beams.

end will be holding down the end of the beam. The deflection of the loaded span will be smaller than in Figure 7.25a but larger than in Figure 7.25b – $\partial_1 > \partial_3 > \partial_2$. Of course, this phenomenon is not confined to reinforced concrete beams. The longitudinal members in Palladio's drawing of Caesar's bridge (Figure 2.2) are continuous over two spans and would behave in this way.

For a series of simply supported steel beams the worst load condition was one in which all the spans carried their maximum load but, although it may be counterintuitive, that is not true for reinforced concrete. The reason can be demonstrated with a three-span beam. Load the two end spans and the centre span will be bent upwards (Figure 7.26a). Load the centre span alone and it will not have the 'help' of the loads on the two side spans (Figure 7.26b) and will deflect more than when all three spans are loaded. The result of this is that a range of load conditions needs to be considered when designing continuous beams.

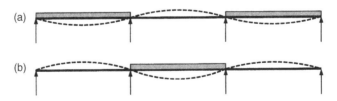

Figure 7.26 Deflection of a three-span beam with different loads.

The task now is to relate those shapes to the pattern of bending in the beam because the reinforcement must be placed on the tensile side of the beam. Which side that is is shown by the curvature of the beam. Looking at Figure 7.25b we can see that it curves downwards at the ends but upwards in the middle. There is tension on the bottom of the beam towards the ends but in the middle there is tension in the top, rather like a cantilever, or more accurately rather like the two cantilevers back to back of Figure 7.21b. Therefore it would be possible to divide the beam into three parts: two simply supported beams and a double cantilever in the middle, the lengths of these components being determined by the points at which the curvature of the beam changes from downward to upward, the points of contraflexure. At these points there is no bending, and since we know what the bending moments look like for a beam and for a double cantilever, we can add these together to give a bending moment diagram for the complete beam (Figure 7.27). The bending over the central support is sometimes referred to as negative bending, or perhaps more simply as hogging, while the bending in the beams either side is, reasonably enough, called sagging.

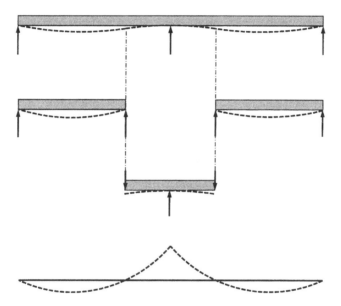

Figure 7.27 A continuous beam can be divided into separate beams at the points of contraflexure.

Prestressing

If concrete is unable to take tensile stresses there is another way of coping with this apart from using reinforcing bars. That is to prestress the material by applying a compressive stress to the beam so that it never goes into tension. We have already seen how to do this. Pick up a number of books from the shelf to move them briefly and the simplest way to do so is to squeeze them between your hands. We all know this requires a certain pressure and if we relax that pressure the books will fall as a heap on the floor.

A number of matchboxes or dice can be simply held together with a rubber band around them and these might be used as a simple beam between a pair of supports. The prestressing in these simple models is external to the beam, while concrete is normally prestressed by wires or cables within the beam. A model of this can be made with a few cotton reels, drawing

Finding the deflection of a beam

The other way of looking at this, which is the way that the support forces are found, is to imagine a long beam with two different kinds of loading. If we know how to calculate the deflection of a beam we first calculate the deflection at the centre of a long beam with a uniformly distributed load. We then calculate the upward deflection of a beam with a point load acting upwards at the centre. Adjust the magnitude of the central upward load until the deflections are the same and one has the vertical force at that point for a three-span beam.

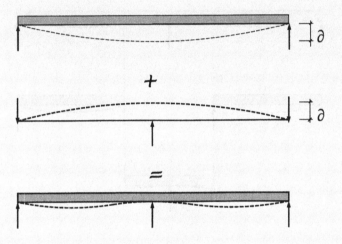

Figure 7.28

For those who might want to try this, the formula for the deflection of a beam with a UDL is:

$$\partial = 5.W_1.L^3/384.K$$

and the deflection of a beam with a point load is:

$$\partial = 5.W_2.L^3/48.K$$

where W_1 is the total UDL, W_2 is the point load and K is a measure of the stiffness of the beam, which is of course the same for both. If the deflections are the same the relationship between W_1 and W_2 can be found. From this the central support force is ⅝ of the total load on the beam.

a rubber band down the centre and anchoring it at the ends with a match or some similar device.[6] This replicates one form of prestressing. Tubes are built into a concrete beam through which cables are passed. Once the concrete has reached an adequate strength cables are anchored at one end and hydraulic jacks braced against the other end pull them tight. The steel is then fixed into the anchor at the jacking end, usually by wedges, and as it tries to return to its original length it puts the concrete into compression. However, the cotton reel model perhaps best illustrates its common use in bridge construction where large concrete elements are precast, brought to the site and then stressed together in this way.

There is another way of prestressing commonly used in the manufacture of standard components. In this method wires are first stretched in tension between anchor blocks and the concrete cast round them. Again when the concrete has gained sufficient strength the wires are released from their anchorages. In this technique the concrete grips the wire along its length and so the same effect is achieved except that this technique depends upon developing a sufficient bond between the concrete and the steel prestressing wires.

> There is some potentially confusing terminology to deal with here because of these two ways of prestressing. Both are prestressing in that the concrete is under stress before it is loaded, the distinction depends on the time when the stress is applied to the steel. In the first method the stress is applied to the steel after the concrete has been cast and this method is called *post-tensioning*. In the second method the stress is applied to the steel before the concrete is cast and this method is called *pre-tensioning*. Nevertheless both are prestressing.

To explain why prestressing works first consider the stresses that develop in a beam in bending. We know that there is tension in the top and compression in the bottom as in Figure 7.15 and in the top diagram of Figure 7.29. Now apply a compressive force to the beam

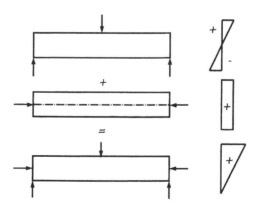

Figure 7.29 Simple axial prestressing to eliminate tensile stresses.

---

[6] American readers should note that a cotton reel is not some celebratory dance from Dixie but what the British call the spool on which sewing thread is wound.

adding that to the bending stresses. If the compressive stress is exactly the same as the tensile stress produced by bending alone the result will be zero stress at the bottom of the beam. It should be clear from this that the prestressing force required is equal to the area of cross-section of the beam multiplied by the stress required.

Compressive and bending stresses

The stress diagrams on the right of Figure 7.29 can be obtained by simple arithmetic. The vertical lines on the diagram represent the zero line on a graph with the stress at any point in the beam plotted horizontally. Assume the bending stresses produced by the applied load are +a and –a. A uniform compressive stress a is then 'added' to the bending stresses produced by prestressing to give 2a at the top and zero at the bottom. Of course, smaller loads will produce smaller bending stresses.

But rather than use arithmetic this can be done graphically. Draw the diagram for the stresses produced by the prestressing force and the stresses produced by bending under load alongside each other. Compressive stresses are shown shaded. Slide the two together so that they overlap with the two compressive stresses adding together. As tensile stress cancels out compressive stress the result is the shaded triangular distribution of stress. One can see immediately that if the load is below the maximum so that the tensile stress produced in the bottom is less than the compressive stress produced by prestressing there will still be some residual compression in the bottom of the beam.

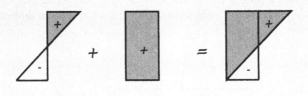

Figure 7.30

Here the assumption is that the prestressing force is applied axially but that is not very efficient. Half of the compressive stress at the top of the beam is produced by the bending induced by the load, and the other half by the prestressing force. Thus, the bending resistance of the beam can only make use of half of the maximum compressive stress that the concrete can take. It would be to our advantage if we could apply the prestressing in such a way that it produces a compressive stress in the bottom of the beam and no stress in the top. If we could do that, the load would be able to make use of all of the compressive stress that concrete was capable of handling. In other words we could double the load on the beam. This is possible simply by moving the prestressing force below the centre of the beam. If the prestressing is at a point ⅓ of the depth of the beam from the bottom then we have the desired result, compression in the bottom and no compression in the top. (Note that we have seen this ⅓ relationship before in the position of the support force on a wall that has no stress on one side of its foundation.) This doubling of the load that the beam can carry has been achieved with no increase in prestressing force.

Applying the prestressing force below the neutral axis is the equivalent of having an axial prestressing force plus a moment applied to the ends of the beam as shown in Figure 7.31. In fact, we can do even better than we have done so far. So far we have ignored the self-weight of the beam, but bending stresses in service result from the live load applied to the beam plus its own self-weight. As moving the prestress below the neutral axis is the equivalent of applying an upward moment to the beam we could move it even lower producing an upward moment that counteracts the downward moment produced by the self-weight. If the additional upward moment produced by this additional lowering of the prestressing force is equal to the moment produced by the self-weight of the beam then it would be as if the beam weighed nothing. Magic! With the prestress applied in this way the beam only has to be sized to resist the live load (see Figure 7.32 and Figure 7.33). As the prestressing force is the required stress multiplied by the area of cross-section of the beam it is to our advantage to keep the cross-section to a minimum. For that reason precast prestressed sections – the kind often used for small bridges – are usually cast as I-sections. Like cast iron, this gives the best bending resistance for the smallest amount of material.

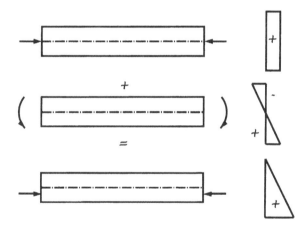

Figure 7.31 Axial prestressing force plus a moment = eccentric prestressing force.

One of the more interesting uses of prestressed concrete in a building was for the floors of Louis Kahn's Richards Medical Research Laboratories, but as that used a two-way spanning system it is sensible to discuss two-way spanning floors before looking in detail at this building.

Two-way floors

A concrete floor slab on just two walls might be seen as being like a series of shallow beams set side by side. It is almost as if we laid a floor of boards next to each other without any

Load, prestress and self-weight

For those who want to follow this through we can draw the diagrams for all of this. We are adding three things together in Figure 7.32. First there is the self-weight of the beam and the bending stresses produced by that (a). Assume the stress is 'a'. Further, there is the useful load applied to the beam and the stresses that would be produced by that alone (b). Finally, there is the prestress that is applied below the middle third line of the beam (shown as a dotted line). The prestress and its position are designed so that if acting alone the prestress would produce a tension stress 'a' to counter the same compressive stress produced by the self-weight and a compressive stress at the bottom equal to the tension stress that would be produced by a + b. Add all three together and we have a compression in the top of the beam and zero stress in the bottom.

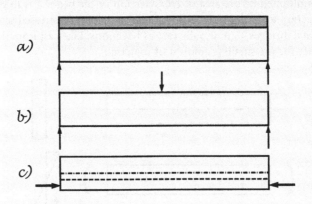

Figure 7.32

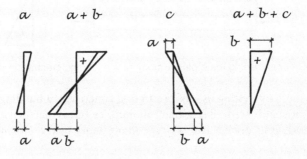

Figure 7.33

joists. Imagine, however, that we have a square opening to span. Which way should we lay the boards, or in the case of a reinforced concrete floor, which way should we place the reinforcement? Why not both ways, and if so how would this work?

Imagine that a plank is placed across the centre of the space in one direction. A load placed at the centre will make this deflect but if a second plank is placed across it in the other direction any load placed at the centre would be shared between the two (Figure 7.34). Both planks will deflect by the same amount and if the opening is square so that the spans are equal the load will be shared equally between them. As a result the deflection would be half that of the single plank. But what if the spans are not equal? Take two planks of different span and arrange them to cross each other as before so that when loaded they too deflect by the same amount. From what we already know about the deflection of beams, it will take a larger weight to deflect the plank with the shorter span by the same amount as the plank with the longer span. Therefore the shorter spanning plank will pick up more of the load than the longer spanning one. Nevertheless it will still be carrying less load than if it had to act alone. A complete floor might be made in this way by having a layer of boards in one direction over another layer running in the other. This is something like double floors where binding and bridging joists run in different directions.

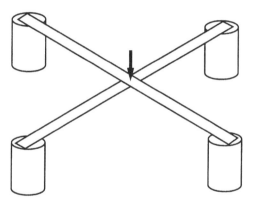

Figure 7.34 Two planks to support a load.

Here is the basis of the two-way spanning concrete slab. In a simple concrete slab reinforcing bars are laid in the bottom of the slab in the direction of the span. If there are supports on all four sides, and the spans are not too dissimilar, reinforcement can be placed in both directions just like the planks imagined above, and the load will be carried to all four walls – or possibly beams depending upon what is supporting the slab. The proportion of the load carried in each direction will depend upon the ratio of the two spans. More reinforcement needs to be put into the shorter span, as this will be carrying a larger proportion of the load.

The next development of the concrete floor was flat slab construction, which eliminated the beams spanning between the columns. The proportions of a beam can be varied; it can be made shallower if it is made much wider. It may then be possible to make a beam shallow enough to be no deeper than the floor slab that it supports. That would be easier to achieve if the floor slab were two-way spanning because this would share the weight out over four beams rather than two. What this would look like before the concrete was cast would be strips of very heavy reinforcement to form the 'beams' between the columns with lighter reinforcement between these beam strips, suggested by the plan in Figure 7.35. The diagram below shows the bending moments across such a slab. Such an arrangement would have the advantage that it would not be necessary to make complex formwork to form the beams; all one would need would be flat formwork and it would be faster to cast. It was for this reason that this so-called flat slab construction became popular for industrial and warehouse buildings in North America, although its uptake in Britain was much slower because of difficulties with the building by-laws.

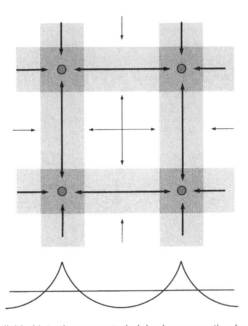

Figure 7.35 A flat slab divided into the supported slab plus supporting beam strips.

In fact the structure has to be a little more than a flat slab because of the problem of shear. The shear in a beam or slab increases towards the supports, i.e. the columns, and the tendency in flat slabs, where there is very little depth of concrete to resist the shear force, is for the columns to punch through the slab. This happened in one building under construction with the floors ending as a pile on the ground. The way to cope with this is to increase the area of concrete carrying the shear force. As always stress = force/area. The concrete carrying the highest shear is that around the top of each column and the area of this can be made larger by either enlarging its perimeter or increasing the depth of the concrete. In practice both were done in turn. The perimeter carrying shear was increased by having a flared head on the column (commonly referred to as a mushroom head), thus giving an alternative name to this type of construction. If the mushroom were not sufficient to reduce the shear stresses to an acceptable level then the depth of the slab might be locally increased with a drop panel (Figure 7.36).

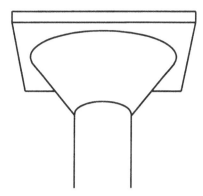

Figure 7.36 A so-called 'mushroom' column head.

The bending moment diagram of Figure 7.35 shows that there is hogging over the columns. For this to be so at the edge of a slab the floor must cantilever beyond the last row of columns. The most appropriate arrangement for flat slab construction is to have the columns set back behind the line of the external wall. This was something realised and made use of architecturally during the inter-war years by architects of industrial buildings. Thomas Wallis, for example, having no need for external columns, developed a horizontal treatment for the elevations of his factories in Britain. Brinkman and van der Vlugt used a curtain wall for their Van Nelle Factory, Rotterdam, with the structure hardly visible. By contrast, Owen Williams's masterpiece, the Boots pharmaceutical factory at Beeston, near Nottingham, has very large square mushroom heads clearly visible through the floor to ceiling glazing.

Two-way prestressing

When Louis Kahn was given the commission to design the Richards Medical Research Laboratories at the University of Pennsylvania he engaged August Komendant as his structural engineer. This was a fortunate collaboration because Komendant had a deep interest in architecture and was prepared to work with Kahn from the inception of his projects.[7] He had also made himself a specialist in prestressed precast concrete, which was a relatively new technique in America, having been imported from Europe. It was this technique that was to form the basis of the floor structures for this building. The first thing to notice is that, although the floor plan is square the masonry service shafts that support the floors are not at the corners (Figure 7.37). This means that the edge beams cantilever from them towards the corners. Just like the double cantilevers of Figure 7.21 bending moments are greatest at the roots of the cantilevers and these are 'expressed' in the increased depth of the section of beam closest to and between the supports (Figure 7.27).

The second thing to notice is that the beams are all designed as *vierendeel* girders rather than as solid beams or the lattice girders of Chapter 2. This type of girder, named after the

---

[7] August Komendant, *18 Years with Architect Louis I. Kahn*, Aloray, Englewood, NJ, 1975.

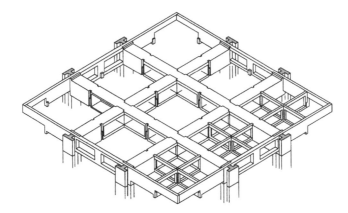

Figure 7.37 Floor layout of the Richards Medical Research Laboratories, University of Pennsylvania.

Belgian railway engineer who developed it for bridges, consists of only horizontal and vertical members. It will be clear from the qualitative analysis of girders in Chapter 2 that such girders can only work if the joints between the vertical and horizontal members are capable of taking bending moments in order to keep the rectangles rigid. Of course, an advantage of such open girders for the beams of a laboratory floor is that they can accommodate services within the floor.

At first it would seem as if the floor is based upon two main beams with the other large beams that were cast in sections resting on them. That is what one might use with steel beams erected in discrete sections, unless they were welded to provide continuity. In concrete this continuity can be provided by prestressing. The separate elements of one pair of beams are made to work together by prestressing, so that the structure is a lattice of four intersecting beams spanning between the columns. The beams in both directions span the full distance between the columns. The arrangement is rather like the beams of Figure 7.34 except that there are two beams in each direction rather than one. The secondary beams, also formed as vierendeels, are then supported by these main beams. It might be worthwhile working out the loads being picked up by each of the beams by producing a drawing for this floor rather like that of Figure 7.2, but I leave that to the reader. Note how the columns, stripped of their brick cladding, are I-sections.

Other structures in bending

Although this chapter has concentrated on the construction of floor structures, it has actually been about members in bending and it is useful to extend our consideration of bending to two other kinds of structures. The first of these is the use of walls as elements in bending. They will bend horizontally if they are resisting wind loads but they might also be used as deep beams, and two examples are shown here. The other aspect of bending is that of frames. In Chapter 6 examples were shown of frames that resisted horizontal loads by bending in the columns and beams, and, while we considered the deflected shapes of these, by using the idea of bending moment diagrams we can make a better comparison of these structures.

Walls as beams

In the eighteenth century large houses presented the problem that small rooms were wanted on upper floors above large rooms below. To achieve this the walls dividing the rooms on the upper floors had at least to be self-supporting rather than transmitting their weight to the structure of the floor. This was done by framing the wall as a timber truss somewhat like the timber bridge trusses. As well as carrying their own weight it was equally possible for such trusses to be used to support floors as well; after all the truss could be very deep in relation to its span. If doorways were wanted through the wall they either had to be arranged where there were no diagonals in the truss, perhaps through the centre of a queen post truss, or the trussing had to be confined to the zone between the head of the doorway and the floor above; both solutions are found. For the latter, iron tie bars were used from the trussing above the door heads to support a plate at floor level.

Forming walls as beams became much easier with the invention of reinforced concrete and might be wanted in buildings where small spaces were wanted on floors above public rooms; bedrooms above the spaces on the ground floor of a hotel is an example. The YMCA building in Manchester, an early essay in reinforced concrete, has rooms above a swimming pool contrived in this way. The trick is to confine openings in the beam to the centre where shear forces are low. The large tension and compression forces there due to bending can be carried in the floor slabs so that the whole construction acts as an I-beam, as deep as the floor-to-floor height.

This is also seen in a more recent building by Marcel Breuer at his student dormitory for New York University. It is clear from the outside of the building that there is something a little unusual about the structure. It is essentially a load-bearing wall structure but the walls subdividing the continuous runs of windows on every floor are discontinuous. This is clear from a section (Figure 7.38), in which it can be seen that the walls are shorter on every other floor. Here it is the second, fourth and sixth floors where the wall is pulled back from the façade, whereas in the walls on either side it is the third and fifth floors that are treated in this way. To achieve this, the longer lengths of wall have to cantilever beyond the shorter ones. But it is not simply the walls that form the cantilever. Figure 7.39 is a section cut out of the building showing that the walls together with the floors above and below are acting as giant I-beams. While the wall carries the shear forces produced by the weight of the cantilever, part of the floor above and below is carrying the horizontal tensile and compressive forces – the hatched areas on the drawing. The width of the floor that can be considered to act in this way is limited by design codes but the compressive stresses in the concrete will be relatively low. Handling the tensile forces is a matter of the amount of reinforcement that needs to be incorporated into the floor slab. Note that each floor slab will have one set of stresses as a result of its spanning between the walls and another set of stresses at right angles to that as a result of its participation in this cantilever action.

A more visually dramatic use of walls as beams can be seen in Eladio Dieste's church of San Pedro, in Durazno, Uruguay, more remarkable because the walls that serve as beams are of prestressed brickwork (Figure 7.40). The task was to replace a burned-out church where

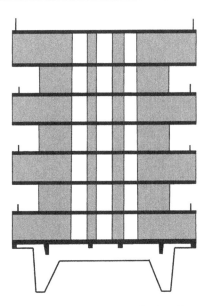

Figure 7.38 Cross-section of the New York University Student Dormitory.

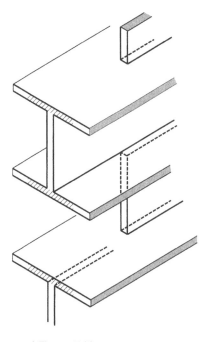

Figure 7.39 Structural diagram of Figure 7.38.

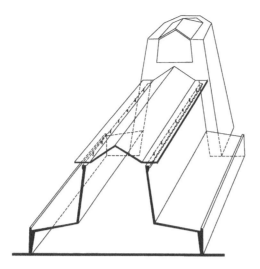

Figure 7.40 Eladio Dieste's church of San Pedro, Durazno, Uruguay.

the original west end survived. The body of the church has a high nave with what appear to be low aisles on either side, although it is in fact all one space with no columns separating nave and aisles and thus supporting the nave walls. The columns have been dispensed with because prestressing the brickwork has turned this wall into a deep beam that spans between the brick box of the presbytery at one end and a concrete portal frame at the entrance. With the wall 8 m high and the length of the nave 32 m, as a beam it has a span to depth ratio of 4 : 1. What is surprising about this beam is its thinness, and one would wonder about the potential for bucking of the top. However, this is prevented by its being connected to the roof by a series of short steel columns. The folded plate structure of the roof, which is also interesting, will be dealt with in Chapter 9, but this is clearly carrying any wind loads on the nave wall.

Bending in frames

In the last chapter we considered possible bending in a portal frame similar to those of the Crystal Palace, pointing out that the frame might sway sideways if either the beam or the columns were relatively flexible. We also noted the quite different ways in which Richard Rogers and Norman Foster had handled buildings in which there were triangulated frames forming both the columns and the beams. Now, using the idea of bending moments and bending moment diagrams we can look at the difference between these frames in a little more detail. First it is worth considering the construction of the frames. In both cases the columns and beams are triangulated frames rather like Figure 6.18. These have the advantage that while the members are relatively small the effective length between restraints is also rather short so that they will take compression forces without buckling.

The Sainsbury Centre at the University of East Anglia was characterised as having a structure like pairs of earth-fast posts carrying beams. The columns are fastened to the foundations in such a way that the latter will carry moments produced by any horizontal forces. The columns of each frame are like a pair of cantilevers fixed at the ground. If we assume a horizontal force P applied at the eaves on one side, this will be shared by the two columns and the moments at the ground will be P.h/2, where h is the height of the structure (Figure 7.41a). The bending moment on the columns is just like that on a cantilever, except that it is on a vertical rather than a horizontal member. Compare this with a complete portal frame with pin joints at the ground and rigid connections between the columns and beams. Now the bending on the columns is the other way up. The restraint against rotation is at the top rather than at the bottom. But just as there is bending in the columns at the top there must be equal bending in the beam. Figures 6.9b and 6.12a. show how the beam must bend upwards at one end and downwards at the other. Remembering that a bending moment diagram must be on the tension side of the beam and that there is zero bending at the centre where the curvature changes from one direction to another, we get the diagram as in Figure 7.41b.

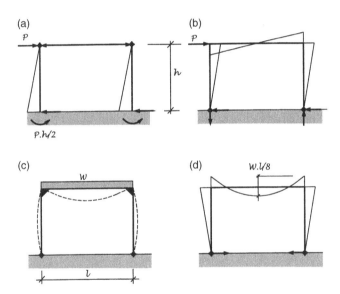

Figure 7.41 Deflections and bending moments of portal frames.

There does not seem to be much advantage in the second kind of structure as there is no less bending on the columns while bending has been introduced into the beam. However, the advantage becomes apparent if we consider the load on the beam. For the first structure a load on the beam will produce no bending in the column and the bending in the beam is just as in Figure 7.23 with a maximum bending moment of W.l/8 at the centre. The second structure can be looked at in two ways. Because it is attached to the columns by a rigid joint, the beam is prevented from rotating freely and so there is some bending moment at the joint. The result will be that the deflected shape will be concave in the centre (looked at from the top) just as with a simply supported beam, but convex towards the supports, and of course points of contraflexure in between. This can be achieved by taking the normal bending moment diagram for a beam and raising it above the line. Figure 7.41c shows the deflected shape as a dotted line while the resulting bending moments are sketched in Figure 7.41d. Note that the difference between the bending at the corners and in the middle of the beam is still W.l/8.

The other way of seeing this is to note that if the feet of the posts were on rollers, as the beam deflected with rotation at its supports, the top of the posts, having nothing to restrain them, would also rotate and the feet of the posts would move outwards. Of course they are not free to move in this way and so load on the beam must result in a horizontal restraining force at the feet of the posts. This results in a bending moment at the top of the post, and the bending moment at the ends of the beam must be equal to that. The bending moment for the beam can now be drawn between these two points. Whichever way you look at this to get the result, the effect is that the maximum bending is much smaller than for the simply supported beam. This is the advantage of an apparently more complex structure.

8 Providing Shelter – Roofs

... the house may now have leave to put on its hatte: having hitherto beene uncovered it self, and consequently unfit to cover others. Which point though it be the last of the art of execution, yet it is always in intension the first, for who would build but for shelter.

Henry Wotton, *The Elements of Architecture*

Henry Wotton used these words in his book on architecture to introduce the subject of roofs. It was something that he had to leave till late in the book because, although a roof over our heads is the object of building, it is the last thing to be put on. Nevertheless it may be the first part of the structure to be designed because it has to be supported by whatever is below, and how we design the roof may well influence the design of the supporting structure. Something of a revived fashion for open roofs, drawing inspiration from medieval carpentry, sometimes leads clients to want the impossible, seeing roof forms that they like without realising that they were dependent upon the kind of support structures that are no longer practical. Today, just as earlier, there can be more to a roof than just a simple shelter. In medieval hall houses and the churches of the time, the open roof was developed as much for its decorative effect as for structural reasons. This was especially so in England, where elaboration of the structure culminated in the hammerbeam roofs prominent in East Anglian churches, but also found in many other buildings. This type of carpentry was described by the French architect and historian Viollet le Duc as the pinnacle of English carpentry; using the roof of Westminster Hall as an illustration of this in his *Dictionary of Architecture*.

The nineteenth century produced its most dramatic roofs for railway stations, and these too were examples of structural art, designed to impress as much as to shelter the trains and travellers. These, after all, were the entrances to the systems and competing companies wanted their customers to see what modern organisations they were entrusting themselves to. Of course, at much the same time church architects were indulging in either a medieval revival in roofs for churches or public buildings or were designing roofs that took their inspiration from medieval carpentry. Most recently Hi Tec architecture took an interest in externally exposed roofs, there are architects who are using roofs as decorative ceilings, and there is something of a revival in green oak roof structures, not only in houses but also for some institutional buildings. The roof is therefore an important architectural element. Some of its structural principles have been dealt with before, but perhaps warrant repeating in this context. Fairly traditional roof forms demonstrate both the relationship between support conditions and the overall behaviour of the structure, and the influence of construction details on the forces that exist, so it is with those that we begin.

Common rafter roofs

As the purpose of the roof structure is to support the roof covering, whose function is to shed the water, the first influence on the roof structure is the nature of that covering. The pitch must be sufficient and the structure strong enough to support the covering's weight. The latter should provoke some caution in the owners of historic buildings. A building with a steeply pitched roof and light scantling timbers may indicate that it was originally thatched so that re-roofing with heavy clay tiles might well result in some structural distress. Similarly Welsh slates weigh less than plain clay tiles so that the substitution of the latter for the former might have a similar effect. Whatever the covering, it is carried by battens that are nailed to the rafters forming the slope and it is with the rafters that we begin.

Imagine first a lean-to roof with rafters spanning between a wall plate on the lower wall, and leaning against a timber fastened to the taller wall. Figure 8.1a shows the overall arrangement and Figure 8.1b the forces on the rafters. To understand the forces in this simple arrangement imagine putting up a ladder against a wall. In the diagrams of Figure 8.2 the weight of the ladder is concentrated at its centre of gravity. We would first stand the ladder upright and raise it to the required height. This has the effect of raising its centre of gravity. As we lean the ladder towards the wall its weight takes over and we have to pull back against its tendency to rotate rapidly about the base. The lever arm of the ladder's weight, d, about the foot is increasing as we lean the ladder further towards the wall, but we cannot increase the lever arm, h, of our resistance to it and so we have to increase the restraining force H that we apply. In this respect the ladder soon has the advantage over us.

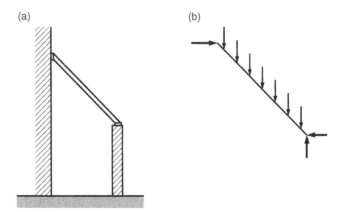

Figure 8.1 Lean-to roof rafters.

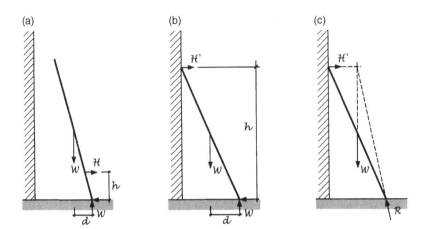

Figure 8.2 Putting up a ladder.

Eventually the ladder comes to rest against the wall and the wall provides the force, H′, that prevents any further rotation (Figure 8.2b). Clearly this force H′ is much smaller than H. Vertical forces on the ladder are its weight acting downwards and the reaction at its foot acting upwards. The ladder is being 'supported' at the top by a horizontal force from the wall and so there must be an equal and opposite horizontal force at the foot. These horizontal forces depend upon the angle at which the ladder is put up; the shallower the angle the greater the force so that if it is put up at too shallow an angle it would tend to slide out at the foot. The same is true of the lean-to roof; there is an outward force acting on the wall plate; the shallower the roof the larger the force.

Finding the support forces is a simple matter of taking moments about the foot of the rafter using the same method as in Chapter 1. Taking moments about the foot of the rafter we have H.h = W.l/2 (Figure 8.3b), and for a 45° pitch where l = h the horizontal thrust is half the weight of the roof. In fact many medieval roofs were just a little steeper than that, commonly 48°, the result of making the rafter length three-quarters the length of the span. Note that the whole exercise can be carried out to find the horizontal force using triangles of forces, the starting point being the diagram of forces in Figure 8.2c. This assumes that the rafters have a plumb cut where they are fixed to the plate on the wall, shown by the detailed sketch in Figure 8.3. The aisle rafters for the barn of Figure 6.5 are also lean-to roofs and may well have the same detail at the arcade plate, i.e. a plumb cut. But there are barns in which the rafters ride over the upper *arris* of the arcade plate, when one would then assume that the support force was at right-angles to the rafter, as in the detailed sketch of Figure 8.4. In that case, when taking moments about the foot of the rafter, the support force must be multiplied by the length of the rafter. Thus, R.a = W.l/2 (Figure 8.4). Note that for the same rafter length and weight of covering the force R is less than the force H in the previous example. The force H′ at the foot of this rafter will be even smaller because it is equal to the horizontal component of R. Also V is no longer equal to W because it will be reduced by the vertical component of R.

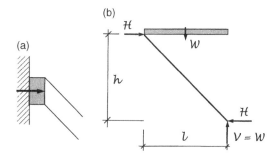

Figure 8.3 Rafters with a plumb cut at the top.

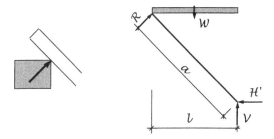

Figure 8.4 Rafters riding over the arris of a plate at the top.

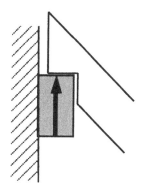

Figure 8.5 Rafters with a birdsmouth at the top.

A further possibility is that the rafter is notched over the plate at the top with what is called a *birdsmouth* (Figure 8.5). In that case the support force will be vertical and there will be no horizontal thrust at the wall plate. This may be rather difficult to contrive but it is a further example of how the forces on a structure depend upon the support conditions and how they can be altered by altering the nature of the construction.

A roof of simple coupled rafters, i.e. pairs of rafters joined together at the apex, has the same forces acting as the lean-to roof leaning against the wall. Each rafter leans against its fellow, i.e. the horizontal force on each rafter at the apex is provided by the one to which it is coupled. It is rather like leaning a couple of playing cards together on a table, and again we know from common experience that it is more difficult to lean them at too shallow an angle. If we try this, the cards slide apart because there is not enough friction between them and the table. In just the same way the rafters thrust outwards at their feet, and as they do so the timber wall plate to which they are attached is being pushed outwards. Either this thrust must be resisted by the wall being massive enough, or the wall plates on either side of the building must be tied together with tie beams.

For any reasonable span the weight of the roof is sufficient to produce unacceptable deflections in small rafters and they need to be assisted in some way. As noted briefly in Chapter 4, there are two ways of doing this: either they are stiffened with some form of bracing between each pair of rafters or they are assisted by using purlins. The two types are called *common rafter roofs* and *purlin roofs*; the former results in the rafters imposing more or less uniformly distributed loads on the top of the walls, whereas in the latter the *principal rafters* also deliver concentrated forces onto the wall. We shall take these two types of roof in turn.

The simplest way to stiffen common rafters is to strut across between each pair of rafters with a collar. This has the effect of enabling small timbers to be used at the cost of some increase in the outward thrust. Adding the collar force C (Figure 8.6) will reduce the apex force so that $H_1 < H$ (H_1 is less than H of Figure 8.3) but $C + H_2 > H$, i.e. the addition of a collar has increased the horizontal force at the wall plate. We cannot find these forces simply from equations that describe the state of equilibrium; this is a statically indeterminate structure.

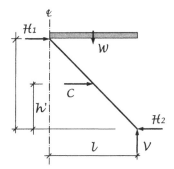

Figure 8.6 Rafters braced by a collar.

For those who might be interested in calculating the forces, it can be done fairly easily for a collar halfway up the rafter using what we have already discovered about two-span beams. The component of the vertical load perpendicular to the rafter is W.cos Ø, where Ø is the pitch angle. The collar provides the same restraint as the central support in a two-span beam. Therefore the component of the collar force perpendicular to the rafter must be 5/8.W.cos Ø (see Chapter 7). Hence the force in the collar can be found, and given this so can the remaining forces. Other positions of the collar will, of course, produce different results.

In a common rafter roof strutted in this way, the roof might depend upon the mass of the walls to resist the outward thrust and this can be determined by the method outlined in Chapter 4. In such a structural scheme the roof and the walls must be considered together in the design. These roofs were also used in timber-framed buildings and then the wall plate had to be stiff enough to act as a beam in the horizontal plane spanning between tie beams. As spans increased so did the complexity of the strutting, but this carpentry was sometimes used for decorative as much as structural effect,[1] and early church roofs often had more structure than was strictly necessary, something that is immediately apparent if they are compared with barn roofs. This is especially apparent when structures with collars, *ashlar pieces* and additional braces were used in porches where the small span could not possibly justify all that timber.

The simple porch roof of Heckington Church, Lincolnshire (Figure 8.7), has what are called soulaces below the collar, and ashlar pieces. The latter are small vertical timbers from the inside face of the wall, either carried on another long plate or, as here, connected to short timbers across the wall forming a triangle with the rafter. The closely spaced rafters with the additional timbers almost give the appearance of an unbroken surface. Such roofs, often found over the chancels of churches, are referred to as *wagon roofs*. Of course laths are sometimes nailed to the underside of these timbers to produce a 'vaulted' plaster ceiling, often painted; many examples of these decorative ceilings survive, their shape determined by the structure hidden above.

Figure 8.7 The porch of Heckington Church, Lincolnshire.

---

[1] It seems to have been the open roof that attracted the Victorian architects of the Gothic revival. It was this that gave rise to the book by the Brandons that was intended as an inspiration to Victorian church architects and from which illustrations in this chapter are taken. R. & J.A. Brandon, *Open Timber Roofs of the Middle Ages*, Batsford, London, 1860. Figures 8.7 and 8.10 are taken from this book.

This kind of strutting was effective enough that small scantling timbers could even be used on the long spans of cathedral roofs. However, simple collar strutting is not very effective in resisting wind loading on a steeply pitched high roof. Wind forces would tend to deflect the rafters more than the weight of the covering and the collar would do little or nothing to prevent this. With the wind producing positive pressure on the windward slope and negative pressure (suction) on the leeward slope, the roof would simply sway sideways like a tent in a wind (Figure 8.8a). The rafters would bend just like the canvas – if not as much. A collar brace alone would simply move with the rafters. The solution was to use scissor braces, which provide better resistance to wind loading by producing internal triangulation within the roof. A little consideration will show that such a roof cannot be distorted without some failure of these braces.

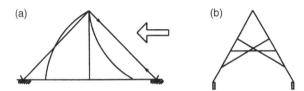

Figure 8.8 (a) Wind loads on a tent. **(b)** Scissor bracing.

Purlin roofs

Purlins are simply beams, horizontal timbers part way up the slope that the rafters lean against. There might be one or more pairs of such timbers within the roof, depending upon the span, but obviously these also need to be supported by something. In a small building the purlins might simply span between the gable walls, or be supported by, or strutted from, cross walls within the building.[2] However, it is more usual for them to be supported at intervals by some form of frame or roof truss that has large rafters called *principal rafters*.

The behaviour of purlin roofs is rather complex and illustrates the need sometimes to simplify the situation in order to make any calculations of the forces. It follows that the results of the calculations will be approximations of the actual forces and so it is sensible to have some idea of the degree of accuracy and to make sure we err on the side of caution. Figure 8.9 shows the deflections in a purlin roof. The purlins will deflect under load and as they do so the rafters will deflect with them. The rafter is a like a two-span beam with a central support, but where that central support is a spring rather than being rigid. As the spring deflects downwards under load so will the beam, and the beam will be compelled to carry more of the load back to the end supports. The central support is shedding load, via the beam, to these two end supports. In the roof the purlin is the spring but it is not loaded by a single rafter but by a whole series of rafters along its length. It is not able to shed much of

---

[2]In the typical British semi-detached house of the inter-war years they were supported by the gable walls and the party walls.

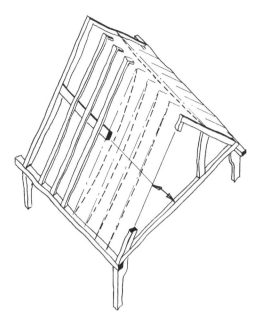

Figure 8.9 Deflections in a purlin roof.

the load of the rafters close to its support because it deflects little there. It sheds more load from the rafters near the centre of the span where the deflection is greater. In fact in some roofs the purlin deflects so much that the rafters located towards the middle of a bay might find themselves completely unsupported by the purlin. The effect is that the load on the purlin is not uniform but falls off towards the middle. To analyse this would be a very complex procedure and it is common to assume in calculations that the purlin is rigid. This clearly overestimates the load on the purlin but rather underestimates the work that the rafters have to do.

One needs to be careful about these assumptions. Someone had a floor over a workshop and the span was so large that the floor was rather lively. He was given a steel beam, which he proposed to put across and under the joists at mid-span. When he discussed this with an engineer he was told that the beam would not be strong enough. But, he reasoned, he had added some structure so the floor must be stronger and could not understand this advice. What the engineer must have assumed was that the beam acted as a rigid, mid-span support for the joists and had calculated its load based on that assumption, presumably finding that with such a load the beam would be overstressed. But of course the beam would deflect just like the roof purlin and the actual load would be less than he had assumed.

Heavily loaded timbers are subject to creep deflections, their deflection increasing with time even though the load remains the same. This effect is more severe if the timber is loaded while still green, i.e. before it has dried out completely. This is what has happened in a large proportion of early timber roofs. Purlins were often rather undersized for the task they had to perform and the timbers were used while still green. The result is the rather wavy roofline that one sees in old buildings as the purlins have deflected between their supports. It means, of course, that one can tell from the outside of the roof where the purlins are supported.

Unless they span between cross walls or gables, purlins must be supported by a pair of principal rafters, usually placed at about 10 ft (3 m) intervals along the building. As with common rafters, the outward thrust of principal rafters must be contained by something, either by a buttressed wall or a tie beam, so that roofs might be divided into those two types. In those that rely upon a well-buttressed wall to resist the outward thrust the principal rafters were normally strutted across, just like common rafters, although whether this was seen as a device to assist the principal rafters or simply to form a frame that could easily be erected is not clear. What is certain is that it was necessary to ensure that the outward forces at the feet of the principals were transmitted into the wall and the principals did not simply slide off. One of the ways this might be done was to use arch braces connected into a wall post, but eventually such arch-braced principals seem to have led to the development of the hammerbeam roof. The hammerbeams are short pieces of timber projecting from the wall looking as if there had been a tie beam, but most of which had been cut away.

The roof of Little Welnetham Church, Suffolk (Figure 8.10), suggests this transition, having arch-braced and hammerbeam trusses alternating. The arch braces are joined into

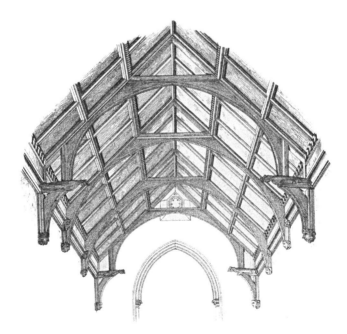

Figure 8.10 Roof of Little Welnetham Church, Suffolk.

the principal rafters with long tenons so that if the principals tend to slide outwards they must take the braces with them. But this cannot happen as the braces but against the wall usually via a wall post. Structurally this seems to be very efficient as there is a fairly direct, and clearly visible, transfer of forces from the principal rafters into the wall. The disadvantage of such a structure is that rather large timbers are required for the braces and the insertion of a hammerbeam divided the brace into two pieces, which might be easier to obtain. The elaboration of this arrangement was to separate the arch brace into two distinct parts with the upper part pulled out to the end of the hammerbeam and the lower part formed as a kind of bracket under it. The post on top of the hammerbeam is called the hammer-post. Now the sequence of load transfer is less obvious because it begins with the principal rafter thrusting against the hammerbeam. This is prevented from sliding off the wall because the wall post is tenoned into it. Occasionally one finds structures much as shown in Figure 8.11, in which there are no more than the essential elements, the hammerbeam and the wall post.

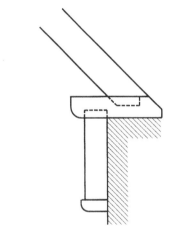

Figure 8.11 Hammerbeam and wall post.

How much support is given to the principal rafter by the bracketing under the hammer-beam and the hammerpost is a matter for some conjecture. The behaviour of hammerbeam roofs was something that intrigued twentieth century scholars, with many competing theories. The problem is not helped by the fact that there are two kinds of hammerbeam roofs, some of them like Little Welnetham that clearly seem to be derived from the arch-braced roof, and in which the purlins are orthogonal to the roof surface. The others appear to be derived from aisled construction because the purlins are rather like the arcade plates of such roofs. Imagine that in the aisled structure of Figure 6.5 the posts are cut off below the aisle tie. Add bracketing members under the aisle tie and the result is a hammerbeam. This sequence of development is suggested by those hammerbeam roofs in which the purlins are set vertically just like the arcade plate, with the aisle tie extended to come under the posts so becoming a hammerbeam. Westminster Hall roof is an example of this type and has generated quite a little industry of scholarly endeavour in attempting to discover how it works.[3] It seems important to recognise that carpenters had two tasks: to support the purlins adequately and to contain the outward thrusts of the rafters. A collar will achieve the former while the timbers shown in Figure 8.11 will serve for the latter. The rest of the timbers may pick up some load, and arch bracers may stiffen the principal rafters, but I find it difficult to imagine that carpenters working on buildings such as Westminster Hall were privy to some structural secret that present-day engineers cannot fathom.

Loading of purlins

We need to be careful about the assumptions that we make about the loading of purlins and the frames that support them. With purlins set orthogonal to the roof slope and the shorter dimension perpendicular to the slope two conditions of loading are possible. Assume first that the rafters are fixed at the foot to prevent outward movement but simply rest on the purlins. If there is deflection of the purlin it is likely to be perpendicular to the slope, which means that the forces are acting in the same direction rather than vertically (Figure 8.12a).

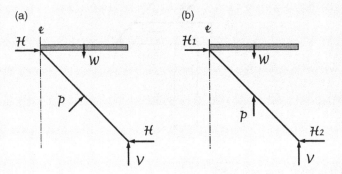

Figure 8.12

However, if the rafters are nailed to the purlins, or pegged as they sometimes were in medieval roofs, and if the wall plate moves outwards the rafters following it will try to take the purlin with them. Restraint against outward movement will therefore be shared between the purlin and the wall plate, with a force on the purlin in the plane of the roof. The magnitude of this force will depend upon the relative stiffness of the purlin and wall plate, and it is usual to assume for simplicity that the force on the purlin is vertical. Assuming one pair of purlins and depending upon which assumption is made gives one or other of the two diagrams of Figure 8.12. If the rafters are divided at a

---

[3]For a discussion of this and some of the papers written see David Yeomans, *The Development of Timber as a Structural Material*, Ashgate, Aldershot, 1999.

purlin set vertically like an arcade plate, then the combined effect of the two lengths of rafter, one leaning against the side of the purlin, the other standing on it, will certainly be a vertical force on the purlin.

At a 45° pitch the relationship between the forces of Figure 8.12a is such that the horizontal force at the wall plate is unaffected by the presence or otherwise of the purlin. That is if p, the reaction from the purlin, is zero the force H remains the same.

Naturally the two different assumptions also affect the forces on the principal rafters. The force from the purlins on to the principals will be either as Figure 8.13a or 8.13b, the former ignoring the small effect of the purlin's own weight. The first assumption produces a slightly odd result. If initially the collar force is ignored, i.e. C = 0, and the pitch is at 45°, the horizontal force at the feet of the principal rafters is also zero. The horizontal force will in practice be equal to the force in the collar, which is there to prevent the principal rafter from deflecting. With fairly stiff principal rafters this force might be quite small. That is not so if the force P is vertical, when $H_2 = H_1 + C$.

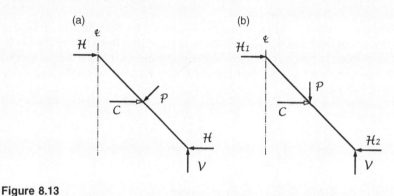

Figure 8.13

Today, people's desire for collar-braced roofs presents problems. People seeing either medieval roofs or Victorian church roofs using this device have tried to use it in modern houses where an open carpentered roof is wanted for visual reasons. Doubtless this, or a variation on it, seems to be the ideal roof, simple in form but allowing a reduced roof height as long as the collar is high enough. Unfortunately, without a buttressed wall the only thing that can prevent the roof from spreading is the collar. While this acted as a compression member in early roofs (Figure 8.14a) where buttressed walls restrained the feet of the principals, it now has to do duty as a tie (Figure 8.14b), and making joints between the collar and the principals to handle the tension forces is very difficult. Neither is it simply the force in the collars that presents problems in constructing a roof like this. It should be clear from Figure 8.14b that there will also be considerable bending in the rafter, the maximum value of which will be just where the connection with the collar needs to be made. The difficulty with this roof form in today's buildings is that it is based upon an image of an earlier form without any understanding of the principles involved.

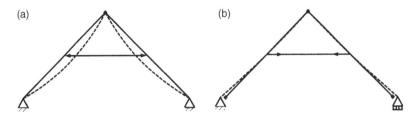

Figure 8.14 Collar as **(a)** a compression member or **(b)** as a raised tie.

Containment by the collar

The force that has to be produced by the collar to contain the tendency for outward movement increases with the collar's height. With no restraint at the feet the A-frame becomes a statically determinate structure.

   This can be seen simply by drawing a free body diagram for the principal rafter and taking moments about the apex of the roof. Assuming a vertical force P from the purlin halfway up the principal rafter, $V = P$, and the clockwise moment, $V.a = P.a$, while the anticlockwise moments are $P.a/2 + C.h$, from which $C = P.a/2h$, the smaller the value of h the larger C will have to be.

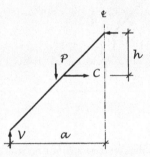

Figure 8.15

   More basic in their behaviour are those roof trusses that depend upon tie beams. A beam across the building at intervals served the function of preventing outward movement of the wall plates under the thrust from the common rafters and was large enough to support struts that assisted the principal rafters. Some roofs had king posts supporting a ridge purlin as well as a pair of inclined struts to assist the principal rafters where they carried the side purlins. In other places queen struts were used, there was no ridge purlin and in the most common arrangement the purlins were supported by a collar, which in turn was carried by a pair of vertical posts. This is called a clasped purlin roof (Figure 8.16), the purlins being clasped between the collar and the principal rafters. It should be clear that this is structurally

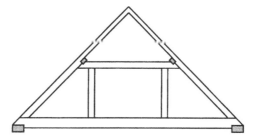

Figure 8.16 Clasped purlin roof.

the better arrangement because as loads are not brought down onto the middle of the tie beam the bending on this member is less.

Nevertheless the need to find tie beams both long enough to span between the walls and large enough to carry the forces from these struts was a limiting factor in the design of buildings. This had not been a problem in Italy where a quite different form of roof truss had been in use for some time, but the obstacle was not to be overcome in Britain until the Italian type of structure was introduced in the seventeenth century. However, before dealing with the behaviour of this improved type of roof we need to consider the longitudinal stability of roof structures. The importance of stability in the design of frames was demonstrated in Chapter 6. But it is equally important in roofs. In fact, although medieval carpenters were generally careful to ensure the stability of their roofs, forgetting this important consideration led to some failures in Britain in the 1980s.

Longitudinal stability

Stand a tall thin object up and it will easily fall over – and this is true for a number of roof trusses standing on a wall plate. Even if they are connected together they will simply fall over like a row of dominoes so that some bracing must be provided to prevent this – bracing that would also resist the wind forces on the gables. For purlin roofs carpenters simply provided braces between the principal rafters and the purlins, so called *wind braces*, and these were more than adequate to ensure the roof's stability. They also helped during erection of the roof, keeping the principals upright as soon as a single pair of braces had been inserted between principals and purlins. They had little wind load to carry, as the exposed area of the gable is relatively small, especially compared with the bracing provided.

It was in earlier common rafter roofs that there might be a problem, especially in high-pitched cathedral roofs. In the lower pitched domestic or agricultural buildings a *crown post* arrangement was used (Figure 8.17). A plate, called a *collar plate*, was placed under the collars and supported by posts, called crown posts, which stood on the tie beams. If the rafters were to rack over they would all have to do so together and take the collar plate with them. Braces between the crown post and the collar plate prevented this from happening. This presented an obvious problem during construction because the crown post had to be held upright while the rest of the roof was assembled. A brace between the crown post and the tie beam

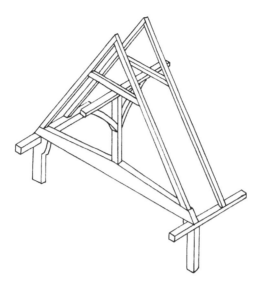

Figure 8.17 A crown post roof.

served this purpose. In barn roofs this brace might be left in place after completion of the framing, while in houses or churches, where appearance was important, it would be removed once the roof was complete, or a pair of braces might be used whose symmetrical arrangement would be acceptable in the completed building. As roofs were open, the crown post was again an opportunity for decorative treatment.

Crown posts could not easily be used in the more steeply pitched cathedral roofs where the posts, and so presumably the braces, would have had to be rather long.[4] One might suppose that this was less of a problem in roofs that were contained by masonry – the central tower at one end and a masonry gable wall at the other – but it was seen to be a serious problem in roofs when they were surveyed in the seventeenth or eighteenth centuries. James Essex, reporting on Lincoln Cathedral in the 1760s, described the problem well:

> Before I leave this part it will be proper to observe that all y upper roof have an inclination to run from the tower in the middle, which is a defect common to all roofs framed in this manner, where every pair of principals is designed to stand alone & have'g no connection with each other they are easily put into disorder by y falling of any one from y perpendicular, whereas if they had been properly united to each other by braces as they ought to have been, nothing could have hurt them, but for want of such braces they are not only in danger of falling themselves, but are likely to throw down the gable of the nave and both crosses, as is nearly the case at present with the north end of the great transept.[5]

---

[4]The only cathedral in which there is any record of a crown post being used is Exeter, where the crown post stands on a collar about one-third of the height of the roof above the wall plate with the collar plate under a still higher collar (see Cecil Hewett, *English Cathedral Carpentry*, Wayland, London, 1974, pp. 27–28).
[5]BM Add. 6761, f.73.

Racking of the nave roof was also occurring at Salisbury when Wren made his structural report on that cathedral over half a century earlier, and his suggested measures for restraining the movement of the roof frames involved strutting from the gable wall.[6] Whether or not his recommendations were taken up, the problem was eventually solved in the eighteenth century when Francis Price carried out extensive re-roofing of the building.[7] At Westminster Abbey, Hawksmoor introduced longitudinal braces in the roof to restrain it against racking.[8] This seems not to have been fully effective because the problem was eventually tackled in the twentieth century by using diagonal boarding over the rafters rather than the original horizontal boarding. This provides resistance against racking in much the same way as braces because the diagonal boarding nailed to the rafters effectively triangulates the roof surface.

Racking of roofs again became a problem in the second half of the twentieth century. Timbers large enough for purlins became difficult to obtain in Britain following World War II, and various other types of roof construction were tried. Close-spaced, light trusses to support small scantling purlins was the first idea, the timbers being fastened together with bolts and toothed plate connectors. Introduced by the Timber Development Association shortly after the war, these TDA trusses are still sometimes used. But the most dramatic change was the adoption of trussed rafter roofs that had been developed in the United States. The key to the large-scale use of trussed rafters was the invention of the truss-plate, a thin steel plate with teeth formed in it. The plates are laid over the junction between two or more timbers and are then pressed in so that the teeth embed in the timbers and fasten them together. The truss plates are effectively gusset plates. Plates are placed over both sides of each joint and this simple factory process joins members together: rafters, ceiling joists and struts forming stiff trusses able to carry the weight of the roof covering. Roof trusses of various forms (see, e.g. the king post truss described below) can be put together with small timbers all in the same plane.

Simple to erect, at first it seemed that they needed little or no site carpentry. Unfortunately British roofing practice differs from American construction, where lightweight asphalt 'shingles' are laid over plywood sheeting to form the covering. The plywood is necessary to support the so-called shingles (in effect no more than strips of patterned roofing felt), and is nailed down to the rafters so preventing them from racking. One can see that if there is any racking of the roof a rectangular shape on the surface would have to distort into a parallelogram – not possible for a sheet of plywood. When first used in Britain it was assumed (if anyone actually thought about it) that the tiling battens would be sufficient to serve the same purpose. This was a mistake.

The kinds of forces on a roof as a result of the wind and the connection with the walls have already been illustrated in Figure 5.3. The problem in Britain was that the rafters were only connected together with tiling battens so there was no racking resistance; problems began to be noticed during the late 1970s and early 1980s. The wake-up call came when the

---

[6] *Wren Society XI*, Oxford, 1934.

[7] Francis Price, *A Series of . . . Observations . . . upon . . . the Cathedral Church of Salisbury*, London, 1753.

[8] R.W. McDowall et al., 'The timber roofs of the Collegiate Church of St. Peter at Westminster', *Archaeologia* 1966, Vol. 100.

roof of a school gymnasium collapsed during construction. These trusses were originally intended for house building but had proved so economical that their use had been extended to larger buildings. Clearly a little more engineering was needed. The solution was to attach diagonal timbers across the slope of the roof to ensure stability. Those erecting the roofs had commonly nailed diagonal timbers across the top of the rafters just to keep the trusses upright until the roofer arrived. Of course, the roofers had then to remove those timbers so that they could fix the tiling battens. To prevent failures permanent diagonal timbers are now fastened under the rafters. Moreover, the roof had to be more effectively connected to the gables to stop them from failing. The irony is that it was not the first time that a change in roofing practice had led to this kind of failure. When the heavy timber trusses used in long-span roofs throughout the eighteenth century (described below) gave way to light iron trusses in the nineteenth century a similar problem of instability occurred, leading to some failures of railway station roofs.

The roof truss

When plaster ceilings came into general use, the roof disappeared from view, only to reappear in the nineteenth century transformed into iron in the roofs of railway stations and market halls. In the meantime a radical change had taken place in the structure of roofs with a shift to the use of *king* and *queen post trusses*. In these the posts were in tension and the function of the tie beam was simply to tie the feet of the principal rafters, and possibly to carry the weight of the ceiling. This change was essential because as spans became larger it would have been increasingly difficult, if not impossible, to obtain timbers large enough to span as beams between the walls and support the weight of the roof. What was needed was something akin to the bridge trusses that we looked at in Chapter 2; and in England the ideas for this type of roof were 'imported' from Italy where this kind of structure was already in use. It was first adopted for a large span building by Inigo Jones, who used a king post truss for roofing the Banqueting House in London, with a span of about 18 m. But it was Christopher Wren who used this structure extensively and also adapted it, developing the queen post truss.

Figure 8.18 shows the king post truss as it was commonly built in England. (Italian roofs were designed on the same principle but used different construction details.) There is a pair of struts to assist the principal rafters in supporting the load from the purlins. These are in compression and push down on the base of the king post, which has an enlarged foot to receive the ends of these struts. While the struts push down on the king post, the post is

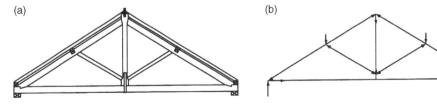

(a)   (b)

Figure 8.18 A king post truss.

unable to move downwards because it has a similarly enlarged head to receive the ends of the principal rafters. Thus trapped between the two principals it is supported by them and so is in tension. The principals pressing inwards and upwards against the head of the king post will press downwards and outwards against the ends of the tie beam. While the beam may well have to support the weight of the ceiling load it is assisted in this by being tied up to the foot of the king post with a metal strap. Thus the king post is helping to support both purlins and ceiling.

This verbal description of the forces can be reduced to a simple line diagram with arrows pointing outwards indicating compression, and inwards showing the members in tension (Figure 8.18b). As the tie beam no longer had large bending forces acting at mid-span it could be made in two lengths providing the joint between them could transmit the tension force. The longest timbers in a roof were no longer the tie beams but the principal rafters. Note that the drawing of the truss shows the form as it had developed by the nineteenth century, in which the purlins are carried on top of the principals rather than being tenoned into them as earlier. With this arrangement the common rafters cannot easily be brought to the wall plate, and a second plate to support them, called a *pole plate*, is carried on top of the tie beam. A simple board is provided at the ridge to nail the common rafters to.

The simple king post truss can be thought of as an arch of two members supporting a central hanger. If the span or the load on the tie beam were particularly large then this timber arch might be made with more than two members, which is what Wren did for the roof of the Sheldonian Theatre, Oxford. His problem was in constructing not only an unprecedented span of nearly 70 ft (over 20 m) but also an attic that was to be used by the university printing press. The first meant that the tie beam had to be formed of several pieces of timber, and the result was an ingenious piece of carpentry (Figure 8.19). To keep the roof to a reasonable height, the pitch was reduced towards the centre so that the principals took the form of an arch of four pieces of timber supporting three posts. The posts were notched at the bottom to support four sections of beam forming the floor. As this would not form a continuous tie, three longer timbers passed under the posts and were jointed into the upper timbers in such a way that the joints would transmit tension forces. The use of so many metal bolts does suggest a somewhat belt-and-braces approach but is understandable in this novel structure.

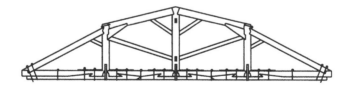

Figure 8.19 Wren's roof for the Sheldonian Theatre, Oxford.

There can be little doubt that Wren used an arch analogy in devising this structure. From this rather complex arrangement it would have been a simple step to combine the two central sections of rafter into a single piece to give a flat-topped roof. If usable space in the attic were not a consideration the central post could be strutted from the feet of the two other posts, the queen posts, although in most cases this would be unnecessary. What is required

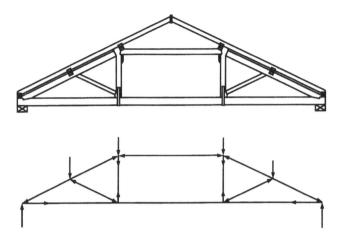

Figure 8.20 A queen post truss.

is a joint at the top of the queen posts to enable them to be carried by the arch-like members: the rafters and the horizontal collar, or *straining beam*, as it was sometimes called (Figure 8.20). Note also that with inclined struts resting on the bottom of the queen posts they would have to be prevented from moving sideways by being tenoned into the tie beam. In large spans where the horizontal force was large, this was not sufficient and a separate timber was placed on top of the tie beam strutting between the bottom of the posts.

By the nineteenth century queen post trusses had become the common choice for longer spans. This type of structure had long been used in Italy, and one finds drawings of this arrangement in Palladio's book on architecture, but it was initially used in England to form roofs with flat tops, keeping the height down where spans were long. Such roof designs later became popular in the form shown in Figure 8.20 for long-span roofs because they provided two points of support for the tie beam and might carry two pairs of purlins more simply than the alternative elaborations on the king post truss.

The coming of iron

Relatively few of these timber trussed roofs can be seen because in houses and public buildings they are hidden above the ceilings they support. They only remained exposed in agricultural buildings, workshops or warehouses and appeared in some early railway stations, but by the mid-nineteenth century iron was becoming the material of choice and at first these timber forms were simply translated into iron, although this happened gradually. At first the carpentry at the ends of members might be replaced with cast-iron shoes bolted to the timbers. With large numbers of trusses this might have been cheaper than the carpentry joints, but for long spans such joints might be more secure. After all it is in the joints that the timber stresses are highest. Iron rods could also be used for the tension members of the truss, replacing timber king posts, queen posts and eventually tie beams. Bolting iron tie rods to castings removed the difficult problem of applying forces to the ends of a timber member that was to be in tension, but the great advantage of replacing the tie beam with iron rods was that the tie no longer had to be a straight piece of timber and this led to the development of new forms of truss. The warehouse shed in Liverpool shown in Figure 8.21 has been long demolished but not before it was illustrated by Newlands.[9] A truss with timber rafters and collar has the tie beam raised up to provide greater internal headroom. The principal rafters are in fact in two lengths sitting in the iron casting, which also takes the ends of the collar, and the whole thing stands on iron columns.

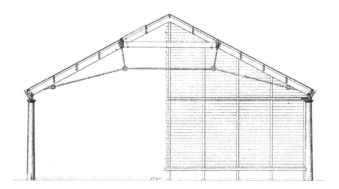

Figure 8.21 A nineteenth-century warehouse shed in Liverpool.

In France Polonceau developed the type of truss that takes his name, and roofs like this in a combination of steel tie bars and timber rafters and struts are still occasionally used today. What Polonceau devised was an arrangement in which the principal rafters were trussed like upside-down king post trusses. Just as the forces in the bridge trussing described in Chapter 2 were reversed by turning the trusses upside down (Figure 2.18), so the king post truss forces are reversed here. What was the tie becomes the principal rafter in compression, and the 'king post' has also become a compression member. The basic structure is shown in Figure 8.22a with the compression members drawn thicker than the tension members. Possibly the longest of the Polonceau roof trusses are those over the Gare St Lazare, Paris. Variations on this form are possible; Figure 8.22b shows a warehouse roof in which only two pairs of purlins were used and in which all the compression members were timber. Timber had, and still has, an advantage for use in rafters and struts because its fairly large

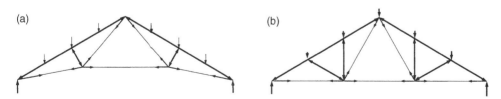

Figure 8.22 Polonceau roof trusses.

---

[9]James Newlands, *The Carpenter's Assistant*, n.d. – facsimile edition, Studio Editions, London, 1990.

bulk means that it does not buckle so readily under compressive forces, which is possible with the relatively slender wrought iron or steel sections.

Three-dimensional roofs

With the coming of purlins supported by trusses the roof was inevitably a three-dimensional structure with loads carried first in one direction and then in the other. The coming of iron freed the truss from the rigid discipline of straight tie beams but for some time it remained as a series of unidirectional structures joined together, the purlins in one direction and the trusses at right-angles to them. It was only in the twentieth century that designers began to explore the possibility of truly three-dimensional roofs, with folded plates and other three-dimensional structures.

Square plans and intersecting trusses

The simplest variation is to have the trusses spanning diagonally across a square grid. This might not seem very sensible because the span of the trusses is increased but it has the effect of reducing the number of columns and trusses needed. Assume that a simple layout for a 10-m span has columns and trusses at 5-m intervals with one pair of side purlins and a ridge purlin. If every other pair of columns is removed and the trusses span diagonally, their span will be a little over 14 m but the span of the side purlins will remain the same (Figure 8.23). The increase in the span of the trusses will present little difficulty because their depth will still be large in relation to the span; the only disadvantage is the increased span of the ridge purlin. This layout was used for the Bespak factory at Kings Lynn on a columns grid of 13.5 m. With the factory more than one bay wide, reducing the number of columns clearly reduced the number of obstructions on the factory floor. This was built at a time when it was fashionable to expose the structure and a combination of dark-coloured cladding with columns and bracing diagonals painted yellow gave this building a rather striking appearance. 'Factory extension for Bespak Industries', *Architects Journal*, vol. 172 (1980), 17–32.

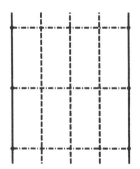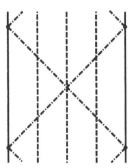

Figure 8.23 Alternative layouts of trusses.

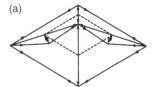 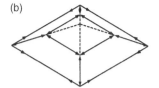

Figure 8.24 Pyramid roofs.

Spanning diagonally suggests a pyramid roof but for such roofs we need to be aware of the possible alternatives. In Figure 8.24a trussing is formed within the principal rafters, the dotted line indicating purlins at the mid-slope. If more purlins are needed then other forms of trussing are possible, perhaps something like the Polonceau based truss of Figure 8.22b. Whatever the form of trussing, the advantage of confining trussing to the principal rafters is that diagonal tie beams across the roof are avoided giving a much more open appearance. This is possible because the trusses can be tied across their feet by a ring of tension members along the tops of the walls. Going back to early roofs using collar-braced principals one might wonder what the principal rafters above the collar are doing. It is the collar that is resisting inward thrust from the purlin load and the upper part of the principal rafters is simply there to form a triangle so that the structure does not become a four-bar chain. Based on that analogy one might do without the trussing below the principal rafters in Figure 8.24a by forming the purlins as compression members, as in Figure 8.24b. In this way there is a compression ring to support the principal rafters at their mid-span. The primary structure consists of the two rings joined by the lower part of the principals.

The external skeleton

All of the roofs discussed so far rely upon structures contained within the volume of the building, but we can hardly leave the subject of roofs without considering the modern tendency to suspend the roof from some external structure. Saarinen hung his roof of Foster Dulles Airport from massive reinforced concrete pylons, as if it were a hammock or suspension bridge, relying upon the stiffness of the pylons rather than the cable supporting side spans that bridges normally have. Figure 8.25 is redrawn from Seymour Howard's book that considers the forces on this roof in some detail.[10] This suspended structure supports heavy precast concrete 'tiles' to form the roof surface so that the forces in the suspending cables must be large with consequently large moments at the feet of the pylons and on the foundations. The pylons must be larger towards their bases to resist the increasing bending moments while at the floor level there are compression forces to oppose the inward pull of the cables. However, this would still leave the moments produced by the cables unresolved, and Howard shows how the foundation forces must act to resist the tendency of the pylons to rotate about their bases. The overall stability of this hammock-like structure is not an issue because these pylons are rooted in the ground. However, overall stability has become a concern for later structures that have relied upon masts, to some extent resembling a ship's rigging.

---

[10] H. Seymore Howard Jr., *Structure, An Architect's Approach*, McGraw-Hill, New York, 1966.

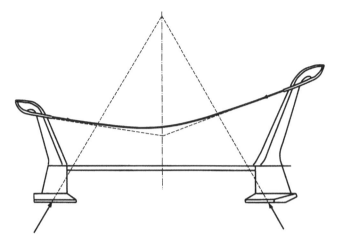

Figure 8.25 Foster Dulles Airport.

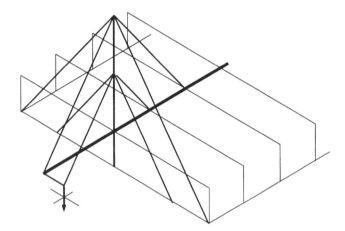

Figure 8.26 Skating Rink at Oxford.

Nicholas Grimshaw's Skating Rink at Oxford is a good example of this type because the structure is so visible and it shows the structural requirements so clearly. The sketch here (Figure 8.26) shows half the structure (not to scale). The enclosed area of the rink is 56 × 26 m, but rather than spanning the short dimension the main span is along the length with a long girder picking up loads from bents, L-shaped structures that support the wall and roof covering. This girder is then supported by a number of cables from tall masts at either end. This is like a cable-stayed bridge except that the back stays are not taken out so far. Naturally the cables pull inwards on the masts and so have to be guyed, but to limit the overall structural length the back stays from the top of the mast are taken to a boom and then brought inwards to the ground anchor. Anyone who has done any sailing will be reminded of the mast, stays, boom and main sheet on a boat. Like the mast on a boat this needs to be stayed to the sides to hold it upright, hence the stays in the plane of the end walls. Additional struts and stays on the masts between the fixings of the main cables have not been shown in this sketch. They are there to prevent buckling of the mast under the large compressive force in it that is produced by the suspension cables.

It goes without saying that the ground must be providing anchoring forces for all of the cables, but only those for the main stays have been shown. It should also be apparent that the external boom must be in compression. The arrangement that combines girders supporting the roof assisted by suspension cables has been used in a number of other structures. While the cables are picking up a large proportion of the roof load the function of the girder is to transmit loads from the roof to these cables so that the girder will be in some bending, the extent of that bending depending upon the spacing of its cable (or tie rod) supports.

What this and other structures demonstrate is that while the roof may be suspended the building still needs a stable frame, and for these buildings it is provided by external stays rather than internal bracing or moment connectors between posts and beams. A more complex, and slightly puzzling example is provided by Richard Rogers's Fleetguard Centre, Quimper, France. The roof is hung from a square grid of columns but in this case provision for the overall stability of the structure is made through struts rather than ties – at least it is along one side of the building. Figure 8.27 shows a corner where along both sides there are booms and tie-down rods, just as in the Oxford Skating Rink structure, except that here the tie-downs are simple vertical members. Along one side bracing is provided by the diagonal struts from the foot of each tie-down to the eaves. What is not clear from the exterior of the building is how provision is made for stability in the other direction. This is described by the architects as a 'dynamic structure' – well, clearly not too dynamic.

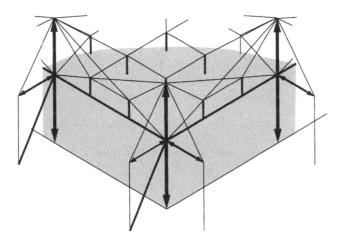

Figure 8.27 Fleetguard Centre, Quimper, France.

This is still a relatively simple structure compared with Foster's Renault Distribution Centre, Swindon, although the concept for that structure began fairly simply. The idea was for a series of upside-down umbrella-like forms (Figure 8.28). This seems simple enough,

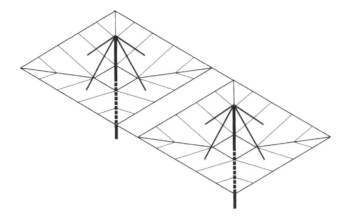

Figure 8.28 Sketch scheme for Renault Distribution Centre, Swindon.

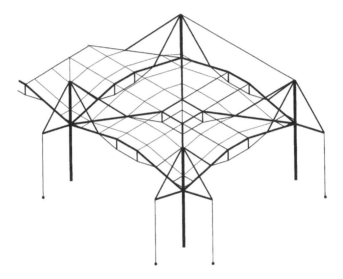

Figure 8.29 Renault Distribution Centre, Swindon, final structure.

but the need to ensure stability of the structure required the umbrellas to be connected together and braced at the edge of the building. This led to the use of half umbrellas along the sides and quarter umbrellas at the corners so that the building ended with cantilever arms and tie-downs (Figure 8.29). These prevent the structure from racking. Of course, these corner and edge columns have to be joined to the others, which accounts for the continuous canted beams between the columns. These are in part suspended from the tops of the columns as part of the umbrella structure but also trussed in the centre with ties and struts under the roof.

The structure is on a square grid of columns and combines trusses orthogonal to the grid and spanning diagonally across it. In each case the central section is a truss. However, the trusses are hung from the masts producing a combination of bracket-like structures and beam trusses. It is not difficult to see what is in compression and what is in tension because the tie members are simple rods, but this only gives a rather simplistic view of the structure because the bracket and the trussed beam are not connected together by pinned joints. Instead the beams of the structure, while connected to the mast-like columns by hinged joints, are continuous between them along the sides of the square. Similar cantilever arms project inwards to a square roof light at the centre. There four short beams form the opening rather like the purlins of Figure 8.24b. Readers might like to speculate on alternative arrangements. Could this central queen-post-like arrangement be removed? Could the short beam be pin jointed to the ends of the cantilevers? What would be both the structural and architectural effects of changes such as these? This is an example of what might begin as a simple idea but which, when all the structural requirements are taken into account, may become rather less than simple. However, we are now beginning to look at three-dimensional structures and lightweight roofs, which is more properly the subject of the next chapter.

9 Structures in a Three-dimensional World

Until we came to the last roof types, all the structures examined could be broken down into two-dimensional elements. A purlin roof is clearly a three-dimensional structure: the rafters are in one plane, the purlins in another, but each element can be described by drawings in separate planes. The forces between them are along a line common to both planes. However, the pyramid roof required thinking about behaviour in three dimensions, and the structures in this chapter all have that characteristic. That is why the subject of vaults and domes has been left so late even though they are some of the most ancient structures. Until the mid-twentieth century these were the most complex forms that had been used, originally in masonry and eventually in reinforced concrete. However, following World War II engineers began to develop other three-dimensional structures to cover large spans, and while the detailed analysis of these may require some complex calculations a simple qualitative under-standing of their behaviour is often possible. Some have even been designed by methods that rely on models rather than mathematics.

Ancient vaults and domes were necessarily compression structures, although strategically reinforced with either timber or iron, but the appearance of new materials in the twentieth century enabled engineers to devise structures that relied extensively upon tension forces. Lightweight membranes for roofing had a further effect in that the whole of the roof surface might be in tension, hung and tensioned to stiff supports against the uplift forces of the wind and relying for their stiffness upon their shapes. Although the forms and materials of both the early and more recent structures might be quite different it is because both require this three-dimensional thinking that they have been left to this late stage in the book and have been grouped together in this way.

Vaults

A simple barrel vault is structurally no different from an arch. Its purpose is to cover a space rather than support a roadway above so its thickness has only to be sufficient to satisfy its need to stand. If it were of uniform thickness then a catenary would be the ideal shape, that being the shape of a hanging chain loaded under its own weight. Some kilns are built like that but normally the requirements of early architecture, or possibly construction methods, demand that vaults have different shapes, often a complete semicircle. But whatever their profile, simple linear vaults hardly provide a convenient architectural device. There was no problem if they were used to roof water cisterns, one of the ways in which the Romans made use of vaults, because vaults could be supported continuously along both sides and enclosed by walls at each end (Figure 9.1a); but rooms require lighting. Moreover, the supporting walls have to be thick enough to resist the outward thrust of the vault. In churches some lower vaulting over side aisles helped to bring the thrust closer to the ground, either in the form of half vaults or complete vaults with a smaller span, but ultimately some form of buttressing was usually needed. One way of coping with the need for horizontal restraint against the outward thrust was to have smaller vaults at right-angles to the main vault (Figure 9.1b).

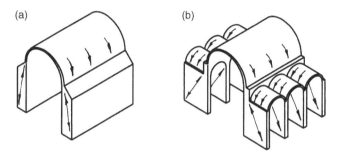

Figure 9.1 Buttressing a barrel vault.

This arrangement could be made even more open if the walls supporting the lower transverse vaults were themselves pierced by arched openings. The Basilica of Maxentius in the Roman forum has side spaces like this on a gigantic scale, side spaces that are now all that survives of the building. However, the main space of this building was not roofed with a simple barrel vault but with cross vaults, the ingenious Roman solution to lighting a vaulted space. It also provided a means of expanding the plan beyond the simple linar form produced by the barrel vault to something supported by a square grid of columns. Geometrically a cross vault is simply two barrel vaults intersecting at right angles. The supports needed are thus reduced to four corner columns (Figure 9.2a).

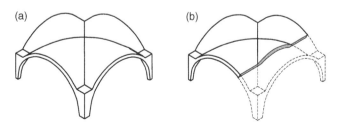

Figure 9.2 The form of a cross vault.

Starting from four corner columns the masons would first corbel out as far as possible and then complete the semicircular vault shape in each direction on some centring. The shape and construction are simple enough, the problem is to explain the way in which this works because while a simple barrel vault can be imagined as a continuous series of arches placed side by side, cut a section through a cross vault and it appears to comprise a number of arches apparently ending in mid air (Figure 9.2b). Figure 9.3a is a reflected plan of the vault with four arches drawn on it forming a square. Any other set of similar equal span arches would meet at the groin as these do, apparently supported by nothing. In fact it is the groin that does the supporting. The horizontal thrusts from the arches on the plan show there are two equal forces meeting at each groin. These thrusts, acting at right-angles to each other, combine to make a much larger thrust along the 45° line, and the groin therefore provides the reaction to this thrust.

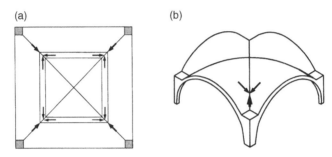

Figure 9.3 Reflected plan and forces in a cross vault.

The reaction must be also acting upwards because, just as the thrusts from the four component arches of a vault thrust outwards, they also thrust downwards. These forces can now be drawn on the upper surface of the vault (Figure 9.3b). Anywhere one looks along the groin there are pairs of forces from the vault surfaces above that are 'supported' by a force along the line of the groin. The groins thus act as a pair of diagonal arches crossing at the centre to support the vault surfaces. The fold in the surface of the vault that forms the groin is, in effect, an arch. A section along one of the groins would show the cumulative thrust from the arches we have imagined to be coming onto it. Of course the groins are not semi-circles; they have the curve defined by the intersection of two semi-circular vaults, and we might well wonder whether the line of thrust in these arches follows their curve or not. We need not consider this in detail because, just as the thickness of an arch ring is sufficient to contain the line of thrust within it so the construction of cross vaults produces sufficient thickness to contain their line of thrust.

A simple variation on this theme is to make the groins semi-circular as well as the arches along either side of the square plan. The eventual vault shape that results from this simple expedient (Figure 9.4) has the vault surfaces sloping upwards from the sides towards the groin. This form does not involve any different structural principles; its shape is merely determined by the process of construction. Roman brick and concrete vaults must have been

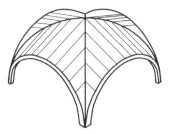

Figure 9.4 Vault with semi-circular groins.

built upon some kind of continuous formwork that carried the weight of the concrete until the vault was complete, not unlike the centring for arch bridge construction.

Choisy produced what has become the classic drawing of Roman construction, an analytical section at the springing of the cross vault of the Basilica of Maxentius with part of the associated side vaults (Figure 9.5).[1] This shows the use of brick and tile that would have been

Figure 9.5 Choisy's drawing of the Basilica of Maxentius.

---

[1] Auguste Choisy, *L'art de batir chey les Romains*, Paris, 1873.

laid on the lagging to form coffered ceilings in the side vaults together with a patterning of brick or tile arches. Roman concrete was then placed over this, a form of construction that required no complex geometry of stone cutting but was something that could be accomplished by a semi-skilled slave labour force.

The pointed vault

Semi-circular vaults result in rather limited plans because they must be built over a square pattern of supports. Semi-circular vaults of different spans would simply be of different heights and to arrange two such vaults to intersect the smaller one would have to be tilted upwards. The groin where the two vaults met would then be curved on plan, hardly an appropriate shape for an arch. The solution to this difficulty was to abandon the semi-circular shape and use pointed vaults where each side of the vault was still a circular curve but of a larger radius. By using this shape builders were no longer constrained by the 2 : 1 ratio of span : height of the semi-circular arch, and the spans of the two intersecting vaults could be different. Figure 9.6a shows a possible arrangement in which the component vaults are all singly curved. What that means is that the shape of each vault is like a piece of curved paper so that a series of horizontal lines drawn across the surface of the vaults would all be parallel. The large arch spans across the width of the building, or the nave of the church, while the narrower arch forms the basic shape of the window opening.

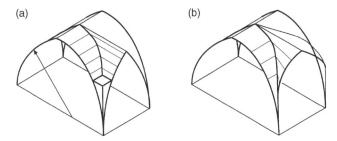

Figure 9.6 Forms of pointed vaults.

With this geometry the window area is restricted, and French Gothic architects carried the springing for the window arch much higher up the columns to produce a vault with a twisted surface in which lines drawn across the surface were no longer parallel (Figure 9.6b). The pointed vault proved to be an extremely flexible device. It was even possible to produce vaults over the trapezoidal plan shapes in the apse at the east end of cathedrals or to slope the ridge of the vault so that the arches on adjacent sides did not have to be of the same height. However, the varying geometry of these vaults need not concern us here, nor the fact that the method of construction varied in different countries. What is of concern is their structural behaviour.

Structurally, the pointed vault is a curious shape because if divided into arch-like strips, in a similar way to Figures 9.2 and 9.3, the arches would be pointed, and a little consideration of the hanging chain analogy for arch forces shows that a pointed arch should have a point load at its centre, which these do not. Nevertheless, these vaults worked and must have used sufficient thickness of masonry so that the thrusts were still contained within the stonework. In part this was achieved by a solid fill part-way up the vaulting, as indicated in Figure 9.6a.

A single rectangular space roofed by vaults in two directions will produce thrusts along the lines of the ribs. The diagonal ribs have horizontal components in two directions, both outward and along the line of the building. Along a building each vault produces equal and opposite thrusts so the vaults support each other. In the major cathedrals the only problems occur at the ends of the transepts. The west end has a grand entrance whose heavy construction is sufficient to buttress the longitudinal thrust of the vaulting, and at the east end lower structures around the choir seem to provide adequate buttressing. However, the gables of the transepts are less well buttressed, especially the north transept gable as the south transept has the cloister built against it. In England the north transept gable at Peterborough has been strapped back to the flank walls with a combination of iron and timber, suggesting that there must have been some concern about its stability. At Beverley, the north transept gable had been thrust so far from the vertical that in the eighteenth century major engineering works were carried out to bring it upright. The gable was cradled in timber shoring both inside and outside the building. It was then cut away from the masonry of the side walls and interior arches and brought back upright by tilting the timber cradle. The columns of the transept still lean today so that the amount of movement that occurred can clearly be seen. Although there were occasional collapses, the balancing of forces within these structures has worked reasonably well. The masonry has even been able to accommodate considerable movement in places, but not within the thin vaulting, where some cracking will often be seen. There movement of the foundations, magnified by the height of the structure, has resulted in signs of apparent distress.

Look up at the under-surface of many vaults and cracks are visible. The vaults have clearly moved over time. With outward thrusts at the top of the piers there will be some outward movement of the structure, either produced by strain within the masonry or movement of the ground. A little consideration will show where hinges will form as a result of this movement of the structure and therefore what pattern of cracking we should look for. Hinges are likely to form where the thin vault joins the relatively stiffer wall structure and also at or near the crown of vault. With hinges in these positions the wall can rotate outwards and the crown of the vault will drop slightly but the structure will still remain in equilibrium – the movement as in Figure 3.12a. However, the wall above the springing of the vault will move out further than at the level of the springing and the vault surface will be unable to follow it. Therefore longitudinal cracks will open up between the vault surface and the wall. Rotation of the vault at the central hinge will also result in a crack in the underside of the vault along the line of the hinge. These cracks were clearly drawn by Pol Abraham in a now often-reproduced drawing (Figure 9.7).[2] Of course there should also be some cracking associated

---

[2]Pol Abraham, *Viollet le Duc et le rationalisme médiéval*, Vincent Freal, Paris, 1934.

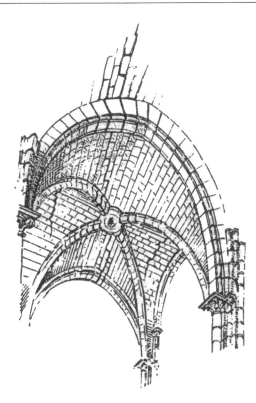

Figure 9.7 Pol Abraham's drawing of cracking in a vault.

with the hinges at the springing of the vault but these cannot be seen because rotation takes place about the lower surface and any cracking will be above the vault.

Elaborations on the basic vault form

English Gothic has little of the buttressing of French Gothic. Externally some of the English cathedrals are little more than boxes with simple buttressing of the walls. Which is better depends upon one's point of view. Is the buttressing to be regarded as a beautiful web of delicate stonework, a magnificent expression of the forces at play, or an unfortunate necessary consequence of all that soaring height inside cluttering up what would otherwise be a pure enclosure of the space? If architects were presented with that kind of thing today would they feel that their engineer had let them down or take delight in all that expression of structure? What English Gothic architects did instead of having such elaborate external buttressing was to use vaulting of a much simpler geometry that allowed them to decorate the under-surface of the vault with ribs (Figure 9.8). As well as allowing intersecting vaults to be of different spans this geometry also allowed vaults of different heights to intersect each other. Thus ribs, built before the surface of the vault and initially a device to aid construction, eventually came

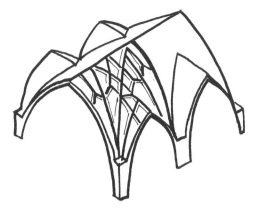

Figure 9.8 English ribbed vaulting.

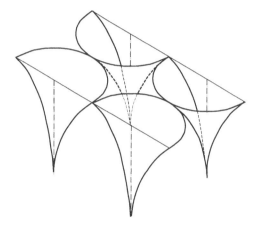

Figure 9.9 Fan vault geometry.

to be used decoratively in English Gothic churches where the vault surfaces were covered with ribs that served no structural purpose.

Elaboration of the ribs eventually led to the fan vault, which had no ribs at all; structurally it was a shell of masonry. The way to imagine a fan vault is to start with an arch spanning between a pair of columns. Then imagine a number of identical arch ribs set radially on each column. These will describe a funnel-shaped surface between which will be flat areas with curved sides (Figure 9.9). This is the basic shape of the fan vault but it does not describe its construction. The 'ribs' that one sees on such vaults are simply carved into the pieces of masonry that are arranged to form these stone shells. Structurally this can be seen as if the form comprised a series of arches leaning in towards the centre where there is a flat panel of stone that is compressed by all the arches. The flat panel is held in place simply by the compression forces from the shell surfaces leaning against it, just like the prestressed structures discussed in Chapter 7. Some fan vaults, such as those in the cloisters at Gloucester Cathedral, are on a fairly small scale but where the scale of the building is much larger the size of the flat panels can be reduced by intersecting the fans, as at Peterborough Cathedral and Bath Abbey, or the panels can themselves be arched as at Sherbourne Abbey.

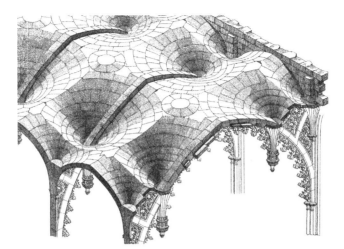

Figure 9.10 King Henry VII's chapel in Westminster Abbey drawn by by Willis.

As if this were not decorative enough, fan vaulting was taken even further by having fans that seem to spring from within the space. This was a structural *tour de force* because it is as if the vaults were supported on air. One set of fans rises from the columns along the wall while another set is carried on hanging stones and intersects these. The best known example is King Henry VII's chapel in Westminster Abbey (Figure 9.10), but the Divinity School at Oxford uses a similar structure and, as the room is much lower, is perhaps even more striking. In this type of structure the vaulting is supported in part by an arch that begins below the ceiling and passes upwards through it. Within this arch is a stone pendant, projecting downwards, and from it springs the fan vaulting that intersects the vault springing from the columns along the wall.

Building vaults

The classic study of the construction of Gothic cathedrals is by Fitchen, who considered the process in some detail.[3] He imagined something like the centres for bridge arches but built in halves with each half spanning from the springing to some central boss at which they would all be connected. This boss would thus transmit the compressive forces between the sections of the centring. This makes a good deal of sense and in most cases the roof timbers provided some sort of platform from which such temporary supports could be hoisted.[4] The ribs could then be built upon these centres and the masonry of the vault surfaces possibly built on lagging boards. One of the problems of that arrangement would be the strength

[3] John Fitchen, *The Construction of Gothic Cathedrals*, Clarendon Press, Oxford, 1961.
[4] This was not always the case as some Spanish cathedrals, for example, have no timber roof above the vaults. Presumably the climate is dry enough for a roof to be unnecessary.

required of the lagging. Towards the springing of the vault the span of the masonry between the ribs is small and the load would in any case be largely transmitted down through the steeply sloping surface. Towards the crown the span of the vault between the ribs is much larger and lagging would have had to carry a large proportion of the weight of masonry.

Fitchen did not consider how the rib centres would be removed once the work was complete. With access to roof-mounted hoists now denied by the completed vaults this process of dismantling could not have been a simple task. If folding wedges had been used at the base of the centres, these could then be knocked out to lower the centres away from the masonry but there would still be the problem of either dismantling them from some form of scaffold or lowering them to the floor. Readers who enjoy speculating about the construction process would be well advised to begin with Fitchen's book and to consider the forces that might be imposed upon the various supports that he suggests.

Domes

A hemispherical dome is semi-circular in cross-section, just like a semi-circular vault, and so appears to be a related structure. If one were to analyse it in the same way there would be a difference in that 'slices' of the dome would be wedge shaped so that the distribution of its weight, and therefore the shape of our analogous hanging chain, would be slightly different. But for a dome this simply cannot be the whole story and, while it can provide an adequate test for the stability of a dome it is fundamentally wrong, as simple observation shows. Buildings roofed with domes have been built by people because they have no timber with which to build a roof, let alone to provide temporary support. The Inuit people build igloos of snow without any temporary support. In the Truli of Italy houses are roofed with rather pointed domes, almost conical structures, constructed of the small stones that are readily available (Figure 9.11).

Figure 9.11 Truli houses of Italy.

When partially complete no arch can be drawn across such structures, and many domes are similarly 'incomplete'. The Pantheon, Rome, is famously lit by a hole at its centre, and the cupolas that crown so many domes that have been built since, stand over an opening at the top of their domes. Clearly, if a complete arch cannot be drawn through the dome there must be some other system of forces supporting it. What these are can be easily demonstrated by a simple experiment. Either imagine, or act out the following. A group of people stand in a circle each placing their arms over the shoulders of the person next to them. They then all move their feet backwards until the weight of each person is no longer over his or her feet. They will in fact be leaning in on each other like a kind of circular rugby scrum (Figure 9.12). Here is a model that represents the kinds of forces that are acting in a dome with the hole in the middle because there is nothing in the middle of this circle of people. No one is leaning directly against the person opposite; each is supported in some way by the person on either side. Try this and it will be obvious what is going on because there will be noticeable compression between your shoulders and those of the people each side of you. It is this ring of compressive forces that is preventing the circle of people from falling inwards, and hence downwards, and similar forces act to prevent a dome from collapsing. That is how it is possible for there to be a hole in the middle of a masonry dome. It also shows how it is possible to build a dome without temporary supports.

Figure 9.12 Sensing the forces in a dome.

This is not a complete description of most domes because this human model relies upon friction forces from the ground. Just as the group are leaning in on each other their feet are thrusting outwards on the ground. If it were done on an ice rink, without the friction forces, as people moved their feet backwards they would begin to slide outwards – with painful consequences. This could be prevented by tying their feet together with a piece of rope. The rope resisting the tendency to outward sliding is obviously in tension, and again the plan shows the forces that are acting (Figure 9.13). Thus there is now a tension ring at the bottom

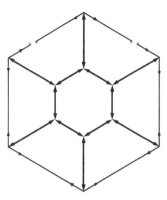

Figure 9.13 The forces acting on a dome.

corresponding to the compression ring at the top. In many cases domes are raised on drums that would be unable to resist such outward forces unless heavily buttressed, so they must have something like the rope around the feet of our human model to contain the outward thrust. Many have chains of timber or iron built into the masonry towards the base to provide this tensile restraint.

It is fairly easy to translate the human model into a force diagram because each person is separately leaning inwards. Their weight is not over their feet and they are all supported by a simple pair of outward horizontal forces at their shoulders with their feet pushing out against the ground just like an arch or a rafter. We could therefore work out the magnitude of the forces required from the weight of the person and the geometry. As the outward force in the centre is provided by the compressive force across the shoulders from the people either side we need to draw this in plan to see what is happening. The compressive force on each person's shoulder will be at a slightly different angle adding together to produce the outward force. Similarly the presumed rope joining their feet will change angle as it goes around producing the inward force in plan (Figure 9.13). Although this is only drawn in plan it might be instructive for you to draw the forces on one of the participants in this circle showing the components of the forces in the vertical plane. The weakness of this analogy is that the people forming this model are only connected together at the top and bottom whereas a dome is continuous. Rather than there being discrete forces acting at the top and bottom there are varying stresses in the material of the dome.

At any level within the dome there will be circumferential stresses, called more simply *hoop stresses*. These are in tension towards the bottom and in compression towards the top, varying from a maximum tension stress at the bottom of the dome to a maximum compressive stress at the top. The consequence is that some reinforcement needs to be provided in a masonry or concrete dome in the bottom zone where the hoop stresses are in tension. In the top no reinforcement is required.

A dome analysis

Finding the forces in a dome

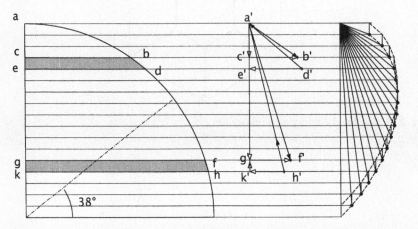

Figure 9.14

The forces in a thin hemispherical dome can be found using the triangle of forces. If a dome of uniform thickness is cut horizontally into number of slices of uniform height it can be shown that they all have the same weight. This means that the weights of both the whole dome and the individual slices can be represented by a vertical line cut into equal lengths. Thus the weight of the slice cbde is represented by the line c'e'. At the top of the slice there is a force, which is tangential to the surface of the dome, represented by the line a'b', whose vertical component is equal to the weight of the dome above bc. At the bottom of the slice there is an upward force supporting the weight above the line ed. This force is also tangential to the surface of the dome and has a vertical component a'e'. We therefore have two triangles of forces, a'b'c' and a'd'e'. The horizontal components of the forces in the dome, b'c' and d'e', are unequal with the lower force being the larger. This difference can only be accounted for by the compressive hoop stresses within the slice.

If the same exercise is repeated much lower down the dome the tangential force of forces a'f' and a'h' also have different horizontal components f'g' and h'k' but now it is the upper force that is the larger. The difference is now accounted for by tensile hoop stresses within the slice gfhk. The triangles for every slice can be combined into a single diagram in which a short vertical line between the ends of each triangle to the preceding one clearly shows the difference between the horizontal forces. If two lines are drawn, one through the ends of the triangles and the other through the points indicating the differences between the horizontal components, these lines will cross. Above where they cross are compressive hoop stresses and below it tensile hoop stresses. The 'latitude' at which this occurs is 38°.

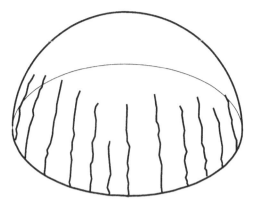

Figure 9.15 Cracking in an unrestrained dome.

The obvious question is what will happen if we try to build a hemispherical dome and fail to provide reinforcement against the tensile hoop forces? Will the dome collapse? The answer is that it will not providing there is adequate restraint against outward movement at the bottom. The feet of the people of our circular scrum need not be joined to each other unless they are standing on ice. On normal ground they will rely upon friction between their feet and the ground to produce the necessary restraint. In fact their only point of contact is between their shoulders. If a dome is unreinforced it will simply crack into a number of slices that will all have arch-like behaviour up to the zone of compressive hoop stresses (Figure 9.15). This perhaps explains the shapes of those domes that are not complete hemispheres, the great mosques of Istanbul for example. While their ideal shape might have been a hemisphere this was not possible without tensile reinforcing and so their builders restricted themselves to domes that were within the zone of compressive hoop forces. However, there is a possible architectural reason for their shapes rather than a structural one.

The architecture of domes

Given the structural constraints of a simple hemispherical dome we need to consider how architects dealt with that and achieved the forms that they did. The Istanbul skyline is renowned for the domes of the city's mosques, which are shallow saucers compared with the domes of so many Christian churches. While a hemisphere might be regarded as the ideal shape it has both architectural as well as structural disadvantages. As an external feature it is unsatisfactory by itself because in many buildings it would not be sufficiently prominent. The solution to that was to raise the dome upon a drum so that it could be seen. But a hemisphere is unsatisfactory as an internal form because its height is such that it cannot be seen clearly as part of the space below. Thus, many buildings, including St Paul's Cathedral, London, have an inner, shallow dome to suit the proportions of the space with a separate hemispherical dome externally, and raised on a drum. The domes of the mosques of Istanbul are confined to the compression zone and simply require adequate buttressing, and the same is true of the inner domes of buildings such as St Paul's Cathedral.

In many cases what we see as a dome in form might not be a dome structurally. At St Paul's, the outer dome shape is in fact formed by timber falsework that is supported on a brick cone. The builders of mosques in Persia, and elsewhere where a prominent dome was wanted, simply built a series of radial walls standing on an inner dome and used them to support the outer shape. That explains the bulbous shape of domes in that part of the world, shapes that are clearly impossible as structures. In the dome of the Pantheon, Rome, it was the inner form that was wanted while the outer form was less important. There the hemisphere is completed by the thickening of the dome and the walls, as its section shows (Figure 9.16). Of course there are other structural tricks that can be played. As well as this strategic thickening of the dome a much lighter material was used for the upper part of the Pantheon's dome.

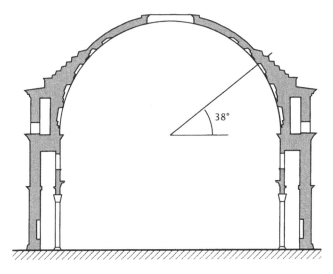

Figure 9.16 Cross-section of the Pantheon, Rome.

The cone that is incorporated into the dome of St Paul's Cathedral raises a question about the relationship between the shape of a dome and the hoop stresses within it. Carrying out the same triangle of forces exercise for a cone as for a dome is shown in Figure 9.17; equal height slices are not of course the same weight but that does not matter as we only need to

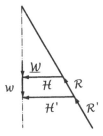

Figure 9.17 Forces in a cone.

consider one slice taken anywhere on the cone. The load on the top of the slice is the weight of the cone above it, W, and this is supported by a force within the masonry, R. At the bottom of the slice the supporting force R′ has a vertical component equal to W + w and acts along the same line as R. The horizontal components of these two forces are H and H′, proportional to the two radii of the cone at those places, and the difference between them can only be supplied by a compressive force within the cone. As this applies anywhere in its height it must be everywhere in compression. It will of course require some constraint at the bottom, in the form of a chain perhaps.

This is, of course, the structure of a church steeple as well as the cone at St Paul's, but the latter suggests an intriguing possibility. Just considering hoop stresses, if a hemispherical dome is somewhere in compression and somewhere in tension, while a cone is everywhere in compression, there must presumably be some dome-like shape, a little more pointed than a hemisphere, that is everywhere in compression. Or, looked at another way, by making a dome a little more pointed than a hemisphere it might be possible to control the tensile hoop stresses to a level where they can be handled.

Some historical examples

Brunelleschi

Brunelleschi used a slightly pointed dome for St Maria del Fiore, Florence (Figure 9.18). Brunelleschi's achievement at Florence was not simply to build a dramatic dome but to do so without using any falsework to support it during construction, although as we have seen this was not such a miracle. His achievement was more in realising that it could be done. The slightly pointed shape of the Florence dome means that the tensile hoop forces are lower than they would be in a hemispherical dome. Roland Mainstone has looked at the develop-

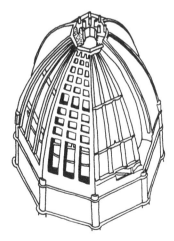

Figure 9.18 Santa Maria del Fiore, Florence.

ment of forces in this dome during the process of construction.[5] (The fact that the dome is octagonal rather than circular in plan does not have any effect on this.) As it stands on a drum it does require a chain to prevent its bursting outwards but Mainstone shows initial compressive stresses near the base of the dome that gradually reduced as the dome was built higher, eventually becoming modest tensile stresses.

St Peter's, Rome

The dome of St Peter's in Rome gave rise to one of the earliest examples of structural analysis. In the eighteenth century there were concerns about the safety of the dome when cracks were noticed in its surface. If the dome was cracking then presumably it was moving outwards and this might mean that the chains that had been built into the masonry to contain the outward thrust were not sufficient. Was the dome in danger of collapse? This was an early example of the application of mathematics to a structural problem and three mathematicians who were commissioned to investigate the problem used the method of *virtual work*, so called because no actual work is done. We simply imagine both deformations of the structure and the work required to produce those deformations.

   The dome is raised on a drum and both the dome and the drum might be imagined as split into sections by a series of radial cuts. If that happened the dome could move outwards by the walls of the drum tilting (Figure 9.19). Some small outward movement at the junction of the drum and dome allows some downward movement of the apex of the dome shown by the dotted lines on the half section of Figure 9.19. As this movement occurred the centre of gravity of the dome segments would move downwards by the distance 'b', the weight W doing some work to produce the movement. As work is defined as the magnitude of the force multiplied by the distance moved the work done would be W.b. As there is a chain to prevent

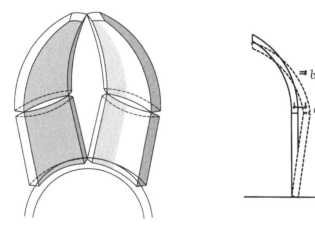

Figure 9.19 St Peter's, Rome, analysis by virtual work.

[5]Roland Mainstone, 'Brunelleschi's dome of St Maria del Fiore and some related structures', *Transaction of the Newcomen Society*, 1969/70; Vol. 42.

this movement and this expands by the amount 'a', work is done on the chain by the movement of the dome. The work done *by* the dome is equal to the work done *on* the chain and the relationship between the two could be determined from the geometry of the dome. An assessment was made of the weight of the dome, so giving the values needed for the calculation. By equating the two values for the work done the required tension in the chain could be found. This analysis did not tell the engineers at the time how much extension would occur in the chain as a result of the force and hence how much cracking was to be expected. The masonry was clearly not able to resist the amount of strain occurring in the chains, so that while a structure might be strong enough to prevent collapse it is not necessarily strong enough to avoid some other undesirable behaviour. More chains with less force in them would have resulted in less cracking.

Hagia Sophia and pendentives

A disadvantage of the dome is that it is circular, presenting difficulties for covering a square shape if that is wanted on plan. A dome might be placed over a square room simply by cutting off those parts that lie outside the square, losing the simplicity of the hemispherical form (Figure 9.20a). A simple hemispherical form can be regained by cutting the top of the dome off and replacing it with a dome of different radius above the circular ring (Figure 9.20b). The four corner pieces left from the original domed geometry that now support the hemisphere are called *pendentives*.

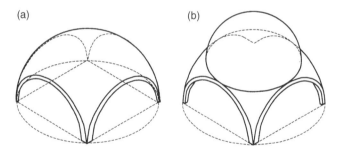

Figure 9.20 The formation of pendentives.

A rectangular space could be produced from this device by simply adding together a number of such forms. This is the structure of the cathedral at Périgueux, but the separate domes break up the flow of the space. A better solution is that adopted by Hagia Sophia, Istanbul (Figure 9.21). This building has a central square space crowned by a dome on pendentives, similar to that of Figure 9.20b but with a flatter dome. The space is then extended in each direction along one axis with the extensions roofed by half domes, which themselves have smaller half domes at their base. This has the advantage that the half domes lean inwards to receive the outward thrust of the main dome. Along the other axis heavy buttresses were used to resist this outward thrust, with broad arches supporting the dome along these sides and transmitting its thrust to the buttresses.

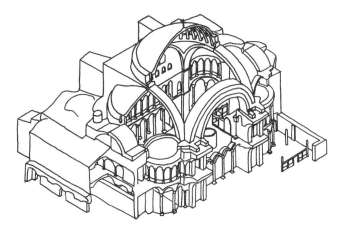

Figure 9.21 Hagia Sophia, Istanbul.

Because this is a brick building, creep in the mortar has allowed the building to move in such a way that its deformations reveal the balance of forces within it. On the two sides where there is only the passive stiffness of arches to resist the thrust of the dome there has been a slight outward bulging. On the other two sides the dome has been pushed inwards slightly, showing that the inward thrust of the half domes was initially greater than the outward thrust of the main dome. Distortion of the structure in this way has involved some redistribution of forces to achieve equilibrium.[6]

The modern three-dimensional structure

Although it is an ancient principle that structures depend upon their shape for their structural integrity, this principle has become important recently both in masonry structures and in reinforced or prestressed concrete structures. One recent example is little more than a continuation of an early form of construction. A method for building vaults was developed in Spain that relied upon thin tiles held together with a quick-setting gypsum mortar. Its great advantages were the rapidity with which the mortar set, and the fact that it had some adhesive strength, which meant that the tiles could be laid into a shallow vault-like form without the need for any centring. Like Brunelleschi's dome, as the vaults were built, compressive stresses developed that held the structure in place. These very thin vaults ultimately relied for their strength on the rigidity of the supporting walls and on their shape; they were used for roofs, floors and even staircases. A Spanish émigré to the United States patented the system there in 1885; he and his son founded the Guastavino Fireproof Construction Company, building extensively both in New York and elsewhere in the country. Many of their buildings have since become landmark structures. This system, variously called Catalan

[6]Roland Mainstone, *Hagia Sophia: Architecture, Structure and Liturgy of Justinian's Great Church*, Thames and Hudson, London, 1988.

vaulting or Guastavino vaulting, has recently been used in Britain for the building of the Pines Calyx Centre, a small conference centre built using such tile vaults and walls of rammed earth. Of course the outward thrust of the vaults used for this building must be contained by tension rings, and reinforced concrete was used for that. The lesson here is that ancient structural types may still be relevant in the twenty-first century.

With the development of reinforced concrete it was clearly possible to build three-dimensional structures in this material. If a dome requires tensile hoop stresses towards its base then either reinforcement can be built in to cope with these or the dome can be pre-stressed around the base. These are the modern equivalents of the chains that were put around the base of masonry domes in the past. But the possibilities go further than that and many twentieth century shell structures might be seen as developments of the barrel vault and the cross vault as well as the dome, all used with a willingness to experiment with different shapes and different support arrangements.

Example of experimenting with different shapes

The simplest place to begin is with the developments of the barrel vault. Consider, for example, Felix Candela's auditorium for Chemical Sciences at the University of Mexico. This comprises two barrel-vault-like shapes, except that they are based on cones rather than cylinders, tapering towards one end (Figure 9.22) but with a series of V-shaped props apparently resisting the outward thrust. The shells are shaped like catenaries in section, the shape following precisely the line of thrust. It seems that the structure could have been built without the raking props, which were added for appearance.[7] If one examines the structure closely the props are not actually a continuation of the shell surface.

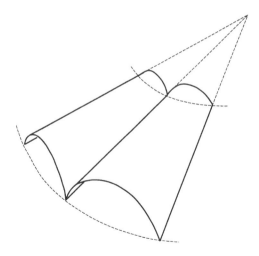

Figure 9.22 Tapered catenary shells of Candela's Chemical Sciences Auditorium.

---

[7]Colin Faber, *Candela the Shell Builder*, Architectural Press, London, 1963, p. 52.

What made that possible is that barrel vaults in reinforced concrete can span between end walls rather than onto side walls. To do this they behave like beams with compression forces in the top and tension forces in the bottom. Try this with a piece of paper and it becomes clear that end diaphragms are needed to ensure that it takes the desired form and that some edge stiffening is also needed but the basic arrangement is as shown in Figure 9.23a. The vault might also be arched in the long direction for even larger spans, have cantilever ends or even be built as long cantilevers for grandstand canopies. There are examples of all of these forms. Three-dimensional structures like this also include some that consist of flat planes – folded plate structures. The simplest of these can be modelled by folding a piece of paper to form a beam. Try this and it becomes apparent that this also tends to bulge out along the bottom edge and Figure 9.23b shows this problem solved by simply folding the paper out along both bottom edges to form edge stiffeners. Therefore there is both arching action in the cross-section and beam action in the long section, the latter shown by the arrows drawn on the diagram.

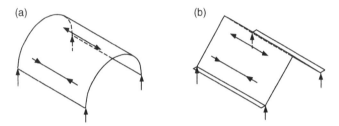

Figure 9.23 Beam action in a barrel vault and a folded plate.

What is so surprising is that these structures can be built in brick. The master of this was undoubtedly Eladio Dieste, who devised an ingenious method for prestressing the brickwork to prevent tensile forces that would otherwise be developed in the structures. Steel wires were first laid parallel in the structure and looped around anchorages. They were then drawn together pulling across them with a simple car jack to obtain the required tension. By this means he built most dramatic structures. The form used for the tribute to Dieste in Salto, Uruguay, is one that he had used for filling station canopies (Figure 9.24). He also built long span roofs for industrial buildings by putting together vaults that were catenaries in cross-

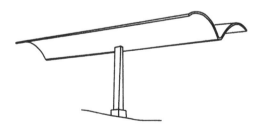

Figure 9.24 The tribute to Eladio Dieste, Salto, Uruguay, a cantilevered brick shell.

section, with stiffened edges but then arched in the long direction to achieve the long spans needed. His folded plate for the roof of Iglesia San Pedro, in Durazno, Uruguay (Figure 7.40), had not only to span the length of the church but also to resist wind loads on the side walls.

Folded plates can also be assembled into crystalline forms relying upon the folds where the plates join to provide stiffening and support in a similar way to the groin of a cross vault, although structures like this have been little used. Much more common has been the assembly of curved shapes with groins between them. This, of course, includes the basic cross vault, a large example of which is the terminal building for St Louis Airport, designed by the engineer Anton Tedesko.

The dome, the other basic form that we have inherited from the ancients, has also been extensively modified with the aid of reinforced concrete. There has not been the same general requirement for hemispherical domes as there was in the past so that modern domes have been designed with different shapes and with quite different support conditions. Eero Saarinen's domed form for the auditorium building at MIT, which used part of a spherical hemisphere, is something of an exception but Saarinen appears to have been rather dissatisfied with the result.[8] If other forms were acceptable architecturally then anything would be structurally acceptable that followed the lines of thrust so that the shell would be either in direct tension or compression, but not in bending. Given that these structures are to be built in concrete rather than masonry a wider variety of support conditions can be adopted and, as we have seen with Dieste's structures; edge stiffeners can be incorporated if necessary. While such structures might be difficult to analyse using numerical techniques, suitable forms can be found by using the inverse of a hanging net. Just as an arch that is the inverse of a hanging chain has no bending in it so there would be no bending in a shell that is the inverse of a hanging net. The weight of the net is uniformly distributed across its surface, as is the weight of the shell.

The engineer who pioneered this method was Heinz Eisler, whose starting point was noticing that an inflated pillow took the form of a shell that he had been painfully attempting to analyse by numerical methods.[9] Inflated forms were difficult in that leakage of the apparatus made it difficult to maintain a constant pressure and hence a constant shape but hanging forms could be frozen – literally. He hung cloth to form the inverse of a suitable shell shape, sprayed it with water and let it freeze outside in winter. Measurements could then be made of the model knowing that the concrete shell would be satisfactory. With this rather primitive method the measurements had to be made rather uncomfortably outside – but who said engineering should be easy? The great advantage of these methods is that one is not confined to shells with regular geometries on regular supports. Figure 9.25 shows a net with edge stiffeners hanging from four supports. Naturally methods have improved since Isler had to measure his models in the winter cold. Today photographic techniques can be used to both record and measure the form of models. Methods have since been developed that replicate these models numerically.[10]

---

[8] Quoted by Joedicke, p. 127, but no source is given.

[9] Heinz Isler, 'Shell structures: Candela in America and what we did in Europe'. In: Guy Nordenson (ed.), *Seven Structural Engineers: The Felix Candela Lectures*, The Museum of Modern Art, New York, 2008.

[10] Kilian, A. and Ochsendorf, J., 'Particle-spring systems for structural form finding', *Journal of the International Association for Shell and Spatial Structures*, 2005; Vol. 46.

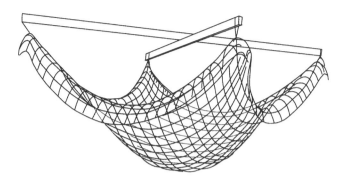

Figure 9.25 Hanging net with edge stiffeners – a model by Heinz Isler.

One should realise that what might appear to be a simple uniform surface conceals a great deal going on within. Although the structure is in simple compression or tension with no bending across the surface that does not mean that the stresses are as uniform as its appearance. If a shell is brought to a series of point supports rather than onto a continuous edge then there must be some concentration of forces at those points. For Gothic structures it was the ribs and the folding of the surfaces that provided the means by which large compression forces were carried, and while it is still possible to do that in concrete it is more normal for the concentration of forces towards the supports to be dealt with by placing heavier reinforcement in those areas.

Apart from the need for edge stiffeners, if a shell is to be brought to a series of point supports then containment of the outward thrust cannot be within the shell itself. In many designs the shells are brought down to the ground so that outward thrusts can be contained by the foundations. For example, in Eisler's Bellinzona supermarket the shell comes down to four points on the ground and is on a polygonal plan. If this were not so it would be necessary to contrive some tension ring external to the shell. Eduardo Torroja did this with his market hall in Algeciras. There projecting edges stiffen the dome between the eight column supports but the outward thrust to these still needs to be contained by a continuous tension ring of steel between the tops of the supporting columns (Figure 9.26).[11] Forces are concentrated at the supports of this shallow dome, one contained within what would be the

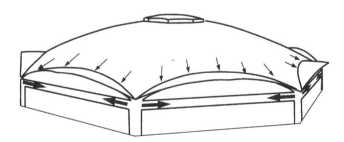

Figure 9.26 Eduardo Torroja's market hall in Algeciras.

---

[11] Joedicke, J., *Shell Architecture*, Reinhold, London, 1963, p. 103.

compression zone of a masonry dome. As there is no continuous ring close to the supports the edge stiffeners must be in horizontal bending between the columns.

Anticlastic forms

So far we have avoided the technical terms describing the geometry of surface structures, but there are two different types. Domes and barrel vaults are all examples of *synclastic* forms, in which the curvatures in two directions are the same, i.e. both convex or both concave; but the availability of materials that take tension has enabled architects and engineers to experiment with *anticlastic* forms. These are forms in which the curvatures are different in the two directions. The simplest, and perhaps the most commonly used anticlastic shape, is the hyperbolic parabaloid, often simply referred to as an HP. The name comes from the fact that sections taken through the surface in two directions are parabolas while sections in the third plane are hyperbolas. In Figure 9.27 the shape is shown by parallel lines in two sets of vertical planes at right angles to each other. All these lines are parabolas, whereas if the shape were to be cut by horizontal planes the lines where they cut the surface, like contour lines on a map, would be hyperbolas.

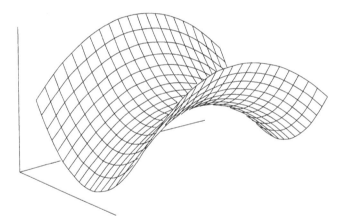

Figure 9.27 The geometry of a hyperbolic paraboloid – an HP.

The surface has another interesting property in that straight lines can be drawn across it in two directions, a property that makes it simple to build. Either straight timbers can be used to create the formwork for a reinforced concrete shell, or a shell could be built up in timber from straight planks laid over each other in the two directions. Because of this the form became popular in both timber and concrete. Figure 9.28a shows how the surface is constructed. Based on a square plan, shown by the dotted lines, the form has two high points and two low points with a straight line drawn across between opposite sides. In Figure 9.28b the structure has been turned through 45° and lines drawn between adjacent sides through the points of intersection of the straight lines to give two sets of parabolic curves. This shows clearly that the lines in one direction take the form of an arch while those in the other are

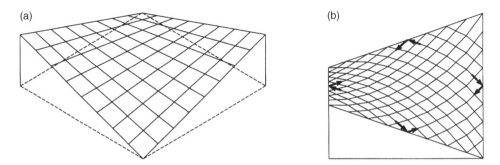

Figure 9.28 (a) The surface of an HP generated with straight lines. **(b)** Directions of tension and compression in an HP.

like hanging chains. This results in compression forces in one direction and tension forces in the other as indicated by the arrows on two pairs of lines. These forces are at 45° to the edges, adding to produce a force along each edge and shear forces perpendicular to it. The edge beams therefore need to be stiff enough to resist these shear forces. They effectively gather the forces from the curved surface delivering them to the supports at the low points.

Perhaps the first of these structures to be widely publicised was the information building for the Brussels World Fair in 1958, not built on the fairground site but in Brussels city centre. In Britain the form enjoyed a period of popularity for roofing in school halls or gymnasia. Single shells clearly produce a concentration of forces at the supports, where heavy buttresses are needed, but as the form has straight edges it is also possible to add a number of such structures together. For example, four HPs leaning together over a square plan produce a roof with horizontal ridges, a simple gable on all four sides and low points at the corners. As the compressive stress in the edge members varies along the length it reduces to zero at the 'gables' of such a roof and with compressive forces being resolved at the centre.

One of the great exponents of such structures was Felix Candela, who assembled them in a variety of ways. A number of such shells brought together produce a fold in the surface that acts as a stiffener to the concentrated forces at the supports. Figure 9.29 shows such an assembly in which each of the surfaces is cut out of a different HP surface. In such an arrangement the lines joining the separate shells are in the form of arches rather than straight lines.

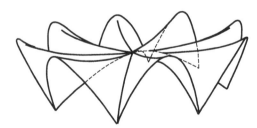

Figure 9.29 Candela's Los Manantiales Restaurant assembled from several HP surfaces.

Structures in tension

The purpose of a roof is simply to provide shelter, and yet this is most often done with quite heavy materials. As the Bedouin and the boy scout use portable shelters made with woven wool or canvas cloth, so we can provide permanent shelters in much the same way. What is needed is a compression structure that supports the cloth at the required height, just like the poles of a tent, and sufficient anchorage at the ground to resist the tension. The difficulty with such a structure, as anyone who has used a tent will be aware, is that they are severely affected by wind. The problem for a roof is that wind loads produce uplift forces, and on a large scale such a structure would have too much movement to be acceptable. Eero Saarinen's Foster Dulles Airport and his Ice Hockey Rink at Yale University avoid the problem of wind uplift by having a relatively heavy roof covering so that the uplift forces are less than the downward forces produced by the self-weight of the roof.

For lightweight roofs, resistance to movement by wind uplift can be provided by prestressing the surface. Imagine that the shape of Figure 9.28b was formed of a lightweight and flexible material instead of timber or concrete. If, instead of the lines that are shown to be in compression, these were to comprise cables to which some tensile force were applied, they would be pulling down upon the material of the covering and preventing it from being lifted up by the wind. Of course the result at the edge beam is two inward sets of forces rather than one inward and one outward, and the edge beam would be in considerable bending. That difficulty can be overcome by changing the shape of the supporting edge members to make them arches instead of straight members. This is the form conceived by the architect Mathew Norwicki for the J.S. Dorton Arena in Raleigh, North Carolina.[12] The sketch of Figure 9.30 omits the verticals that frame the walls of this building so that the form of the main structure can be clearly seen. It comprises two intersecting arches across which the cables carrying the roof covering are strung, those in one direction forming concave curves while those in the other are convex.

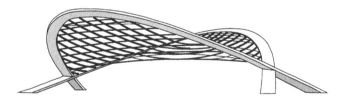

Figure 9.30 Dorton Arena, Raleigh, North Carolina.

Perhaps the best known of this type of structure is the Olympic Stadium at Munich, and because it is much closer to a tent in concept it is much easier to understand. Little explanation is needed of this, or of many others of Frei Otto's designs because the nature of the

[12]Norwicki died in a plane crash but the building was completed by William H. Deitrick using Severud, Elstad, Krueger as structural engineers.

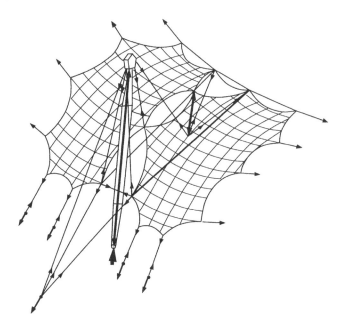

Figure 9.31 Munich Olympic stadium.

forces is clearly visible in the construction. That does not mean that their design has been a simple matter. The pole and the guys at the back of the Munich stadium (Figure 9.31) are rather tent-like, but the front needed to be clear of structure in order not to obstruct the view from the seats. Therefore the covering is held forward by a tensile member that sweeps around the curve of the stadium. Note also the compression member within the covered area, suspended from the main pole and from the main tension member at the front. Frei Otto is another engineer who, like Heinz Isler, worked extensively with models to develop the designs of his structures.

There is an issue of scale associated with this kind of structure, just as with any other. Kenzo Tange designed a couple of suspended structures for the Tokyo Olympics. That for the pool (Figure 9.32), engineered by Mamoru Kawaguchi, brought the cables supporting the roof covering to two long cables running the full length of the building. The cables

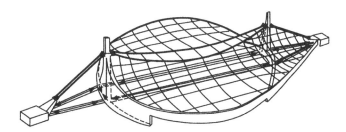

Figure 9.32 Yoyogi stadium, Tokyo.

supporting the roof come onto the rear walls of the building, which have the appearance of deep arches resembling the scheme adopted by Saarinen for the Yale hockey rink, although that is on a much smaller scale. However, the main cables must carry something like half the weight of the roof, a load increased by the downward pull of the bracing cables, and one that is concentrated at the tops of the towers. In this case there are dampers between the tops of the towers and the main cables to control wind vibrations. The anchorages for the stays provide only downward restraint so there are long struts the full length of the stadium. As these struts must diverge to pass either side of the pool there must be tension forces in the end walls. The scale of this required large connectors between the roof support cables and the main cables, the latter deflecting as much as 2 m during construction. The roof covering might be light in weight but the overall structure is hardly minimalist.

Structures for their time and place

Although the scale of the Tokyo structure made it a major engineering project, the use of structures elsewhere that are shaped to conform to the direction of the forces in them has allowed architects and engineers to devise some very economical buildings. This is possible because shaping structure in this way avoids the need to cope with bending moments and their associated stresses. Moreover, this has occurred where and when materials for other types of structures have been in short supply. Dieste and Candela devised their structures for less industrialised countries using indigenous materials and readily available building skills, so avoiding the need to import large rolled steel sections. There was a similar situation in Britain in the 1950s where, in the immediate postwar period, there was a shortage of steel for construction. Reinforced concrete or prestressed concrete used much smaller amounts of steel and this encouraged engineers to explore the possibilities of three-dimensional structures that reduced the requirement for steel even further. This led to the use of shell and folded plate structures. The differences between these new kinds of structures and the early masonry domes and vaults is that they are generally thin structures, closely following the lines of force within them, and they may take tension as well as compression forces. This has led to a wide variety of geometries being used including structures relying upon flat planes as well as curved shapes. Given the reduction in materials required by structures like this there is presumably considerable potential for their use today when architects and engineers are concerned to find building methods with low embodied energy.

Appendix:
Some Elements of Grammar

Algebra

Algebra is not something to be afraid of because it is simply a form of shorthand to avoid long complicated sentences. When you see it, don't panic. All you have to do is to translate the expression into the sentence that it represents. Those who have practised this sufficiently can manage without the translation just as we may know what a certain expression in a foreign language means without the need to translate into English. It's simply a matter of practice.

Suppose that we have the expression $W = r.t.h.l$ for the weight of a wall. This simply means that W equals r multiplied by t multiplied by h multiplied by l. Obviously these letters stand for something, and that will be identified in the text and/or in an accompanying drawing. In this case the weight of the wall (W) equals the density of the material (r) multiplied by the thickness of the wall (t) multiplied by the height of the wall (h) multiplied by its length (l). You might recognise that the weight is simply the density of the material multiplied by the volume (thickness times height times length).

In most cases the length of the wall will not be included in the expression because it is simple to deal with unit lengths, i.e. we talk of a 1 m length of wall. Then all forces will be given in terms of the force per metre length so we can simply eliminate that term from the equation. What we then have is the weight per metre length.

In some cases a term will have a small number above it, such as t^2. Again this is to reduce the length of the expression. The superscript 2 simply indicates that the term is to be multiplied by itself. Thus, t^2 (t squared) equals t multiplied by t. From this, as you might deduce, t^3 (t cubed) equals t multiplied by t multiplied by t.

In some cases to economise on the letters used subscripts are adopted, e.g. R_1 and R_2 or R_a and R_b. This is done when there are two forces that serve a similar function but have a different value. In this case, the most common, it would be the reactions at the ends of a beam. They are both reactions and so are given the letter R, but they are at different ends of the beam and so are distinguished by either a number or a letter.

There are some symbols that are worth noting:

$<$ means 'is less than'
$>$ means 'is more than'
Σ (the Greek letter sigma) means the sum of all the values that follow.

Loads and forces

For our purposes a force is that which tends to disturb a body that is at rest. However, we need to distinguish between external forces acting on a structure and internal forces within the members of a structure. External forces include the superimposed loads, e.g. the loads on a floor or the wind loads on a wall, but also, and perhaps confusingly, the self-weight of the parts of a building, after all something can fall down because of its own weight. These two kinds of external force are sometimes called live and dead loads or the superimposed loads and the self-weight.

Internal forces are the forces within a member. They are the reactions to the externally applied forces. Here it is not the presence of the forces that tends to produce movement in the structure but their absence that would certainly lead to such a movement. If a member were to be cut the force within it would fall to zero and the structure might then collapse as a result.

Static equilibrium

The structures that we are designing must be in a state of static equilibrium. For this to be so all the forces and all the moments acting on the structure, or indeed on any part of it, must sum to zero.

Where forces are inclined to the vertical it is normal to find their vertical and horizontal components, which are then considered separately with a sign assigned to the direction of the forces. Thus downward forces might be considered positive and upward forces negative. However, this is simply a convention and the signs could be the other way round. Similarly we might consider forces that act from left to right as positive and those acting from right to left as negative. The sign of a moment depends upon whether it is clockwise or anticlockwise.

The laws of equilibrium

For those who like the mathematics the statement about equilibrium may be written as:

$$\Sigma V = 0, \Sigma H = 0, \Sigma M = 0.$$

Thus the sum of all the horizontal forces equals zero, the sum of all the vertical forces equals zero, the sum of all the moments equals zero. This is the requirement that satisfies Newton's third law – that for every action there must be an equal and opposite reaction.

Moments of forces

The moment of a force about a point is the turning or rotational effect of that force about the point. The moment of a force can be taken about any point; it does not have to be on the structure being considered, although it often will be. The moment is the product of the force and the distance of its line of action from the point. In practice this means drawing a line to represent the direction of the force and then drawing (or imagining) a line from the point at which we want to take moments and which is perpendicular to the line representing the force (Figure A.1). The length of this line is often called the lever arm. Note that it is not necessarily the distance from the point about which we are taking moments to the point where the force acts on the structure. The moment of the force about the chosen point is magnitude of the force multiplied by the distance – F.a in Figure A.1.

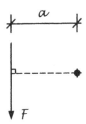

Figure A.1

Components of forces

It is often convenient to divide a force into two components at right angles to each other. These are often, but not always, vertical and horizontal components. In other cases they may be components perpendicular and parallel to the part of the structure being considered, such as a sloping rafter. The relationship between a force and its components is given by the diagram in Figure A.2.

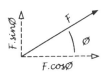

Figure A.2

Triangle of forces

Any three forces that act at a point and are in equilibrium may be represented in magnitude and direction by the sides of a triangle taken in order. In practice this means that if one draws three lines whose lengths are proportional to the magnitude of the forces that they represent, and whose direction is the same, they may then be reassembled to form a triangle in which the arrows representing the direction of the forces all point the same way around the triangle – see Figures A.3 and A.4. In each case the forces drawn on the left hand of the diagram are

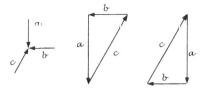

Figure A.3

not to scale but are shown acting at a single point on a structure. They are then represented in an abstract diagram, rearranged to form a triangle and drawn to scale. Clearly two triangles are always possible as shown. Figure A.3 shows two of the forces at right angles to each other, where the relationship between them clearly follows from what has been said about components of forces.

However, the rule applies to forces acting at any angle to each other, as indicated in Figure A.4. You should also note that the theorem can be extended to any number of forces acting at a point. If they are in equilibrium then they can be drawn to scale and arranged to form a polygon. If the magnitude and direction of all the forces but one are known then the unknown force can be found by drawing such a polygon. The unknown force will be that which closes the polygon when all the others have been drawn.

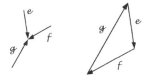

Figure A.4

Parallelogram of forces

This has not been referred to in the text but may be useful. If any two forces are represented by lines whose lengths are proportional to their magnitude they can be added by drawing a parallelogram in which these lines form two of the sides. The sum of the two forces is then the diagonal of the parallelogram. See Figure A.5, in which c = a + b.

Clearly the parallelogram of forces and the triangle of forces follow from each other.

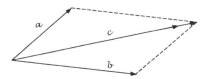

Figure A.5

Stress

In a member that is under simple compression or tension this is the force in that member divided by its area of cross-section. With stress given the symbol f, the force P and the area of cross-section A, f = P/A. However, when members are in bending the stress will vary across the member.

Strain

Strain is the change in length of a material produced by an applied force. It is defined as the change in length divided by the original length. With strain given the symbol ∂l and the original length, l, strain = $\partial l/l$. Both are measured in the same units and the strain in most materials is small so that this is a very small number. The strain will normally be a very small fraction of the original length.

Modulus of elasticity

Sometimes called Young's modulus after Thomas Young, who described this property of materials, it is the stress in a material divided by the strain produced by that stress. It is always given the symbol E. Thus E = stress/strain. This is the property that determines how flexible a beam made of that material will be. With most materials the strain will be very small and so dividing the stress by a very small number results in a very large value for E.

Glossary

Angle of repose
The maximum stable slope of a granular material.

Anticlastic
A surface with the property that sections in one direction are convex while those taken at right angles to that are concave.

Arris
The edge where two surfaces meet.

Ashlar pieces
Short vertical timbers in a common rafter roof flush with the inside face of the masonry and strutting the rafters.

Balloon frame
A system of light timber construction originating in America.

Bay
The structural division of a building frame or roof, the bay length being the distance between adjacent frames.

Bed joints
The mortar joint between successive courses of masonry.

Bending moment
See Moment.

Birdsmouth
The cut-out from a rafter to form a seating onto a plate.

Bond timbers
Timbers built into the coursing of brickwork or other masonry to provide greater horizontal continuity.

Bracing
Structural device to prevent racking of a frame.

Bressummer
A beam set with one face in the surface of a wall – hence breast-summer.

Brick bonding
The method of laying bricks so that that each thickness shall be attached to the one behind.

Buckling
The tendency of a structural element that is in compression to fail by bending at right angles to the direction of load.

Cage construction
The early method of framing in which a cage of iron or steel columns and beams was contained by masonry walls.

Cantilever
A horizontal structure supported at one end only.

Catalan vaulting
A system of vaulting depending upon tiles and a quick-setting mortar built up in two or three layers to form a very thin shallow vault.

Catenary
The shape adopted by a hanging chain under its own weight alone.

Centring – centres
The falsework used to support the masonry of a bridge during construction.

Centroid
The intersection of lines on a surface that divide it into equal areas. It will be the centre of mass (commonly called the centre of gravity) of a solid plane of that shape.

Clasped purlin
A purlin clasped between the principal rafter of a roof and a horizontal collar.

Collar brace
The horizontal timber that struts between two rafters.

Collar plate
The longitudinal plate in a collar-braced roof that runs under the collars, sometimes called a collar runner or a collar purlin.

Common rafter roofs
Roots framed without purlins.

Components of a force
A force may be divided (or resolved) into two forces at right angles to each other. These are called the components of the force.

Contraflexure, point of
The place where the curvature of a structural member changes from one direction to another, i.e. from concave to convex.

Conversion
The process by which round timber is converted into rectangular sections for use in construction. (Lumber is the American term for this rectangular material.)

Corbel
A projection from the surface of masonry, normally to provide a support.

Cord (of a truss)
The top or bottom member of a truss.

Creep
The continuing movement of a material under a constant load.

Cross vaults
Vaults formed by the intersection of two vaults at right angles to each other.

Crown post
The post standing on the tie beam and supporting a collar plate.

Diaphragm
A surface acting to transmit forces in its own plane.

Draw-boring
The method of forming offset holes in a mortice and tenon joint so that a peg driven in draws the timbers together.

Dry-stone walls
Walls laid without mortar.

Effective height or length
The height or length used in calculating the slenderness ratio of a wall or other structural member in compression. This will be the height or length between assumed points of contraflexure.

Extrados
The upper or outer curve of an arch.

Falsework
A construction used to support some visible part of a building or other structure. This can be permanent, as in the timbers that are used to support vaulted plaster ceilings, or it can be temporary, such as the timber structures used to support the masonry of bridges during construction.

Flags
Large rectangular pieces of stone used for paving.

Flange
The top and bottom parts of an I-shaped beam or girder.

Folded plates
Flat surfaces connected together to form a structure.

Folding wedges
Wedges driven together in opposite directions.

Four-bar chain
Theoretically four members joined by pin joints. In practice the ground forms one of the bars of the chain so that there are only three members thus linked. This is an unstable mechanism.

Free-body diagram
A diagram showing one structural member only with the various forces acting upon it.

Friction, coefficient of
The measure of the friction that can be developed between two materials defined as the ratio of the friction force and the force normal (perpendicular) to the surface between the two materials.

Funicular arches
Arches that take the form or the inverse of a hanging chain under the action of the same vertical forces.

Gin pole
A single guyed pole from which a hoist rope is suspended.

Guastavino vault
See Catalan vaulting.

Gussets
Plates used to connect structural members together.

Hardwood
The timber of any deciduous tree.

Headers
Bricks that have their ends (or heads) in the surface of a wall.

Hoop stresses
The circumferential stresses in a dome.

Intrados
The lower or inner surface of an arch.

King post
The vertical post in the centre of a roof truss.

Lagging
The material spanning between the centres of an arch and supporting the voussoirs.

Lintel (or lintol)
The structure spanning an opening.

Lower bound
The lower values for the forces resisted by a structure or structural member.

Lumber
An American term given to sawn or converted timber.

Moment
A measure of the tendency of a force to cause rotation about a point.

Mortice and tenon
A commonly used joint between two timbers comprising a mortice, or slot, cut into the foundation member into which is inserted a projecting tenon formed in the end of the joining member.

Neutral axis
The surface within a member in bending that remains at its original length.

Nodes
In any assembly of members forming a frame the points where the members are connected are called nodes.

Ottoman construction
Construction based on closely spaced timber studs commonly used for the first, or upper floor walls of a house on a masonry ground floor.

Parabola
A geometrical curve that is the shape formed by a hanging chain under a uniformly distributed load (horizontally) and the shape of the bending moment diagram for a uniformly distributed load.

Party wall
The wall between two adjacent properties.

Pendentives
The surfaces, usually spherical in form, that enable a hemispherical dome to be placed over a share plan.

Pisé de terre
A method of wall construction in which earth is rammed between timber formwork.

Plate
A horizontal timber within a timber frame to which members above are attached but which is not required to carry bending.

Plate bande
A masonry structure acting as an arch but whose intrados is a straight line, i.e. it has a flat soffit and is commonly used as a lintel.

Polonceau truss
A roof truss named after Antoine Polonceau, nineteenth-century French engineer and inventor.

Pole plate
A plate within a roof carried above the tie beam to support the common rafters.

Portal frame
A frame comprising two uprights and a horizontal member between them, thus resembling a portal.

Pre-Columbian
The period before the discovery by Columbus of central and south America.

Principal rafters
The rafters forming part of a roof truss and which support the purlins.

Purlins
Horizontal members in a roof. These may either support the rafters in a 'traditional' roof or support sheeting in a modern steel-framed roof.

Putlogs
The horizontal members of a scaffold. Hence putlog holes are the holes left in the masonry when the scaffold has been removed.

Queen posts
Pairs of timbers in a roof truss supported by the principal rafters and straining beam.

Racking
The tendency of a frame to sway sideways in its own plane.

Rafters
Sloping members in a roof.

Reactions
The forces generated in response to the application of a load.

Retaining walls
Walls designed to contain soil.

Romanesque
This term is given to buildings postdating the Roman era but which use semicircular arch and vault forms. There are many churches and cathedrals that have this characteristic. The use of these arch and vault forms is also associated with rather large supporting columns. It is thus a much heavier form of architecture than the Gothic that followed it, heavier because of structural necessity rather than architectural choice.

Sarking
A continuous material placed over the rafters as a secondary defence against rain or snow. This may take the form of boarding or simply roofing felt.

Scantling
The cross-sectional dimensions of something, usually timber.

Scissor bracing
Pairs of timbers resembling scissors fixed between pars of rafters.

Sections, method of
An analytical method developed by Wilhelm Ritter (after whom it is commonly named) that imagined cutting through a truss and replacing the cut members with appropriate forces to restore equilibrium.

Shear
The tendency of one part of a structure to slide relative to another.

Shear legs
Pairs of timbers joined together at the top in the form of an inverted V and guyed so that a hoist can be suspended from the apex, thus forming a simple crane.

Shear wall
Shear walls prevent such sliding by means of diagonal compressive forces. They thus exhibit the action of a diaphragm (q.v.).

Skeleton framing
The type of framing in which the floor loads are carried by the frame alone independently of any external walls.

Slenderness ratio
For simplicity we may consider this to be the ratio of length (or height) to the thickness of a structural member. In design it is the effective height that is measured and for steel sections a property called the radius of gyration is used instead of the thickness.

Soffit
The underside of a structural member.

Softwood
The term given to the timber of coniferous trees.

Soulaces
Short timbers in a common rafter roof between the collar and the rafters.

Spandrel
1. The space between the curve of an arch and the level of the roadway above (sometimes called the haunches). 2. The area of masonry under a window opening.

Strain
The change in dimension of a material under load.

Straining beam
The timber between the heads of the queen posts in a queen post truss.

Stress
The force per unit area on a material. Thus pounds force per square inch or Newtons per square millimetre.

Stretchers
Bricks laid with their long dimension in the face of a wall.

Structural scheme
The method by which the loads on a structure are brought to the ground.

Synclastic
A surface with the property that sections in both directions have the same direction of curvature.

TDA roof
A system of roof construction developed by the Timber Development Association, comprising closely spaced trusses of small scantling timbers joined with tooth plate connectors and carrying purlins also of small scantling.

Truss
An assembly of members forming a framework that will span between two supports.

Trussed rafter roof
A common rafter roof in which every pair of rafters is formed into a lightweight truss using gusset plates. The gusset plates are commonly patented 'truss plates'.

Upper bound
The maximum load carried by a structure or structural member.

Vierendeel
A type of truss in which all the panels are rectangular. This type of framework relies on the joints being able to carry bending moments.

Virtual work
A method of analysis in which small deformations are assumed and the work done to produce such deformations is calculated.

Voussoirs
The tapered stones that form an arch.

Wagon roof
A type of common rafter roof in which all the rafters are braced by both ashlar pieces and soulaces to give the appearance of an inverted cradle of timber.

Wind braces
Braces in the plane of a roof between the principal rafters and the purlins.

Wrought iron
Iron that has been forged after smelting, a process that reduces its carbon content.

Index

Lightning Source UK Ltd.
Milton Keynes UK
UKOW06f0911080514

231321UK00005B/69/P